IMAGES
of America

UKIAH

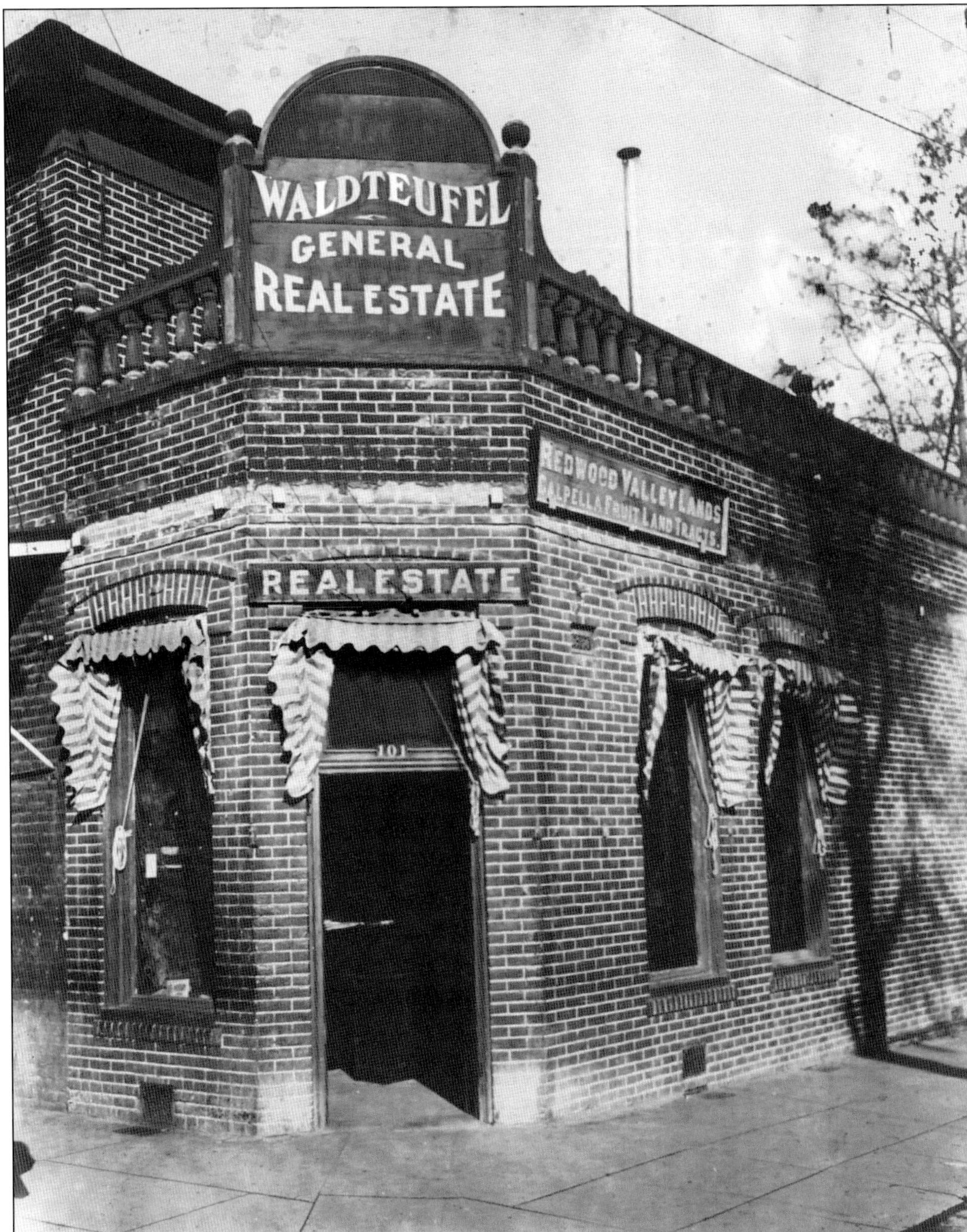

The Waldteufel Real Estate Office is shown around 1912 on the northeast corner of Perkins and State Streets. (Courtesy of Ed Bold.)

ON THE COVER: A 1941 summer band concert is shown in front of the old courthouse. Robert Sharpe, the director, is standing at left. (Courtesy of Ed Bold.)

IMAGES
of America

UKIAH

Darline Bergere

ARCADIA
PUBLISHING

ISBN 978-0-7385-7040-2

Published by Arcadia Publishing
Charleston, South Carolina

Printed in the United States of America

Library of Congress Control Number: 2009921918

For all general information contact Arcadia Publishing at:
Telephone 843-853-2070
Fax 843-853-0044
E-mail sales@arcadiapublishing.com
For customer service and orders:
Toll-Free 1-888-313-2665

Visit us on the Internet at www.arcadiapublishing.com

To my sons, for all the years of unwavering support and encouragement.

Contents

ACKNOWLEDGMENTS

For sharing his personal historical photograph collection and countless hours of assisting me with names and dates, I am forever grateful to Ed Bold, Mendocino County historian, and his wife, Melissa. Without Ed Bold, this book would have never become a reality.

Thank you to Robert and Lila Lee, who allowed the use of their extensive collection of pictures, and to the Grace Hudson Museum, who helped by providing photographs from their archives and information that I could not have obtained elsewhere. Kelly Neighbors, Melody Mack, and Bill Stambaugh came forward with photographs from yesteryear when I put out a frantic call. Thank you to Janis Cox and William French Jr.

Thank you to Bill McMorris and his daughter Susan, who rescued me from my computer incompetence. Thank you to Kelly Reed, my editor at Arcadia Publishing, and my fellow author Kathleen Manning, both of whom always urged me on to complete the book.

INTRODUCTION

From 1859, when it officially became a town, breaking away from being governed by Sonoma County, Ukiah went on to be voted the No. 1 Small Town in California in the late 1990s. Ukiah was where the ranchers came to town to shop, then rode their horses to the nearest tavern, where they were served their libations while still sitting in the saddle. In the 1960s, "the back to the land movement" led the "city folks" to flee to the gentle valley.

Ukiah has always been the refuge of a widely diverse population, including ranchers and farmers working side by side with winery owners, artists, and musicians enriching the local culture, Pomo Indians weaving unique baskets that are sought after throughout the world, and Spanish settlers who put down roots through the Feliz and Yokayo land grants, bringing their rich culture and traditions to the area to be shared with everyone in the valley. Descendants of the original settlers still live in the community.

Nestled in a beautiful valley surrounded by mountains, Ukiah supported the logging industry and pear orchards during the 1900s and more recently wineries and craftsmen. This is the site of Vichy Springs Resort, built in the mid-1800s. Vichy Springs was a favorite destination of luminaries such as Jack London, world-famous author of stories of the Northwest, who enjoyed relaxing at the spa's rejuvenating baths. Presidents Grant and Harrison were frequent visitors, as well as Mark Twain and Robert Lewis Stevenson; boxer John L. Sullivan had his training camp here.

Just on the outskirts of Ukiah is the sleepy little village of Hopland, home to one of the banks of Pomo Indians and where one will find wineries, Bocce ball courts, and the first solar living center in Northern California.

Take a walk back in time though the Grace Hudson/Sun House Museum. There one will find some of the finest examples of Pomo basketry and weavings in the country. The museum is also home to many of Grace Carpenter Hudson's oil paintings of Pomo children and life on the reservation.

Summer months bring the annual Sunday in the Park free concerts with many well-known musicians from throughout the country. Every Fourth of July, descendants of the Johnson and Cunningham families get together for a family picnic, a celebration that has been going on for over 100 years. In September, visitors flock to the Fabulous Flashback Car Show and Poker Run weekend.

During the month of October, the City of Ten Thousand Buddhas in Talmage, on the outskirts of Ukiah, holds its annual Honoring Elders weekend. December brings the Lighted Truck Parade, where local companies and drives of privately owned semitruck decorate their rigs with Christmas lights and decorations. The parade drives down State Street, the main street of Ukiah, ending at Alex Thomas Plaza for the annual Small Town Christmas celebration.

Ukiah is a town where everyone still rides their bicycles, the high school has a homecoming parade before the big game, and the bells still ring on the ice cream truck. In the early 1920s, the local chamber of commerce began promoting Ukiah as "the Gateway to the Redwoods."

One

Early Days and Those Who Shaped Ukiah

Whether in a big city or a small town like Ukiah, there are always people who shape the area with their contributions. Ukiah's beginnings are quite remarkable in the wide diversity of the early inhabitants. Three separate Pomo bands of Native Americans resided in the area. They were the Yokayo band, the Guidiville band, and the Pinoleville band, who all settled in the valley.

The area was home to photographer A. O. Carpenter, who traveled throughout Mendocino County documenting life in the area through his photography. Grace Hudson, another notable resident, was renowned for her portraits of Native Americans and is the namesake of the Grace Hudson Museum. Her studio, called the Sun House, is open to visitors from all over the world. Frank Sandelin, builder and owner of the Palace Hotel, provided certain panache to the town with his elegant hotel. Resident Harry Siems was the owner of the Palm Saloon, the popular "watering hole" where everyone who was anyone met and greeted their fellow citizens.

The Johnson, Cunningham, and Thomas families established farms and pear orchards in the valley. William D. L. Held, a member of the California Legislature for three terms, was honored by having the Held-Poage Library named after him. Frank C. Albertson, the Hofmans, and the Luce family all did their part to shape Ukiah.

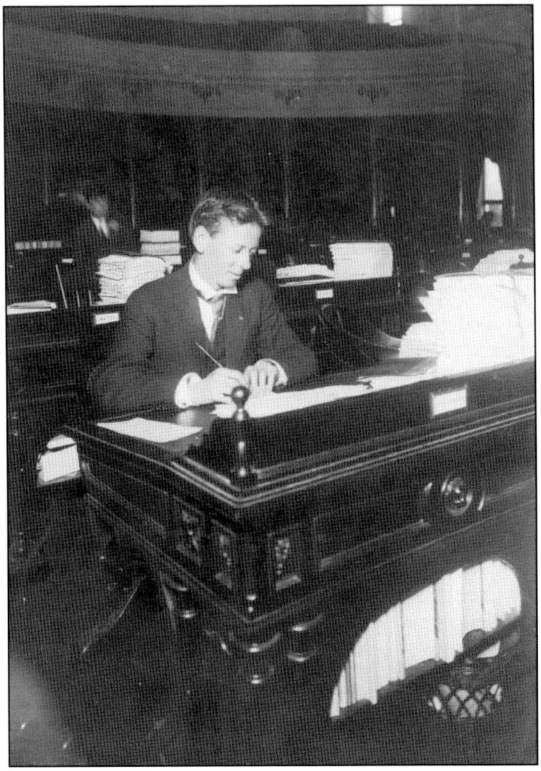

Ukiah resident William D. L. Held was a member of the California Assembly. He was elected to three terms in the California Legislature, from 1904 to 1905, 1906 to 1907, and 1910 to 1911.

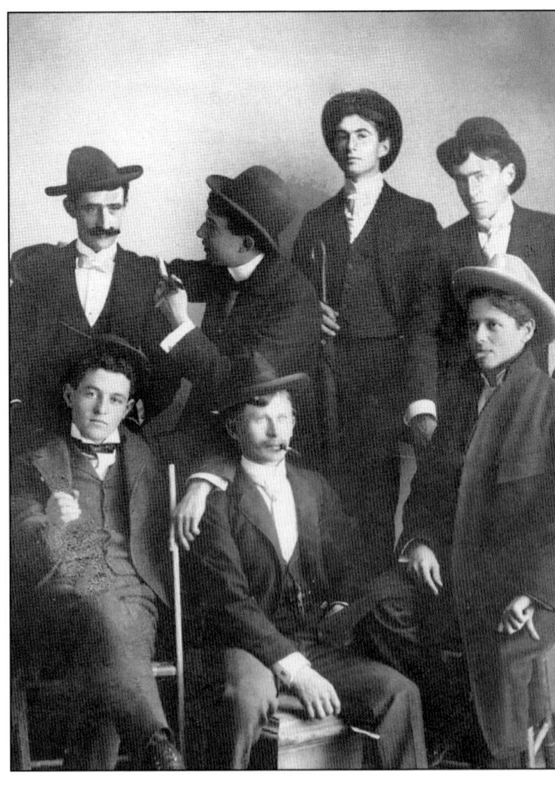

This picture from Christmas 1898 shows (first row) Oscar Weger, Jim Heap, and Billy Held; (second row) Clint Van Allen, Ernest Wheeler, Al Banks, and Bert Cleland.

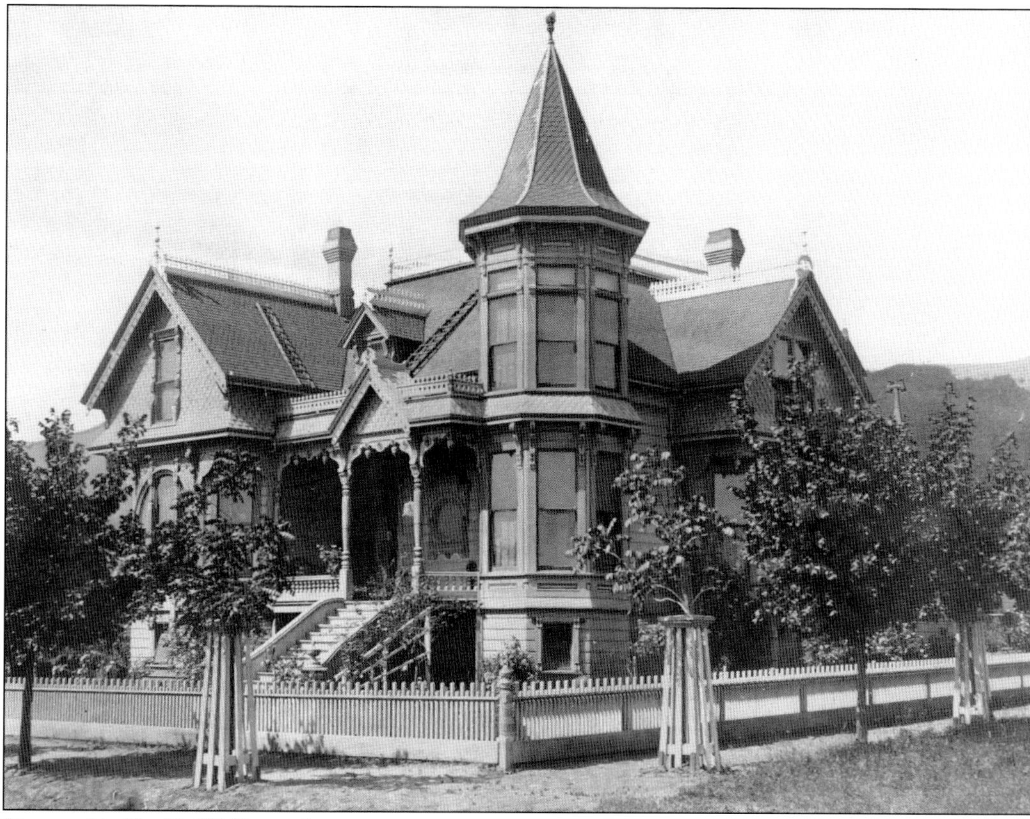

Pictured is Dr. E. W. King's home around 1890. The residence was located at the corner of South Dora and Jones Streets at 600 South Dora Street.

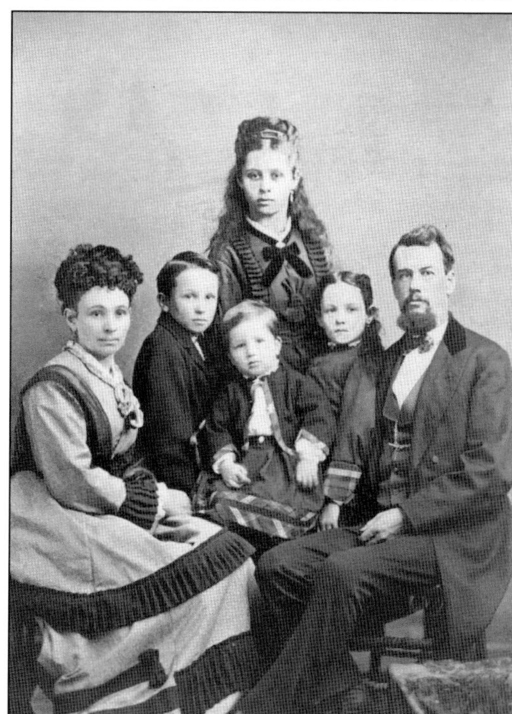

The A. O. Carpenter family is shown around 1873. From left to right are (seated) Helen, Grant, Frank, Grace, and Aurelius O. Carpenter; (standing) May Carpenter. (Photograph by A. O. Carpenter; courtesy of the Grace Hudson Museum.)

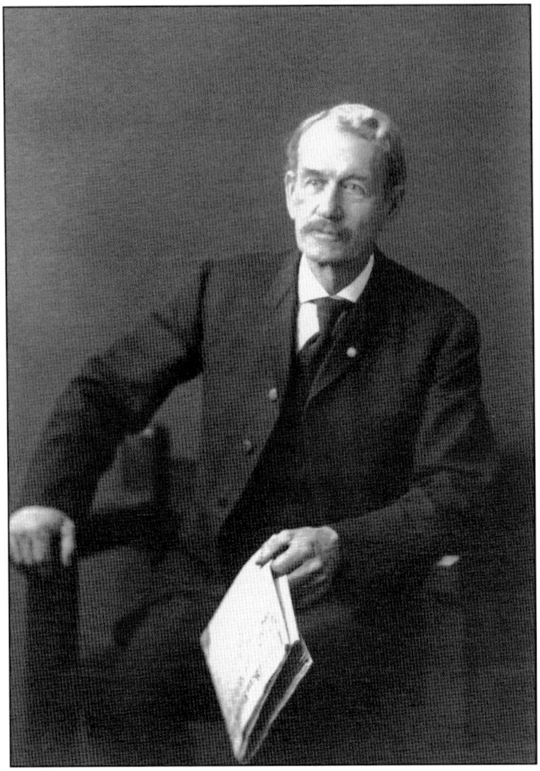

This picture of Aurelius Ormando Carpenter was taken by George Wilcox around 1915. Wilcox was the architect and builder of the Sun House. (Courtesy of the Grace Hudson Museum.)

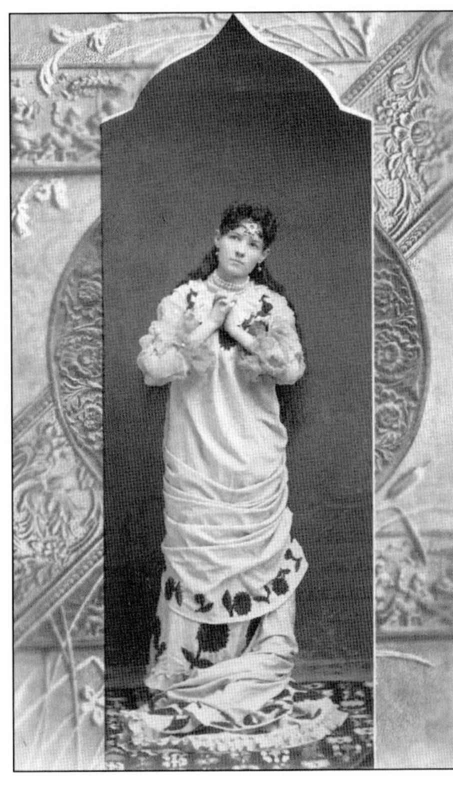

Grace Carpenter, the daughter of A. O. Carpenter is shown in 1885. (Photograph by A. O. Carpenter; courtesy of the Grace Hudson Museum.)

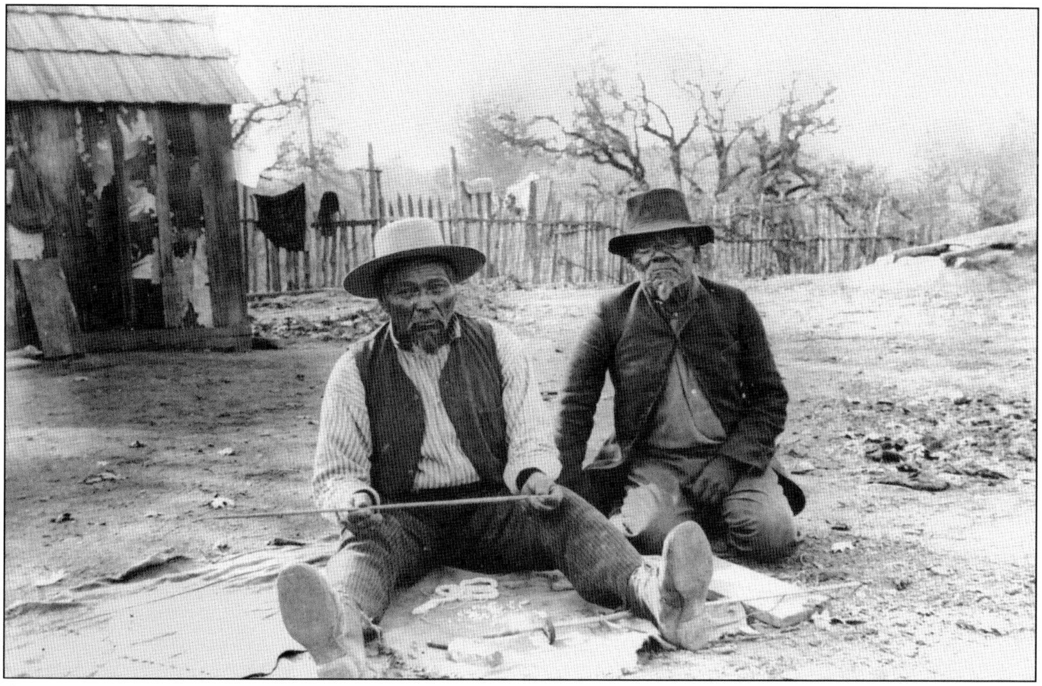

A Pomo man is pictured in 1890 fashioning clamshell disc beads, a strand of which can be seen coiled in the center of the image. Pomo people used these beads as a form of currency in earlier times and still greatly value them today. (Photograph by A. O. Carpenter; courtesy of the Grace Hudson Museum.)

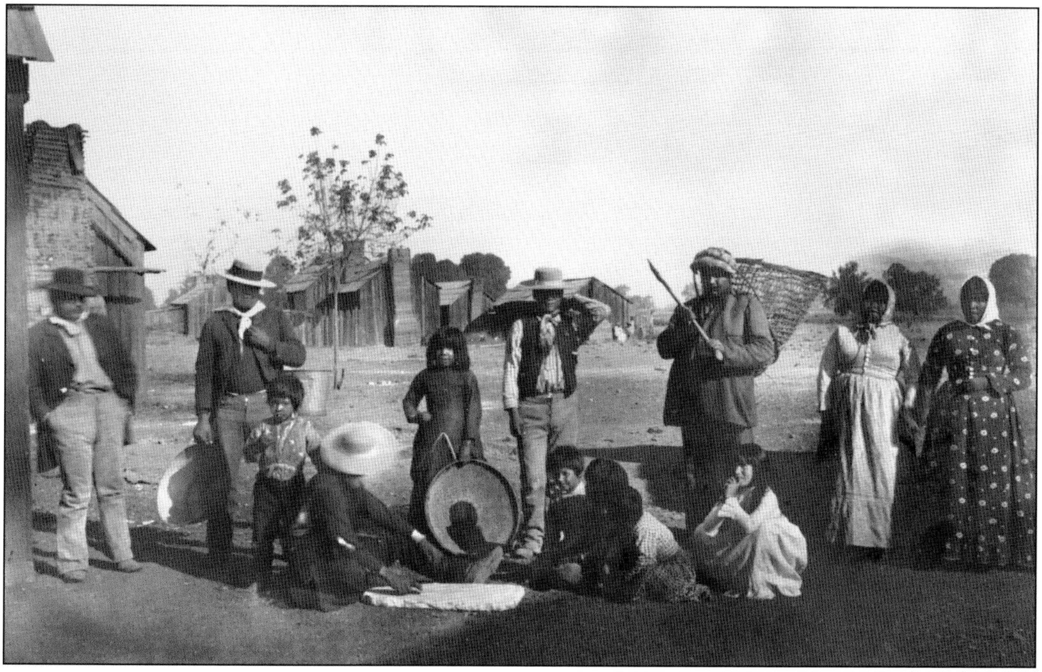

These are the Pomo residents of what was probably Pinoleville Rancheria, north of Ukiah, in 1890. (Photograph by A. O. Carpenter; courtesy of the Grace Hudson Museum.)

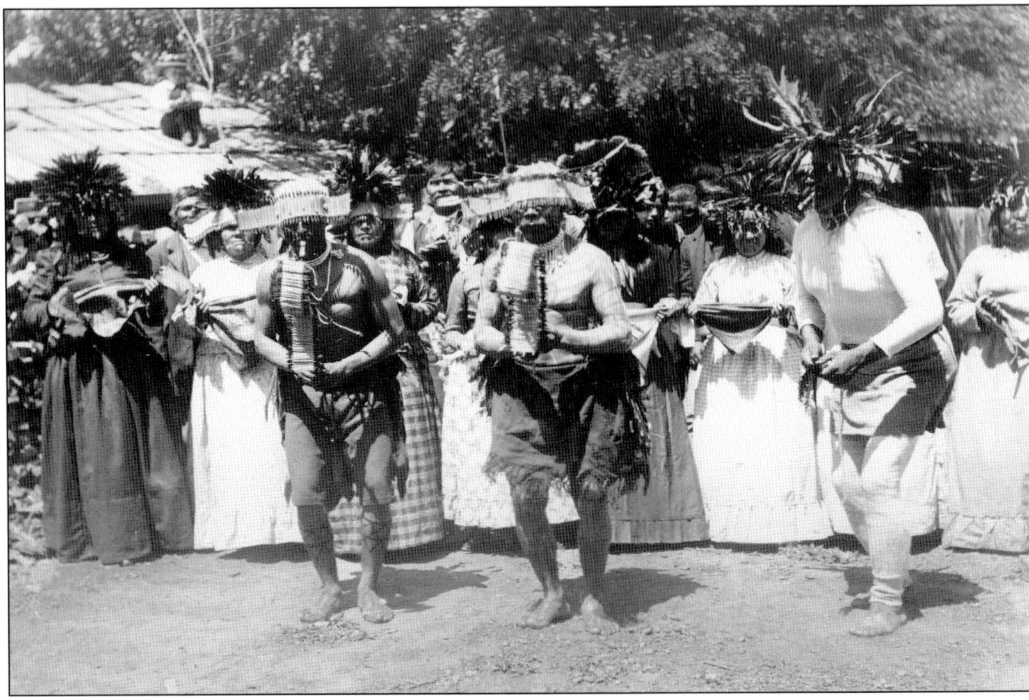

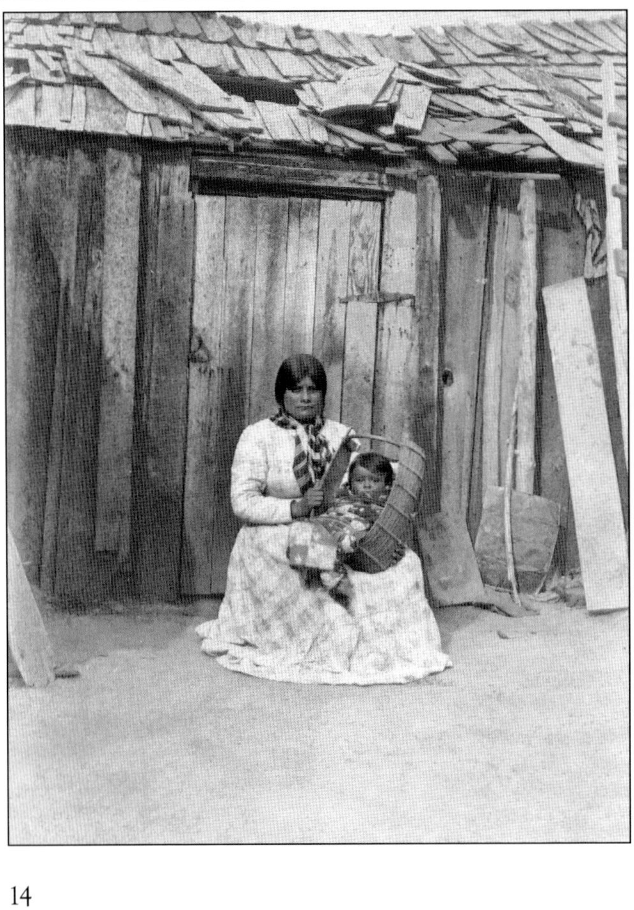

Pomo men are shown dancing around 1895. They were probably photographed outside a roundhouse. The roundhouse was a tribal ceremonial structure where ritual dances were often performed. (Courtesy of the Grace Hudson Museum.)

Pictured in 1892 is a Pomo woman with her baby. The baby is snugly wrapped in a cradle basket in front of a home at the Yokayo, or Beattie, Rancheria, southeast of Ukiah. (Photograph by Henry W. Henshaw; courtesy of the Grace Hudson Museum.)

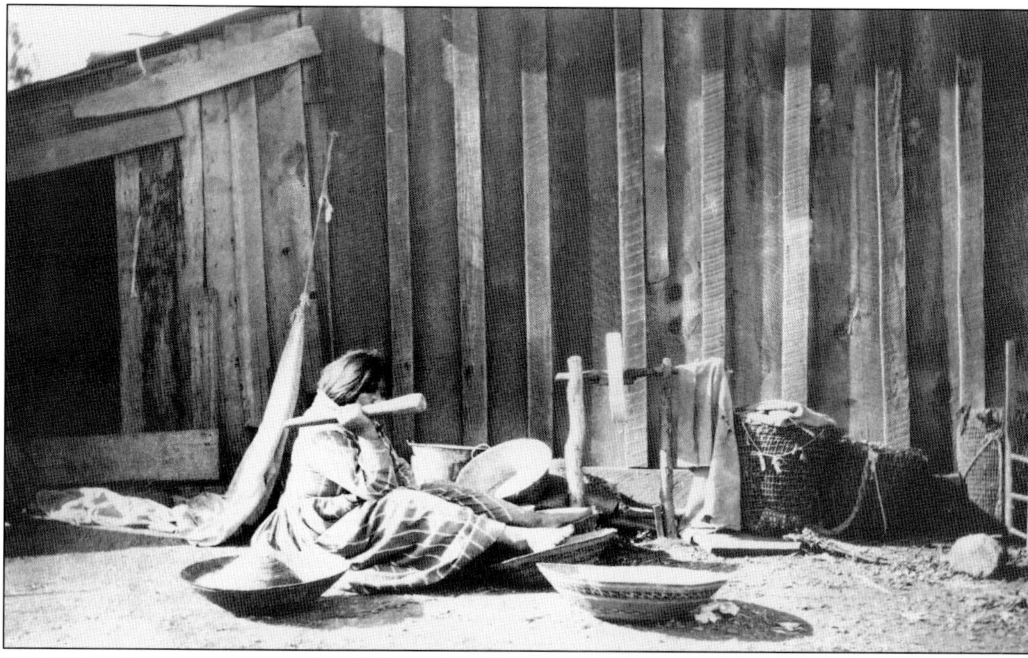

In 1892, a Pomo woman at the Yokayo Rancheria is shown pounding shelled acorn nut meats into a fine meal. Acorn mush and acorn bread provided two of the Pomo people's staple foods. (Photograph by Henry W. Henshaw, collection of the Bureau of American Anthropology, Smithsonian Institution.)

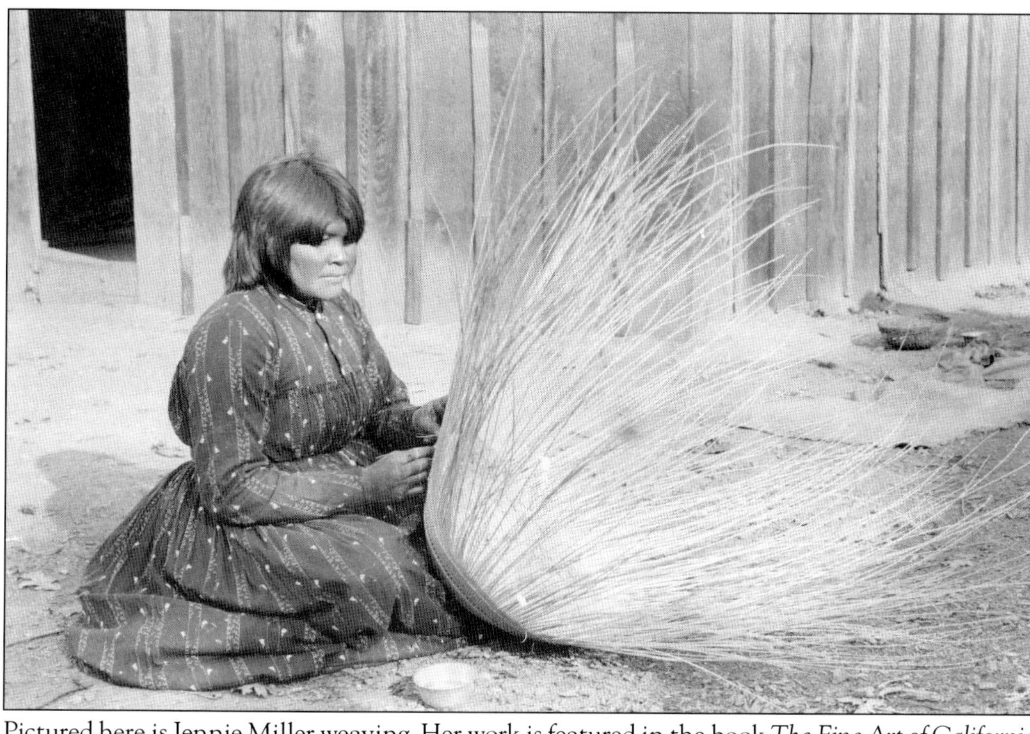

Pictured here is Jennie Miller weaving. Her work is featured in the book *The Fine Art of California Indian Basketry*. (Courtesy of the Grace Hudson Museum.)

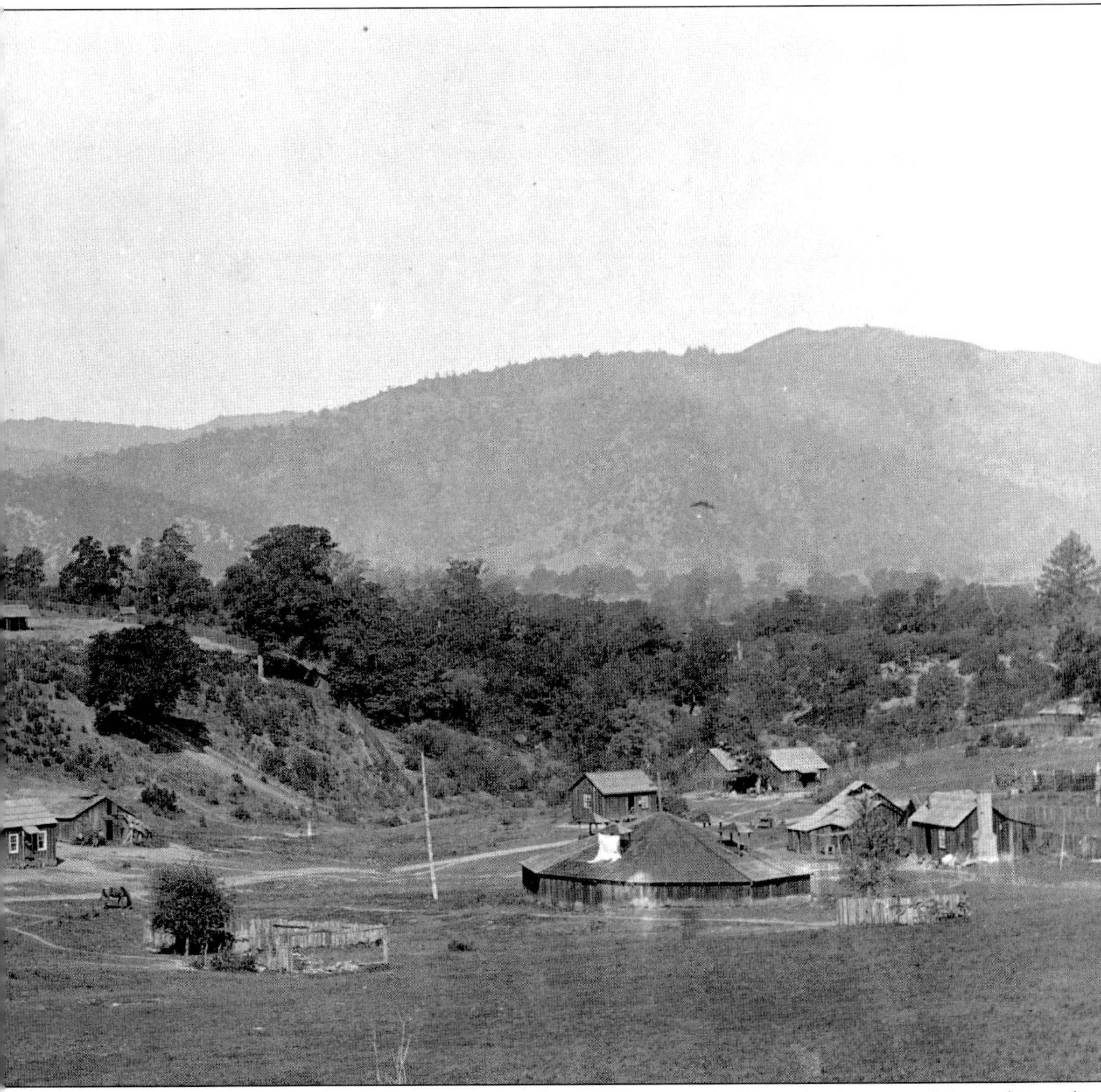

This *c.* 1890 photograph shows the roundhouse that was the Pomo Indian people's traditional ceremonial structure and other buildings at the Yokayo Rancheria. (Photograph by A. O. Carpenter; courtesy of the Grace Hudson Museum.)

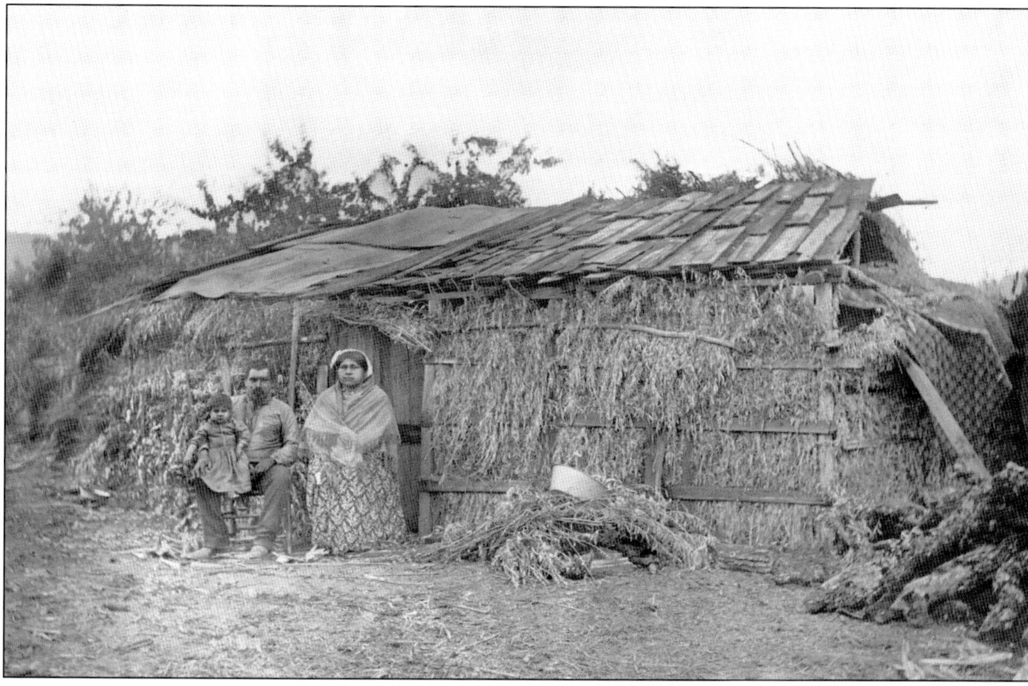

This 1890 photograph shows a Pomo family photographed in front of their brush house. Often Pomo people would construct such temporary structures to live in during the hot summers when working for local ranchers harvesting crops. (Courtesy of the Grace Hudson Museum.)

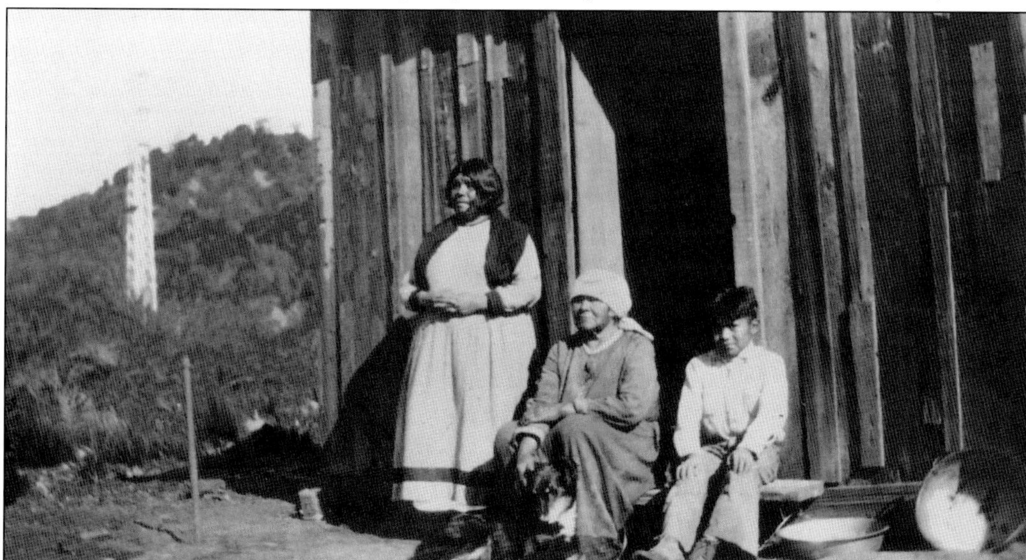

Pictured are Mollie Pettis Duncan (standing), Topsy Pettis (center), and Robert Duncan in 1928. They are shown in front of their house at Coyote Valley Rancheria. Topsy Pettis was a well-known and widely admired healer, or "Indian doctor." Her niece, Molly Pettis Duncan, was one of Grace Hudson's favorite models, along with Molly's son, Robert. A number of years later, the Duncans' home, along with the rest of this rancheria, were flooded to create the present-day Lake Mendocino. (Photograph by Bertha Emery; courtesy of the Grace Hudson Museum.)

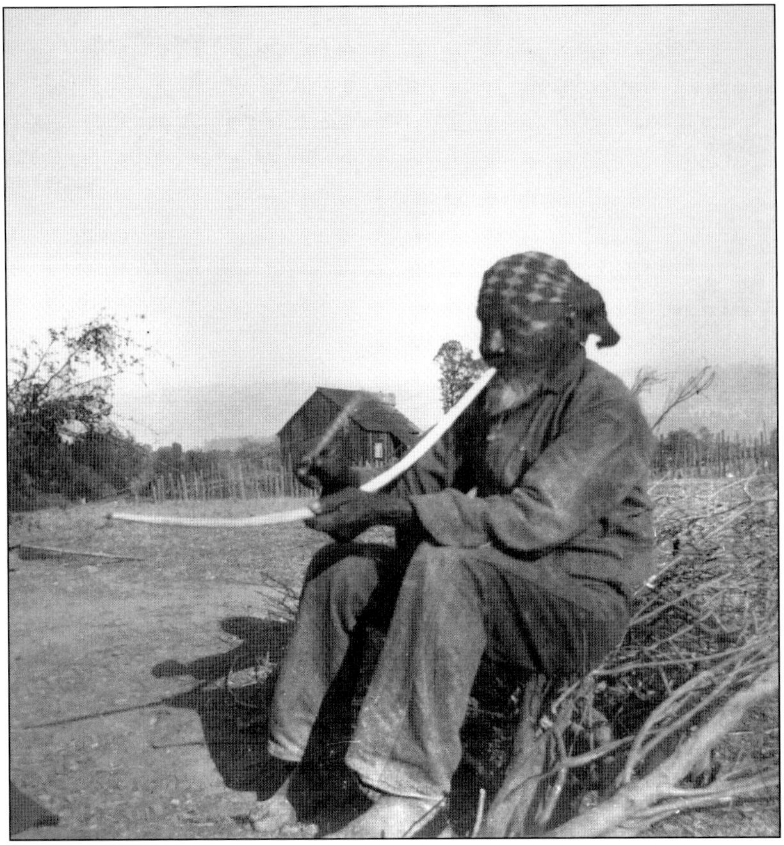

Pictured is John Scott, the leader of the Pinoleville Rancheria. The community was located just north of Ukiah. John Scott is shown playing the mouth bow. (Photograph by John Hudson; courtesy of the Grace Hudson Museum.)

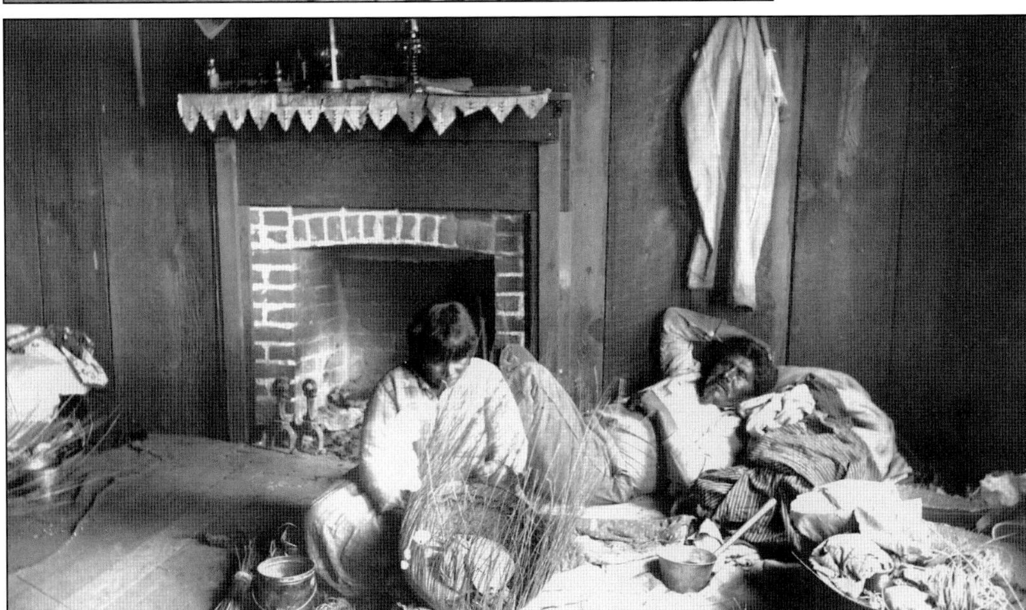

Charley Pinto and Mary Pinto are shown around 1885. They were photographed at their home at the Yokayo Rancheria. (Courtesy of the Grace Hudson Museum.)

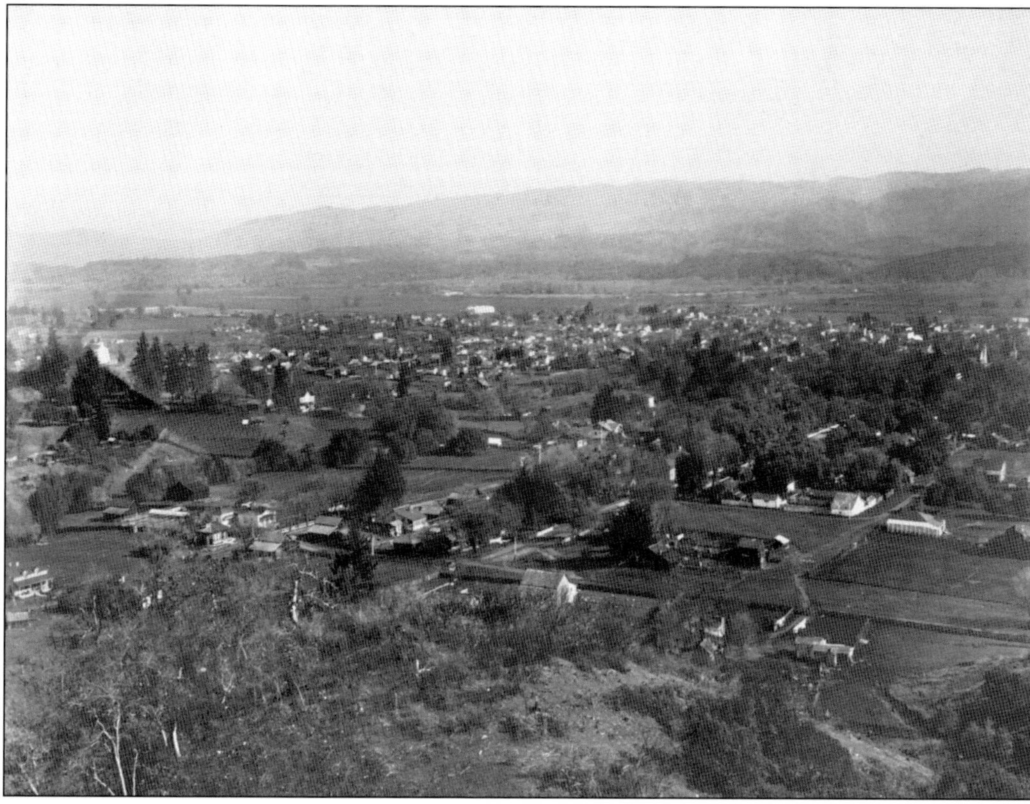

Seen here is an overview of the valley looking east in 1909. The photograph was taken from the western hills.

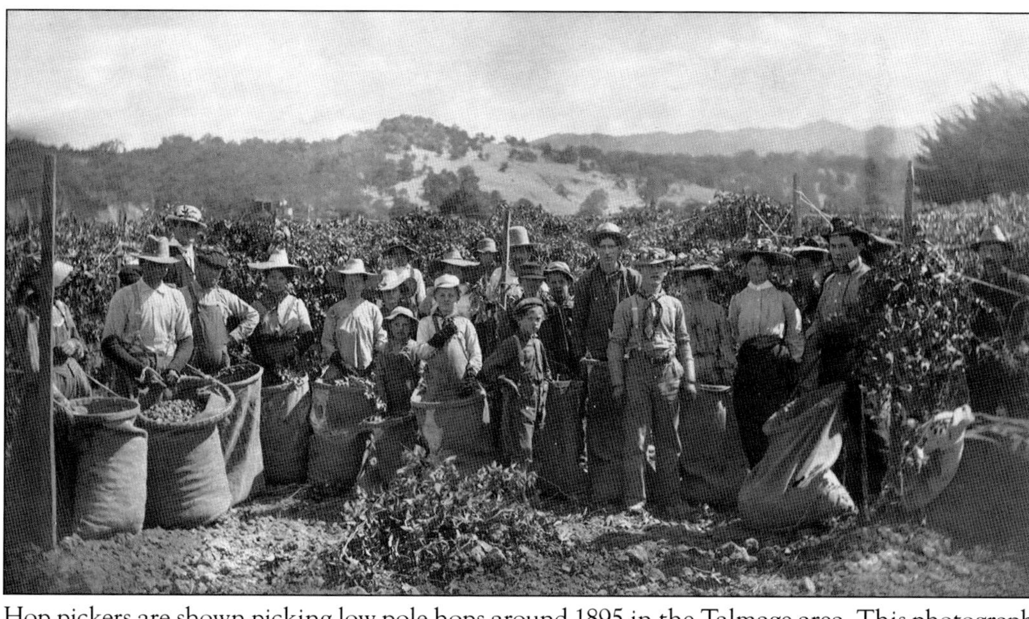

Hop pickers are shown picking low pole hops around 1895 in the Talmage area. This photograph by A. O. Carpenter was taken from a 5-by-8-inch glass-plate negative. (Courtesy of the Grace Hudson Museum.)

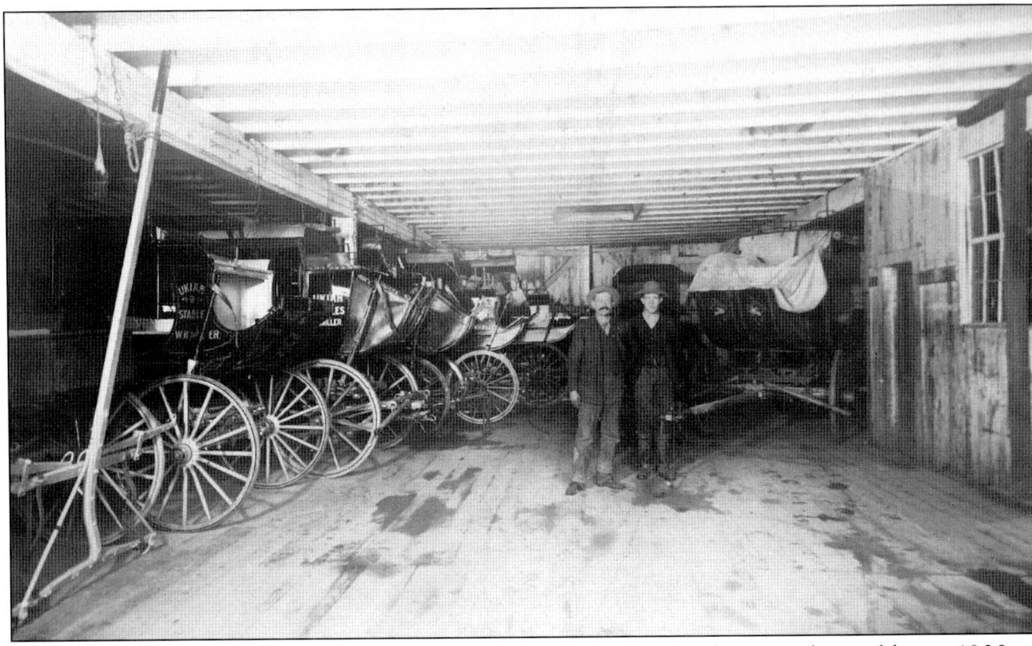

William H. Miller, on the left, and eight of his stagecoaches are shown at his stables in 1900.

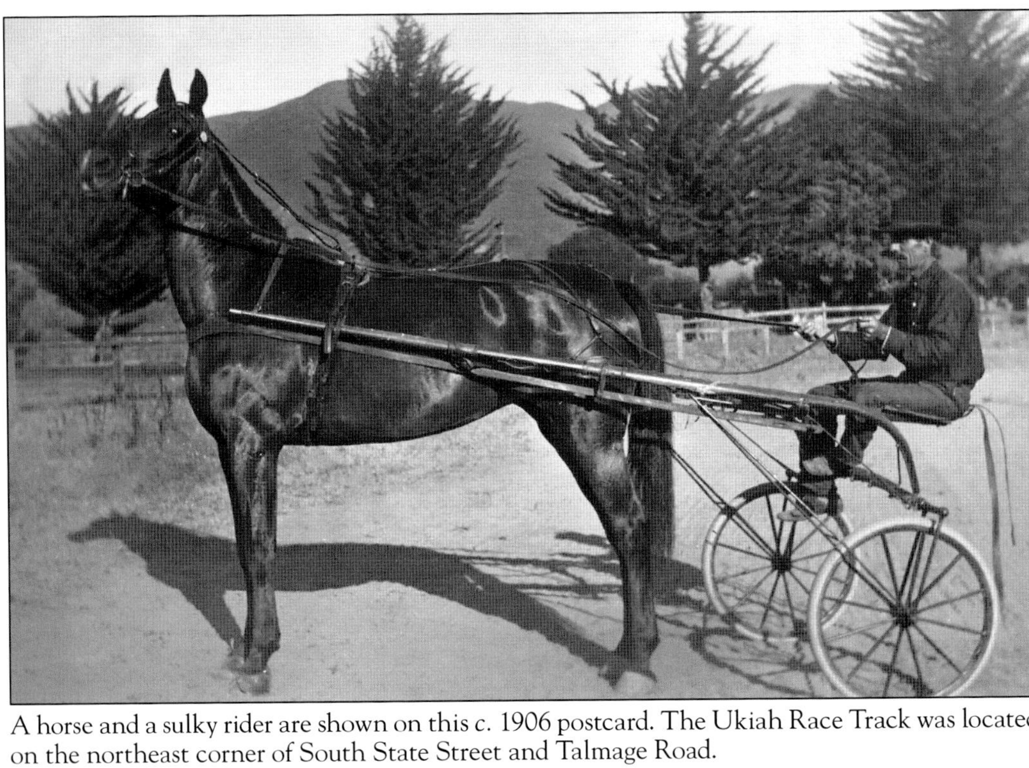

A horse and a sulky rider are shown on this *c.* 1906 postcard. The Ukiah Race Track was located on the northeast corner of South State Street and Talmage Road.

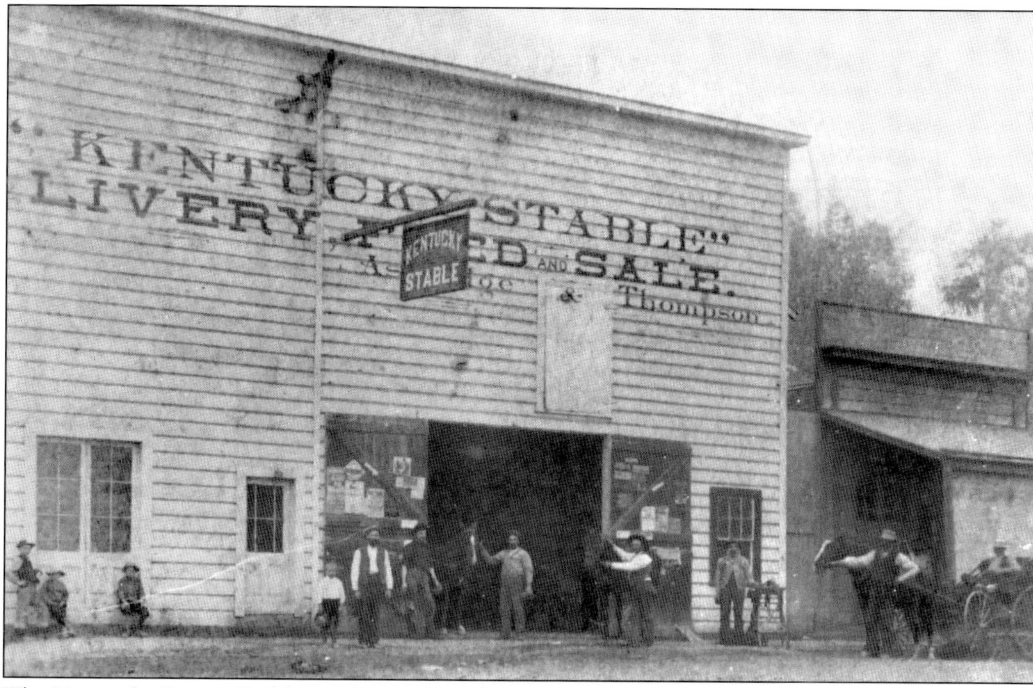

The Kentucky Livery Stable was located on the corner of State and Stephenson Streets. Asbridge and Thompson, owners, were in business from September 1888 to September 1892. This picture shows feed for sale around 1889.

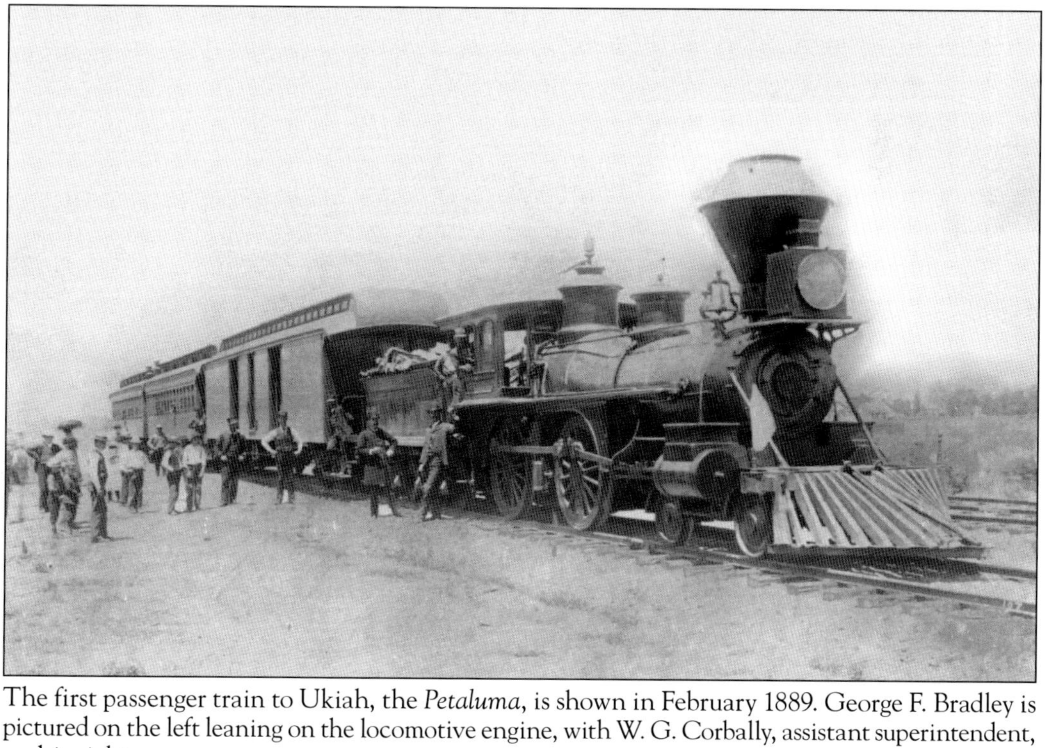

The first passenger train to Ukiah, the *Petaluma*, is shown in February 1889. George F. Bradley is pictured on the left leaning on the locomotive engine, with W. G. Corbally, assistant superintendent, on his right.

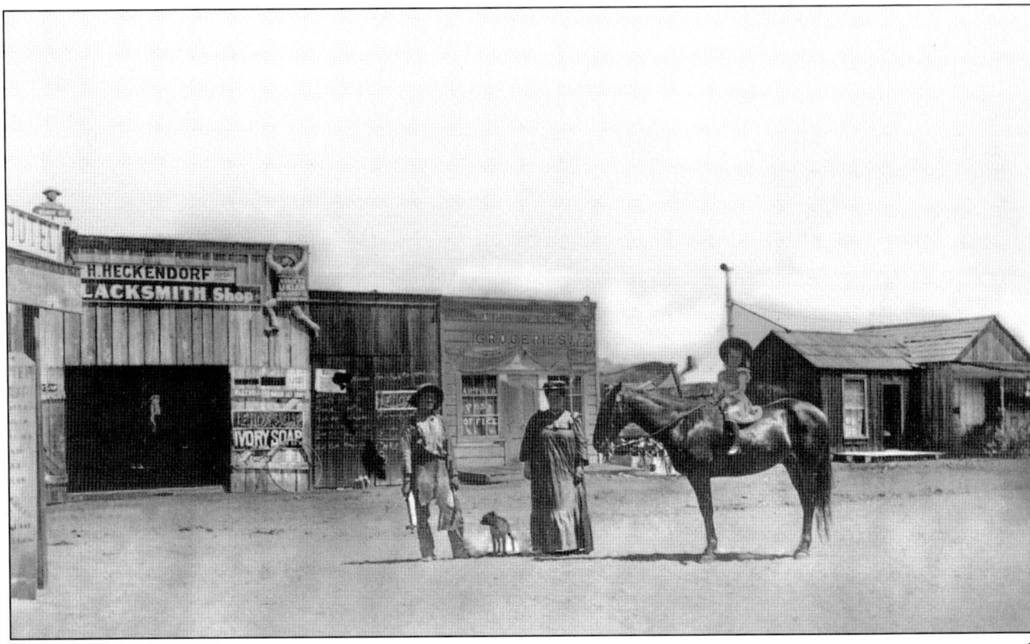

At the Arthur Post Office, Henry H. Heckendorf, the first postmaster, is shown in 1904 with his wife, Ida, and daughter Louella (on the horse). This is now the location of the Forks, a short distance north of Ukiah.

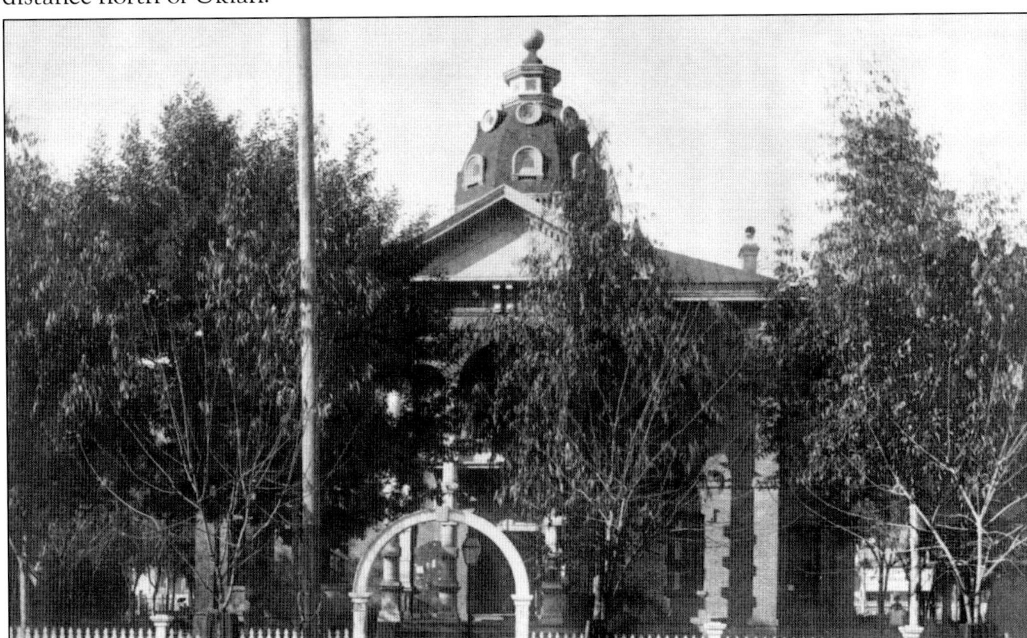

This view shows the Ukiah Courthouse in 1889. The flagpole on the left was erected in 1886. A high wind blew it down on July 4, 1890. The courthouse in this photograph was demolished in 1949.

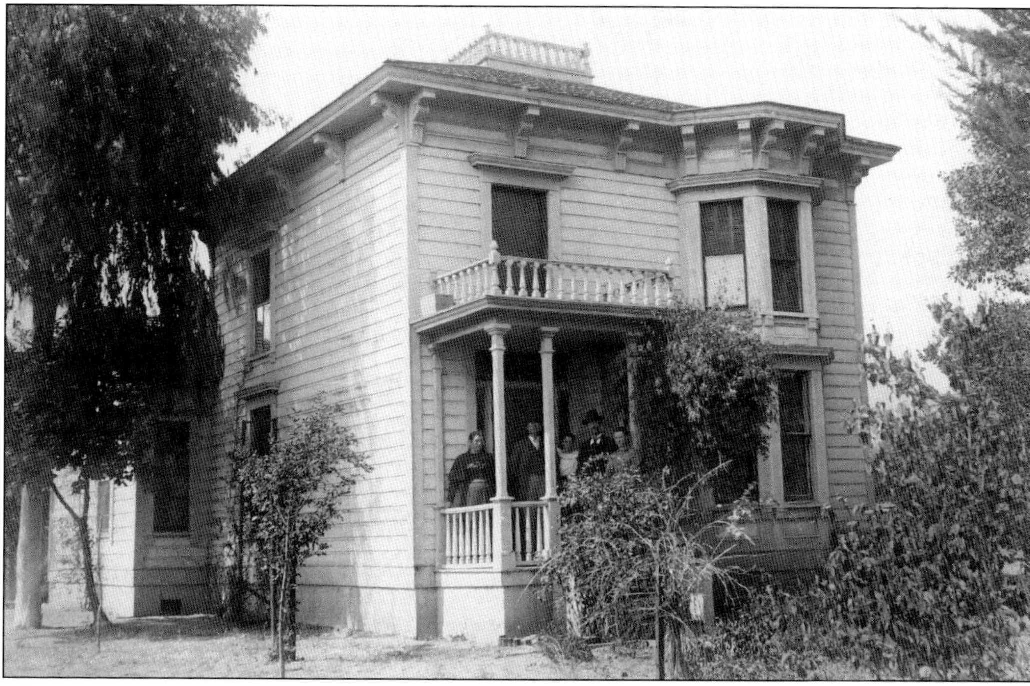

This was the home of Amanda Poage at 1000 North Oak Street. It is an Italianate house built in 1879.

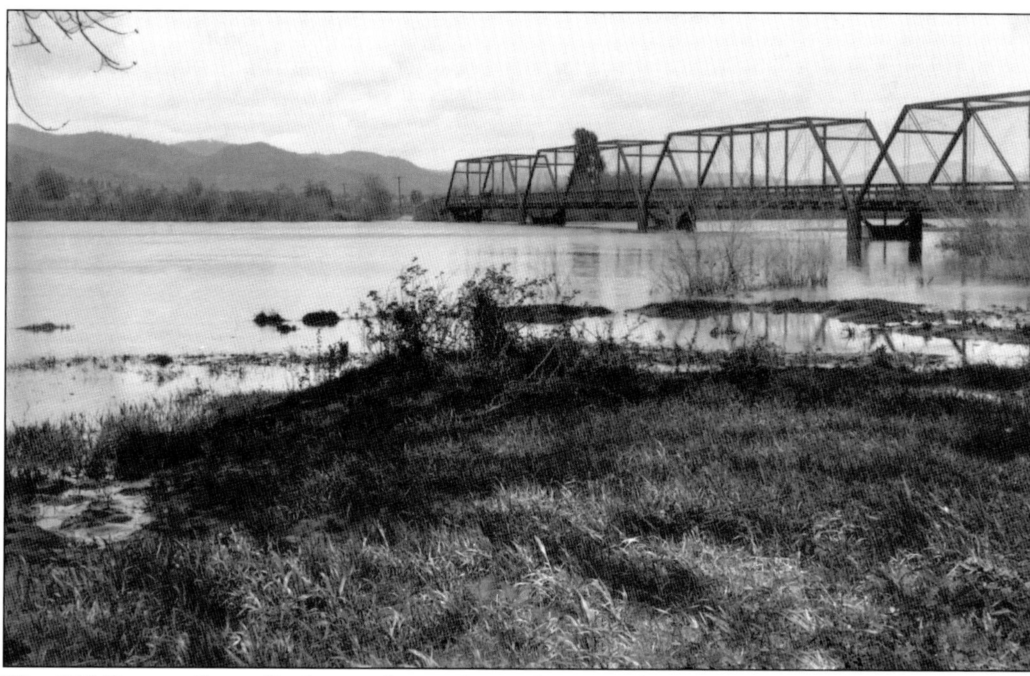

The Old Russian River Bridge on the road to Talmage is shown around 1908 during a flood of the Russian River.

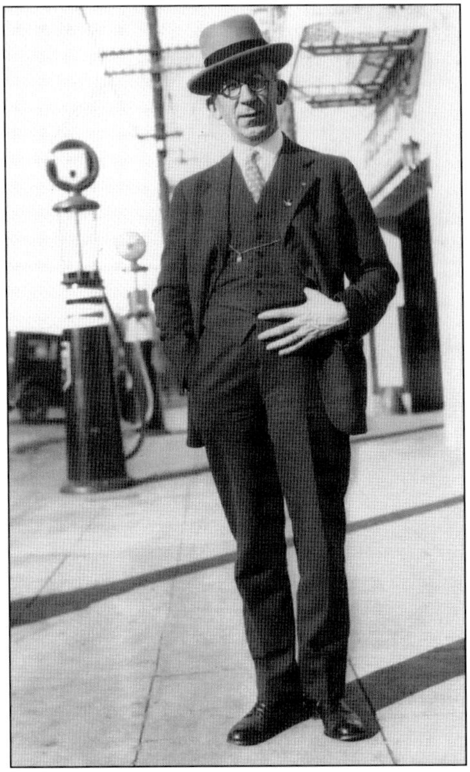

Local attorney Keith Eversole is shown in the 1920s. Eversole was born in Ukiah in November 1888. He practiced law for several years in Ukiah and then moved to San Francisco, where he continued his law practice. He died in December 1973.

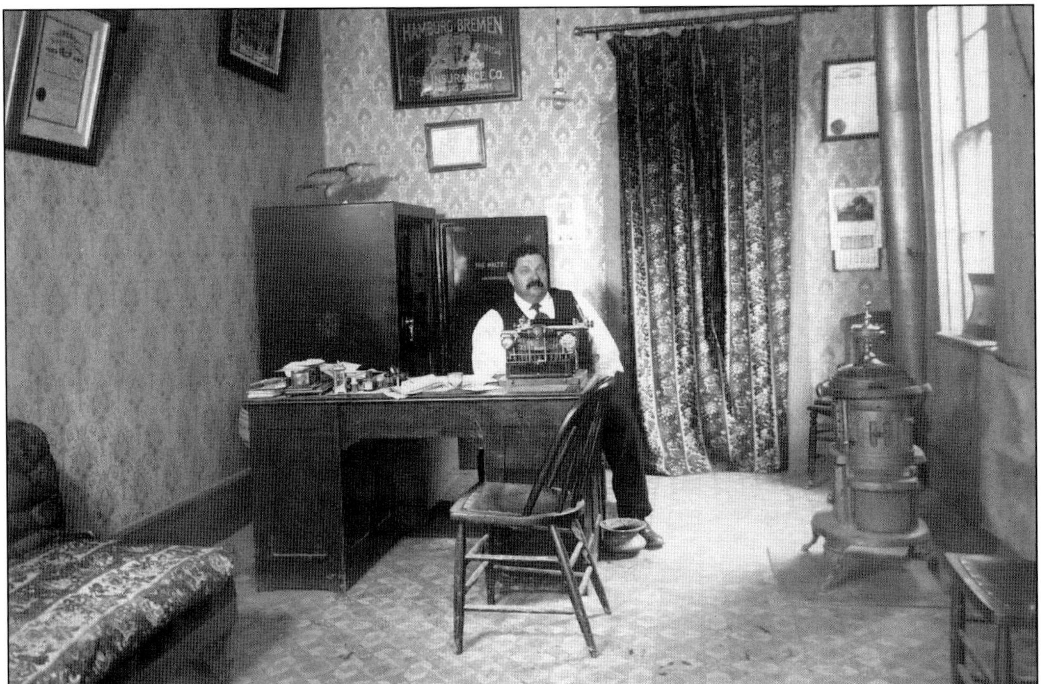

This 1905 image shows the Frank C. Albertson Insurance Office. Albertson's insurance office was located on the northeast corner of South State and Church Streets.

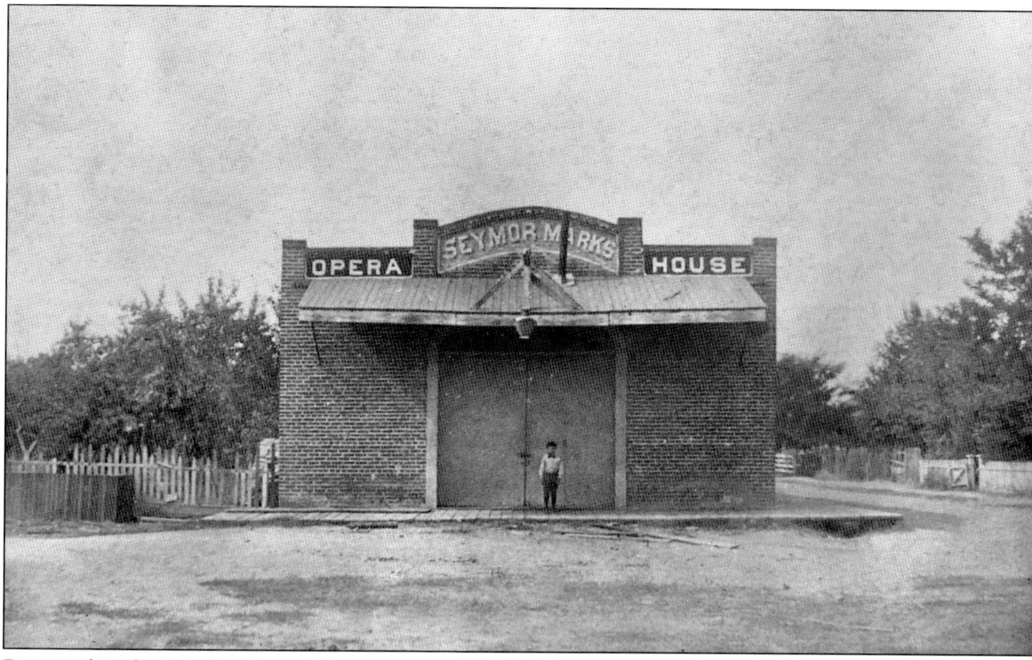

Pictured is the Marks Opera House around 1892. The opera house was located on the northwest corner of School and Henry Streets. The building was torn down in 1912. It served as an opera house, a cultural center, and a venue for roller skating.

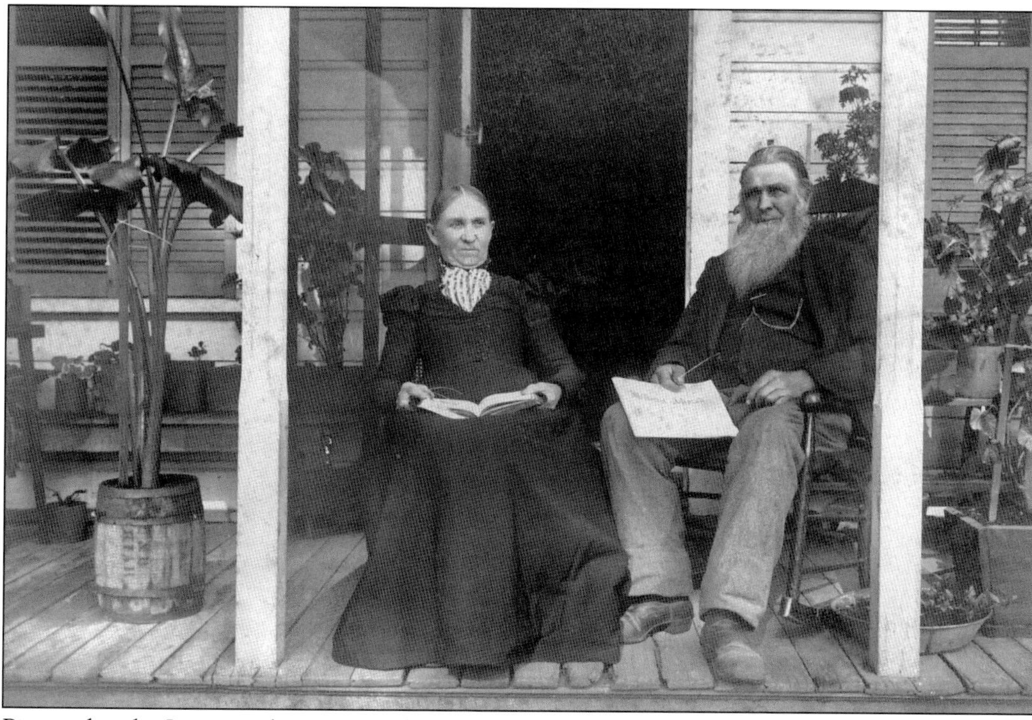

Pictured is the Luce residence around 1900. Charles and Helen Luce are shown in front of their home. Charles Luce was the owner of many acres of land on South Dora Street. Luce Avenue and Helen Avenue were named after the family.

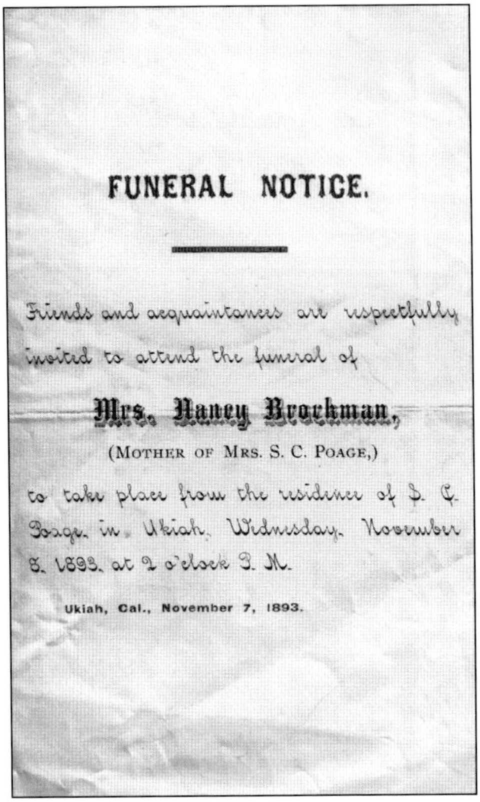

FUNERAL NOTICE.

Friends and acquaintances are respectfully invited to attend the funeral of

Mrs. Nancy Brockman,

(MOTHER OF MRS. S. C. POAGE,)

to take place from the residence of S. C. Poage, in Ukiah, Wednesday, November 8, 1893, at 2 o'clock P. M.

Ukiah, Cal., November 7, 1893.

This funeral notice from November 7, 1893, is for Nancy Brockman, the mother of Mrs. Simeon C. Poage.

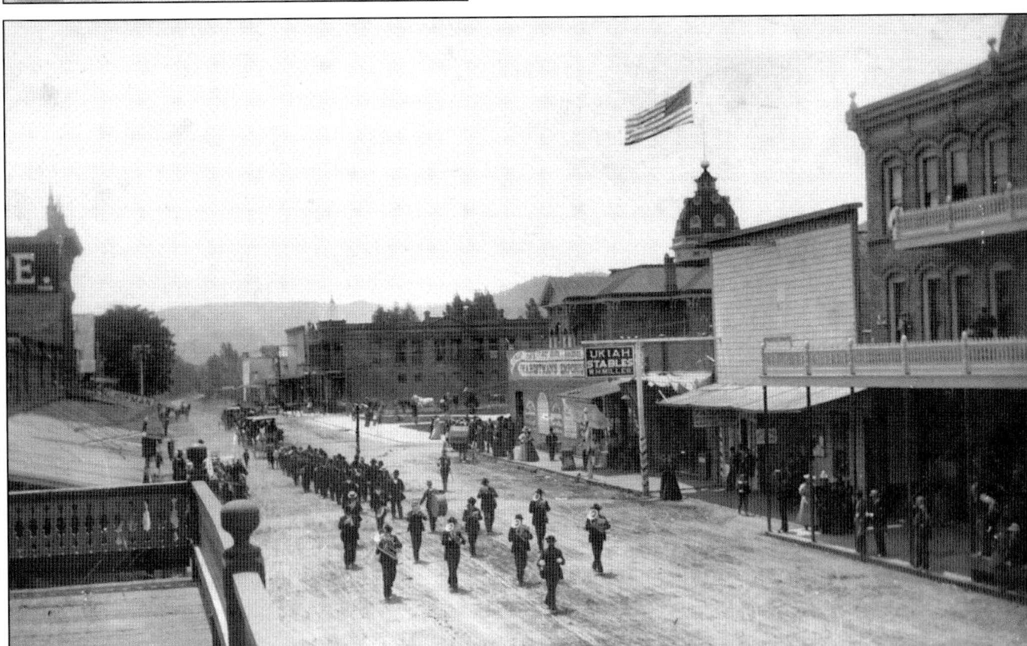

The funeral procession for Rev. Harrison Price is shown on August 8, 1895. Reverend Price was an educator and pastor of the Christian church. He was a member of the board of educators for many years.

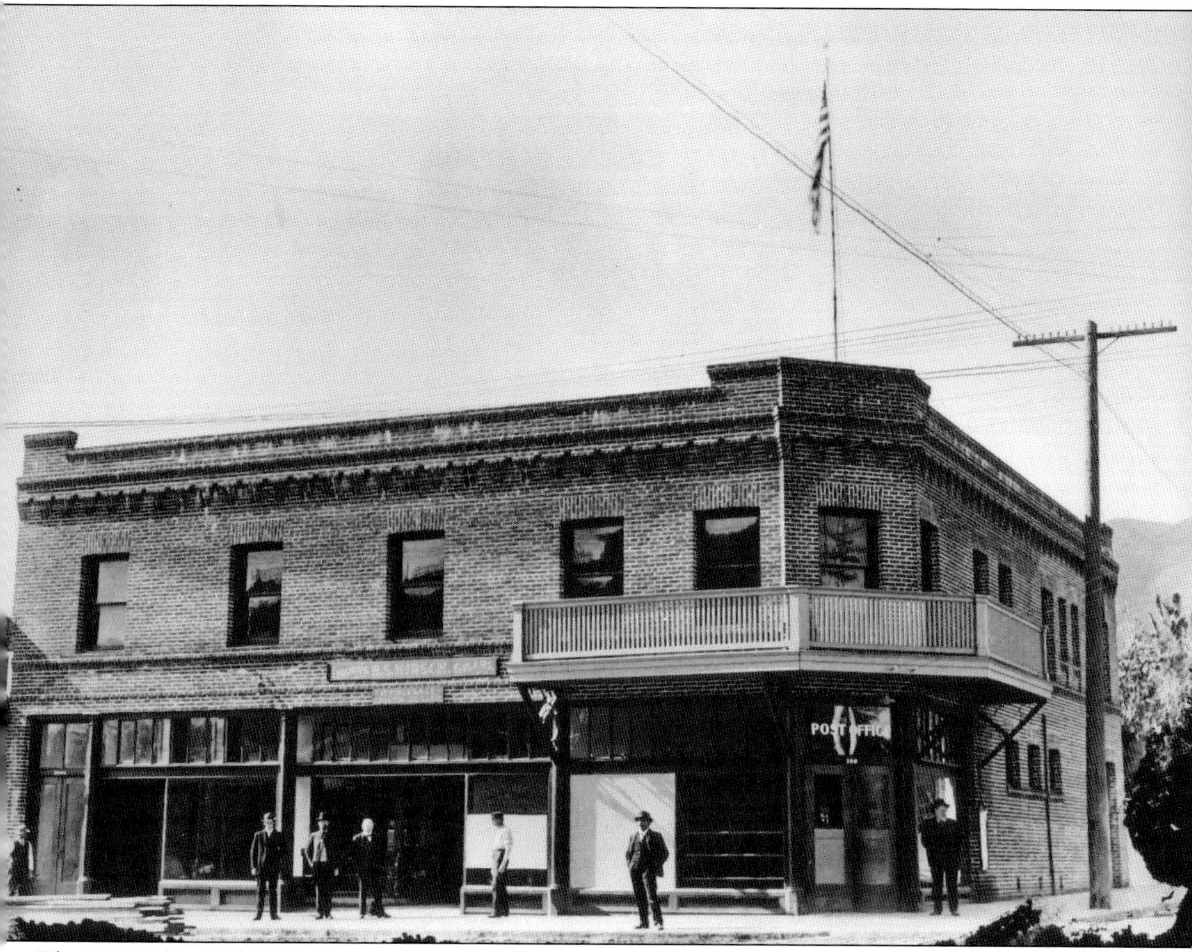

The McKinley Building is pictured in 1909. The McKinley Building was constructed in 1908 and served as the location of the Ukiah Post Office from September 1908 to October 1909.

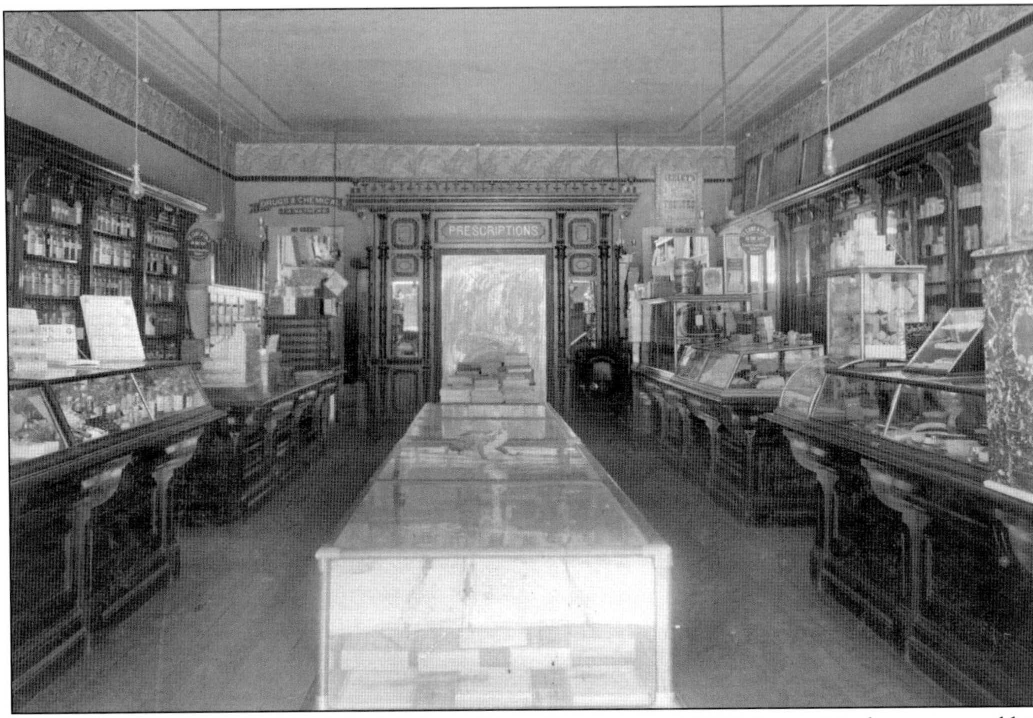

Pictured is the interior of the J. R. Mathews Drug Store around 1900. James Mathews opened his drugstore in September 1882, finally selling out in 1918.

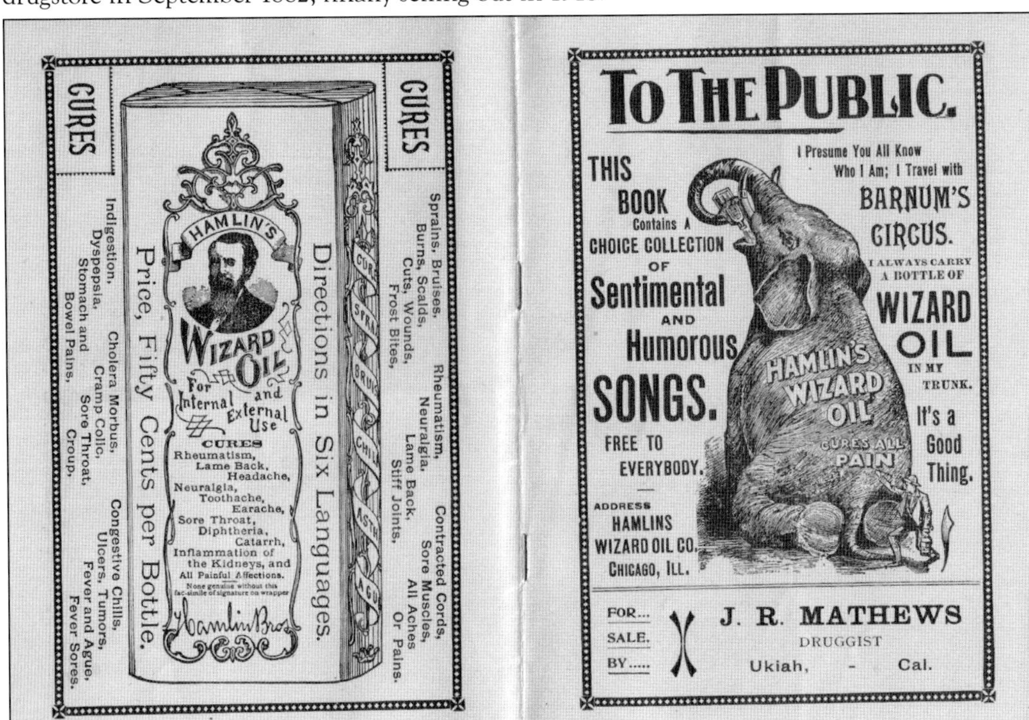

This advertisement from druggist J. R. Mathews features an elephant. (Courtesy of Ed Bold.)

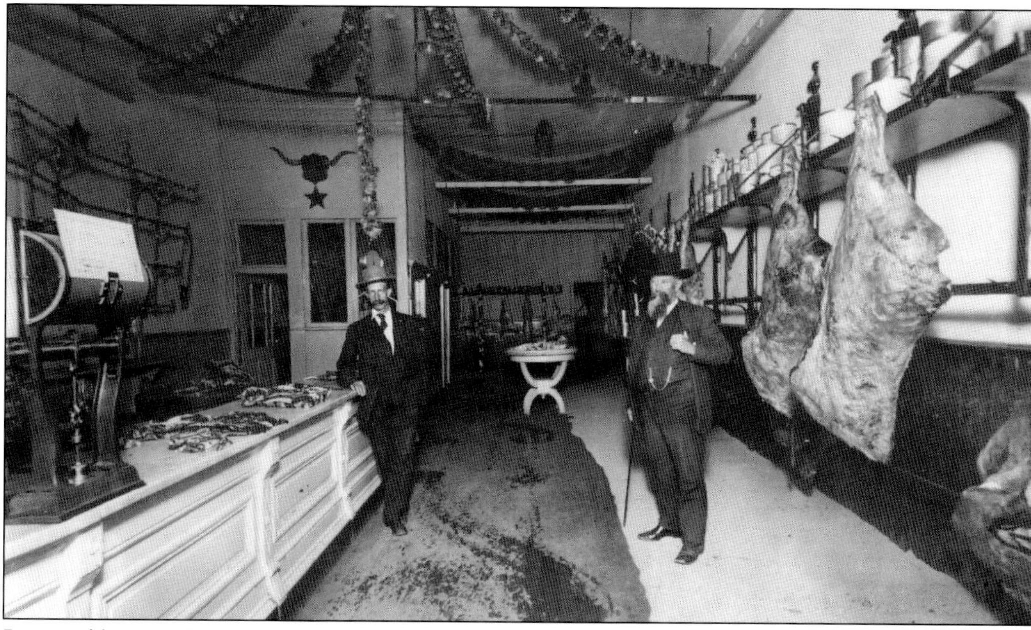

Pictured here is the City Market in August 1909. Fred Smith (left) and L. P. Smith are pictured. This is now the location of the Forest Club on North State Street.

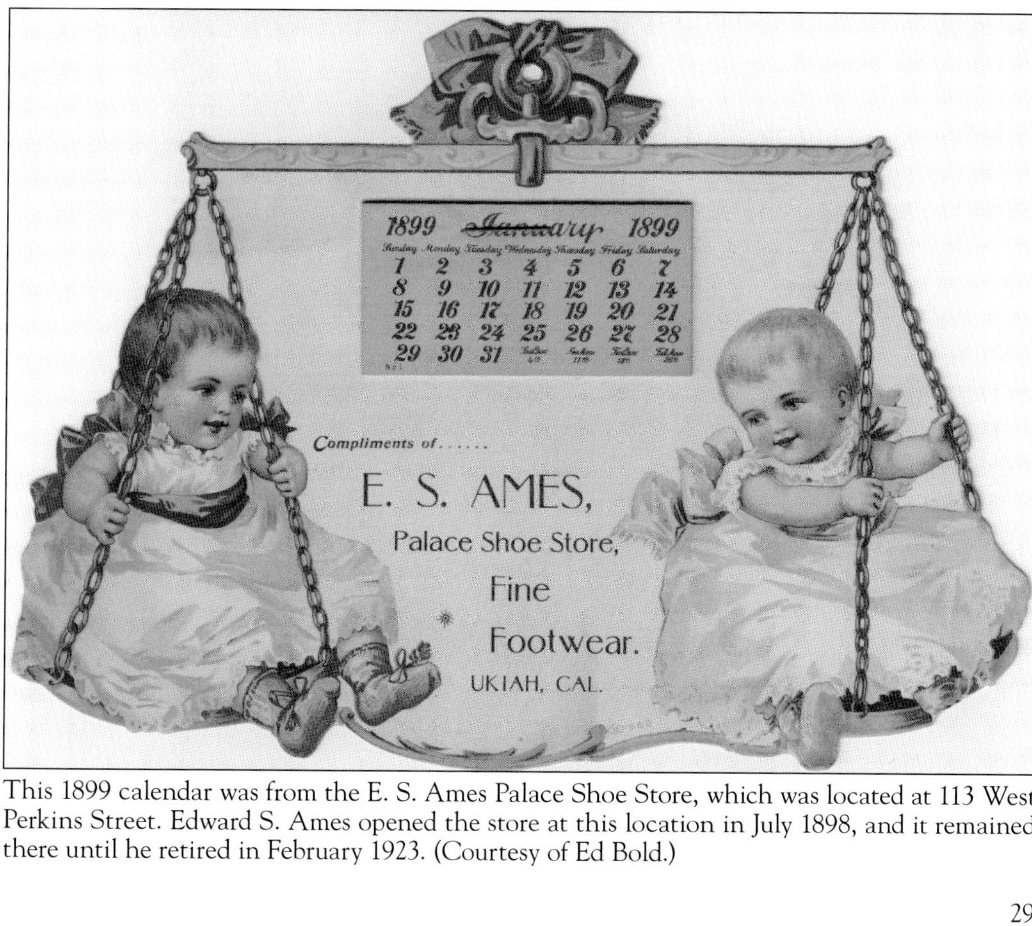

This 1899 calendar was from the E. S. Ames Palace Shoe Store, which was located at 113 West Perkins Street. Edward S. Ames opened the store at this location in July 1898, and it remained there until he retired in February 1923. (Courtesy of Ed Bold.)

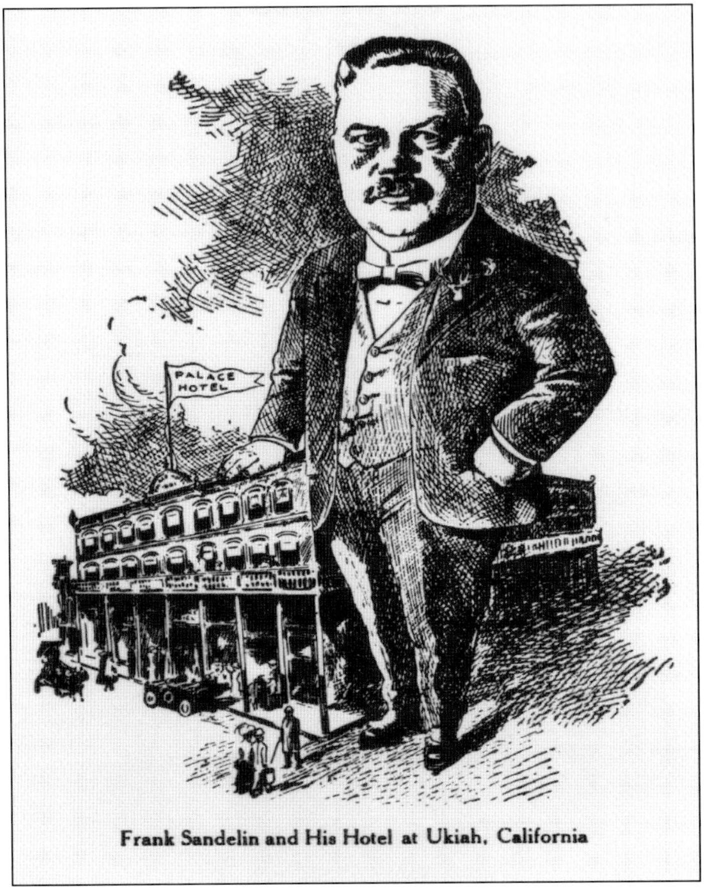

Frank Sandelin and his hotel, the Palace, are shown in 1913. This cartoon of Frank Sandelin was made by a traveling man who came to Ukiah and sold postcards. He would make cartoon drawings of all the local businessmen and then sell them postcards. (Courtesy of Ed Bold.)

The Carpenters' Ukiah Home Gallery is featured around 1872. A. O. and Helen Carpenter build their home on the northeast corner of State and Clay Streets, a short block from where the Grace Hudson Museum and Sun House now stand. (Photograph by A. O. Carpenter; courtesy of the Grace Hudson Museum.)

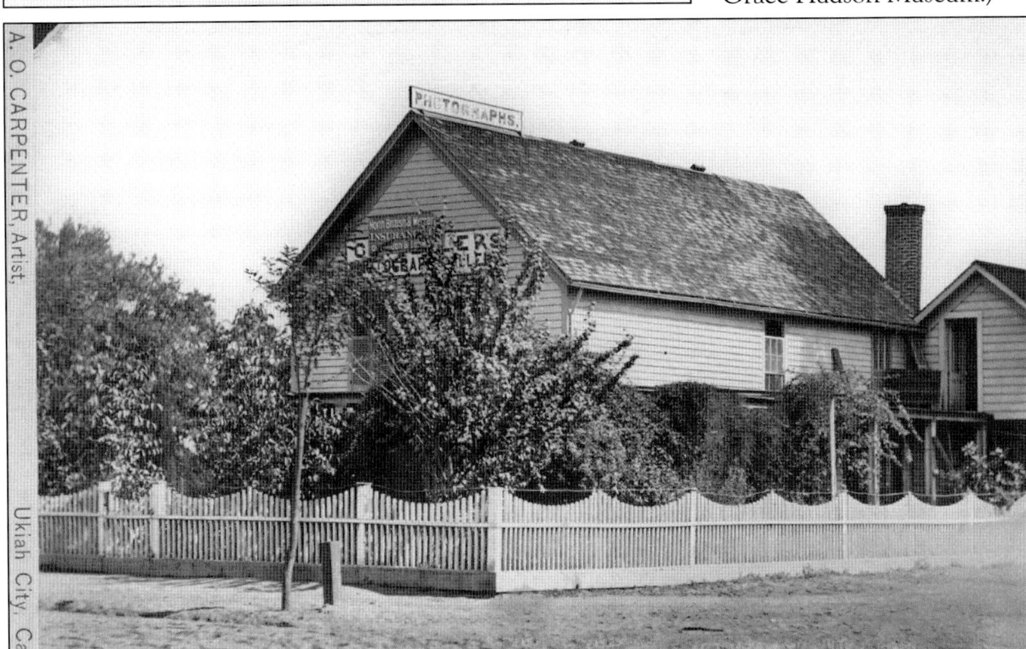

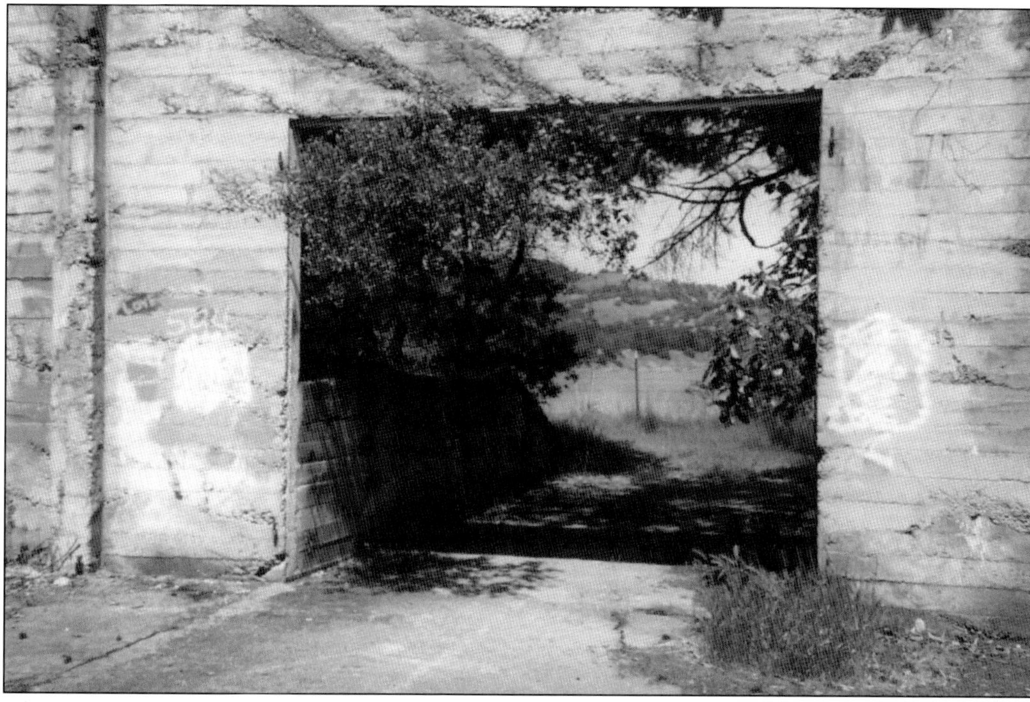

The Garzini Winery was located on Vinegar Hill. During Prohibition, the government forced local wineries to dump their wine down the hill. Hence the area became known as Vinegar Hill, overlooking Lake Mendocino.

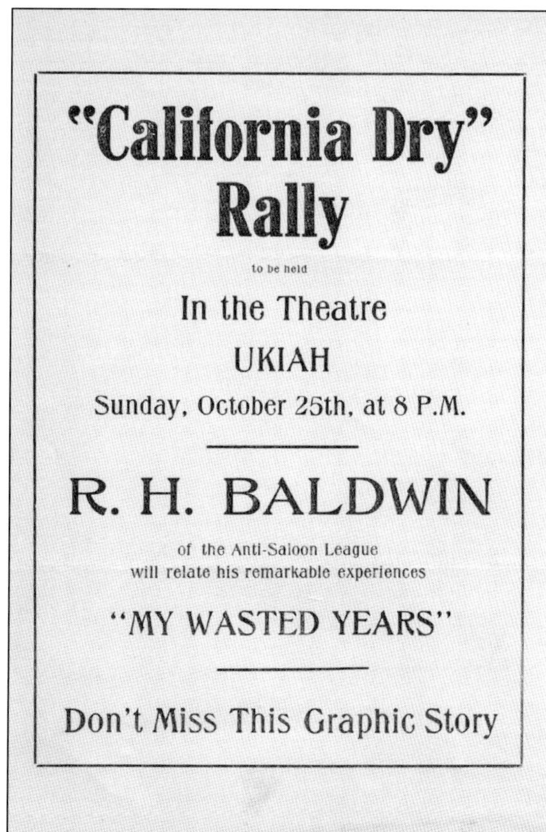

A California "dry rally" was held on October 25, 1914. It was an anti-saloon rally held in Ukiah with R. H. Baldwin speaking on "My Wasted Years" and the evil of liquor. (Courtesy of Ed Bold.)

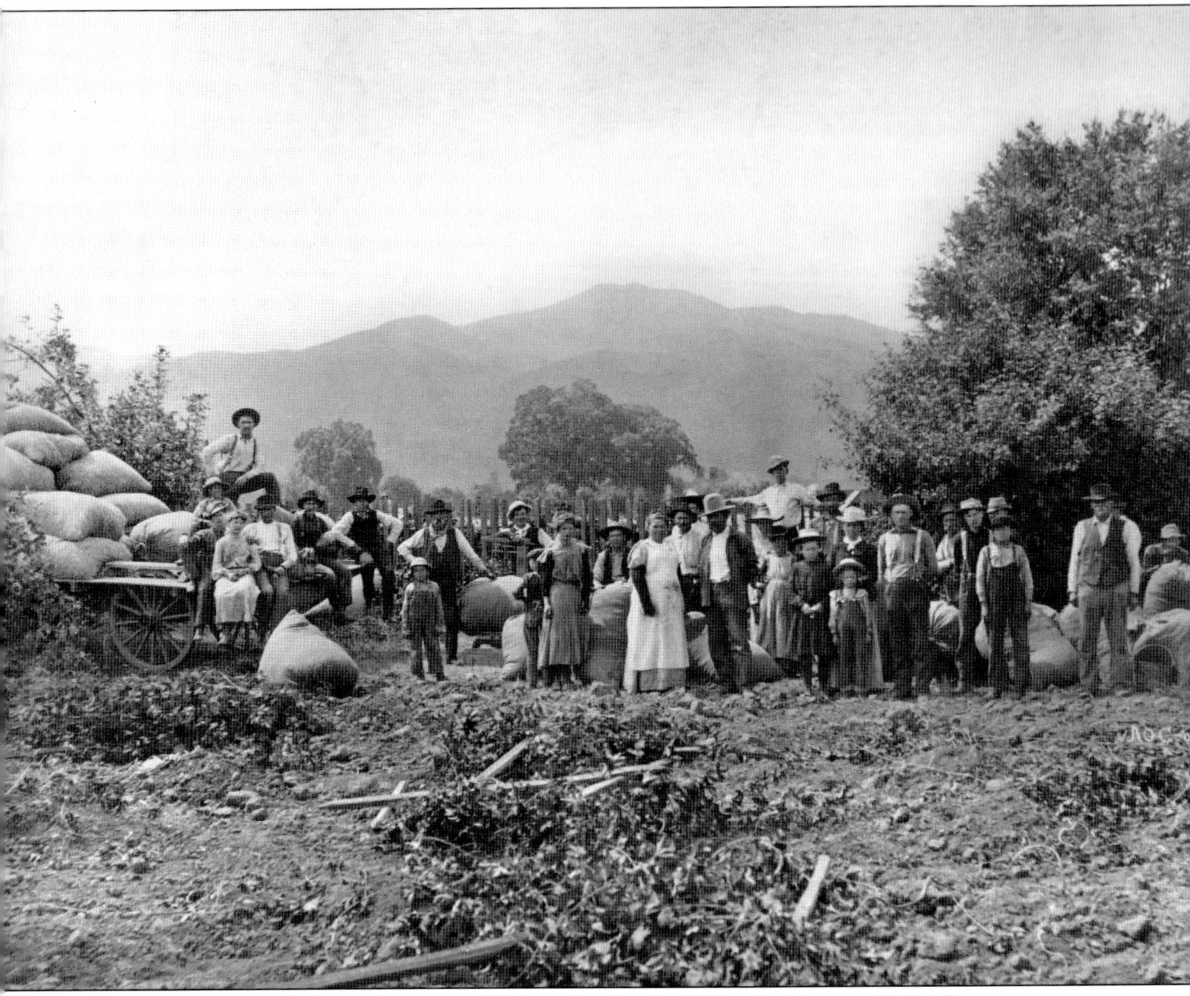

These hop pickers are shown in 1905 at the Sanford Hop Field east of Ukiah.

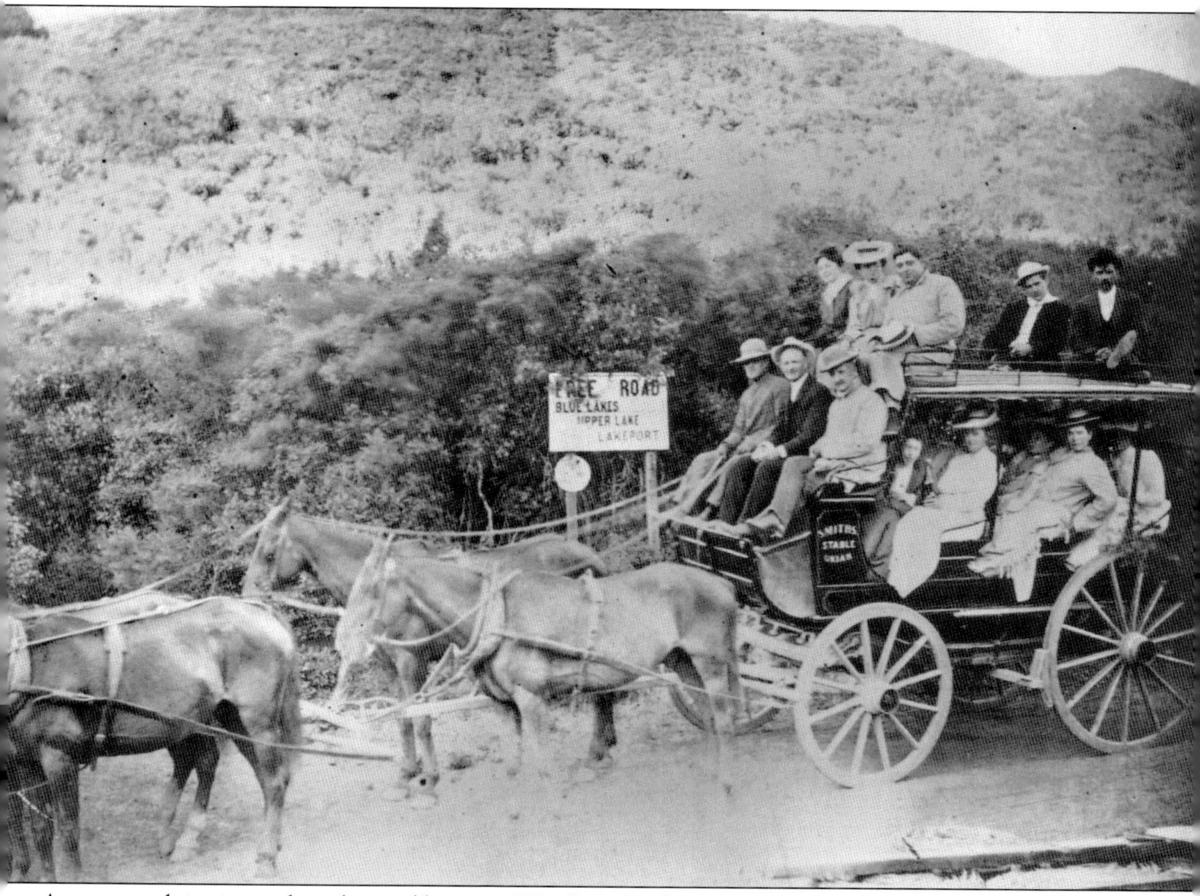

A stagecoach is pictured on the road between Ukiah and Lake County about 1903. The photograph shows the sign "Free Road" and the Smith's Livery Stables stagecoach.

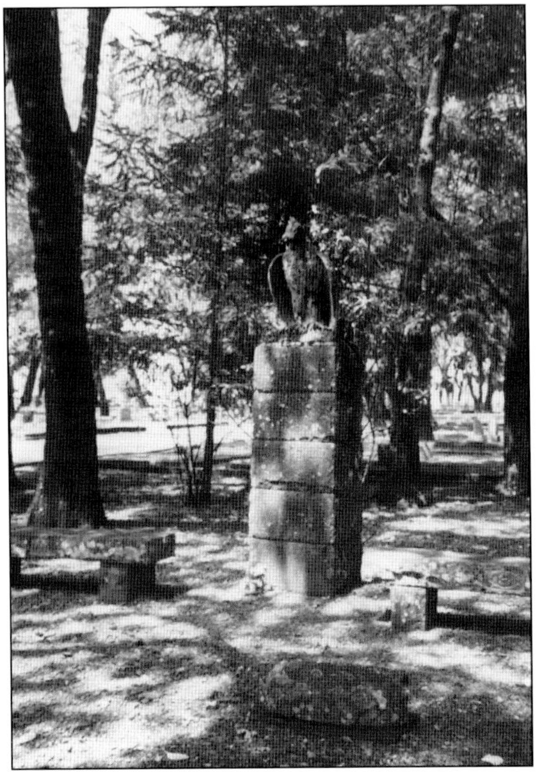

Pictured is the grave site of Grace Hudson at the Ukiah Cemetery. The site was designed by Grace Hudson in November 1934. The phoenix overlooking the grave site was carved by an artisan in Santa Rosa. Grace Hudson died in March 1937.

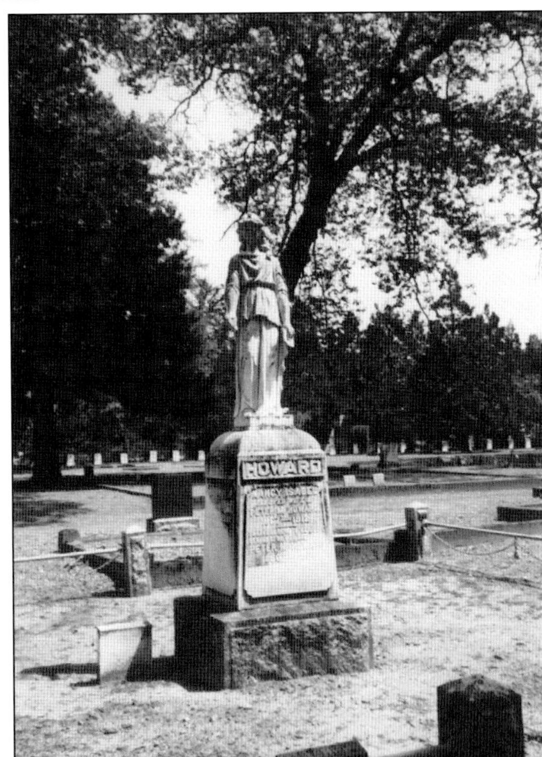

This monument is for Nancy Isabel Howard at the Ukiah Cemetery. She was born February 27, 1876, and died October 1, 1912. She was the wife of Peter M. Howard. This picture was taken in 1997.

Two

Schools, Churches, and Government

When Ukiah was founded in 1856, it was actually part of Sonoma County. In 1859, the state legislature created Mendocino County, and Ukiah was chosen as the county seat. A county courthouse was erected to provide for the entire county. A new courthouse replaced the original structure in 1872, and that was replaced by the present building in 1951, which stands at the corner of State and Perkins Streets.

The State Hospital for the Insane was located east of Ukiah in a town now called Talmage. Eventually the hospital was closed and the buildings and land became the City of Ten Thousand Buddhas, which is one of the largest Mahayana Buddhist communities in the Western Hemisphere. The jail and other county offices were moved over the years to Low Gap Road, where they are currently located.

The original Ukiah High School was built in 1894 and was located on North Spring Street. The present high school is located on Low Gap Road near the county offices. Each October, the school holds its annual homecoming week. Each class competes with rallies, skits, and a parade down State Street. The event culminates with the crowning of the homecoming king and queen during halftime at the football game.

Ukiah is a widely diverse community where one will find churches of all dominations within its boundaries.

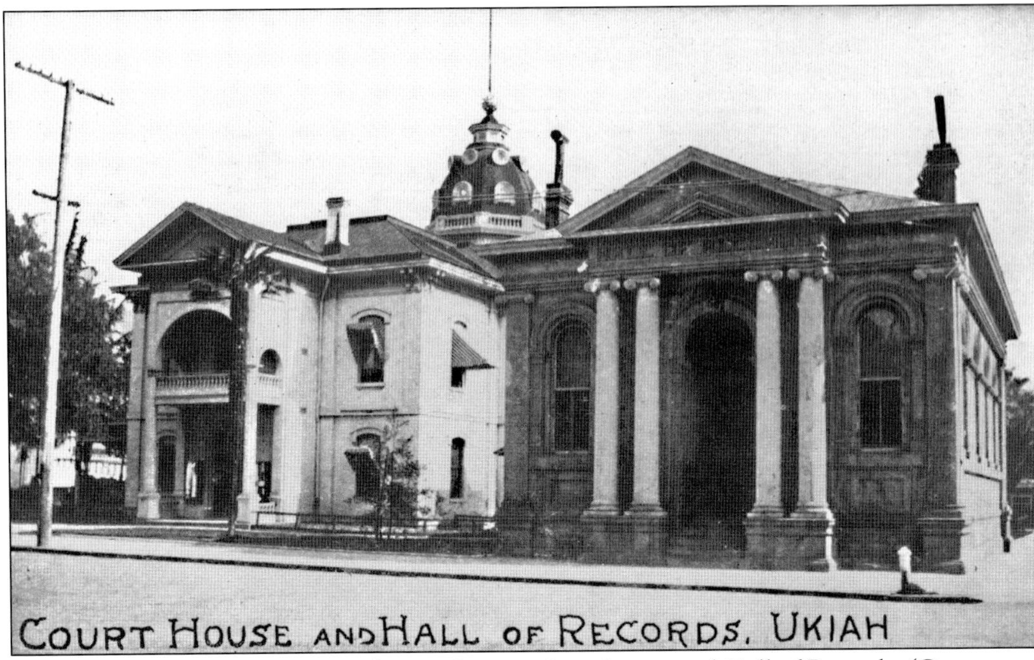

Pictured around 1920 is the Mendocino County Courthouse and Hall of Records. (Courtesy of Kelly Neighbors.)

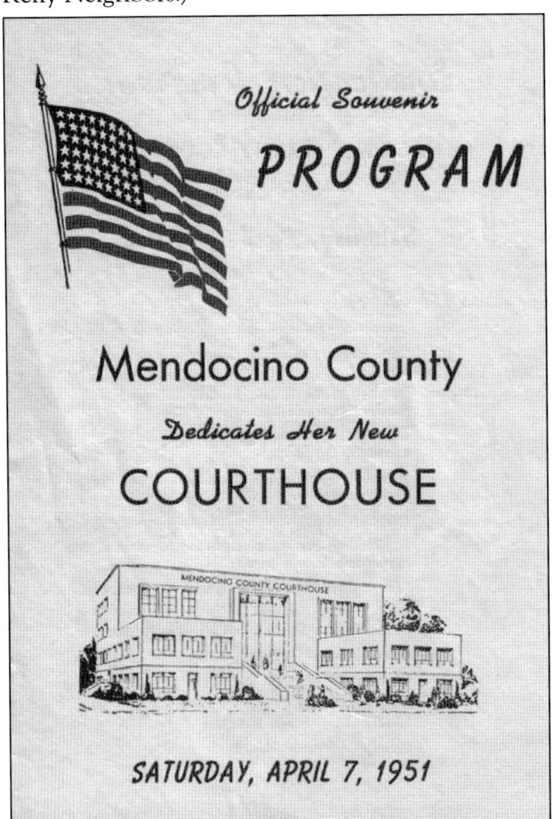

This program is from the Mendocino County Courthouse dedication on April 7, 1951. (Courtesy of Ed Bold.)

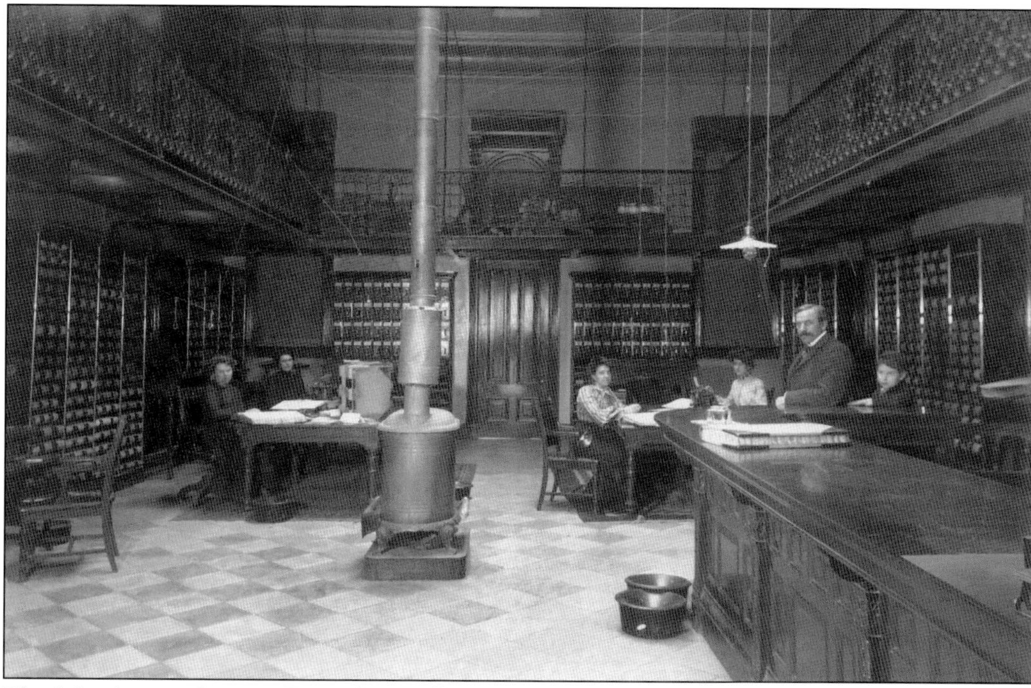

The Mendocino County Recorder's Office is shown about 1904. From left to right are Luella McCracken, Nora Ellis, Cornelia White, unidentified woman, recorder Pat Connolly, and unidentified child.

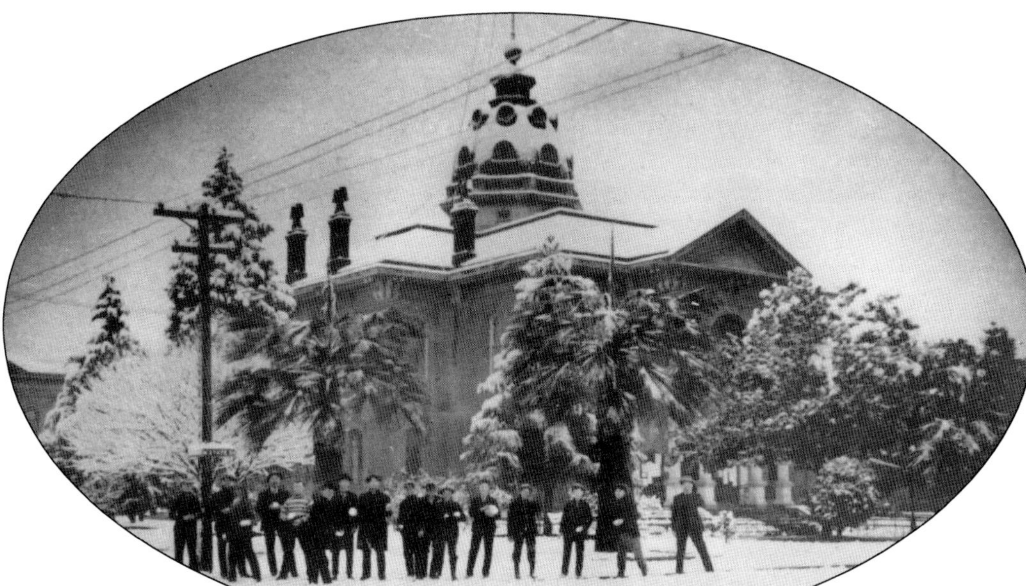

The courthouse is pictured here in January 1907. Ukiah was blanketed with over 6 inches of snow during the winter of 1907.

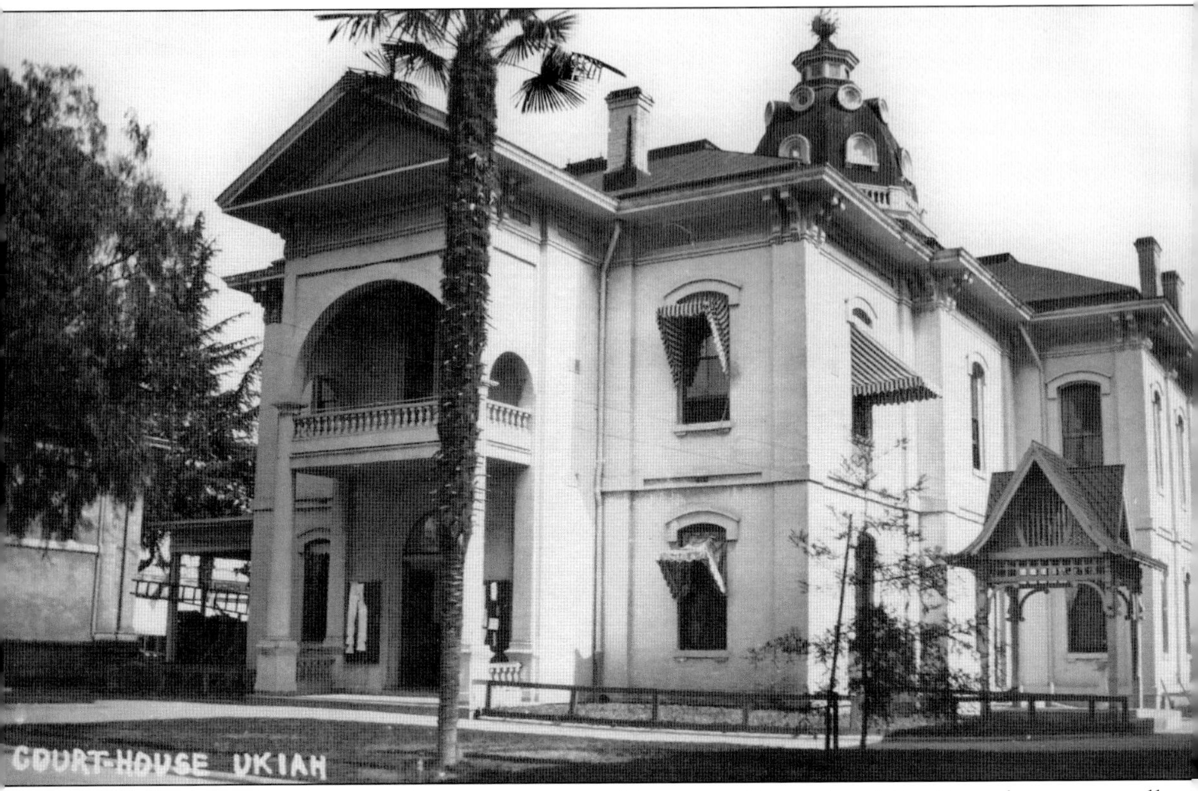

The west side of the courthouse is shown in this postcard from the 1920s. Note the ornate well house on the right.

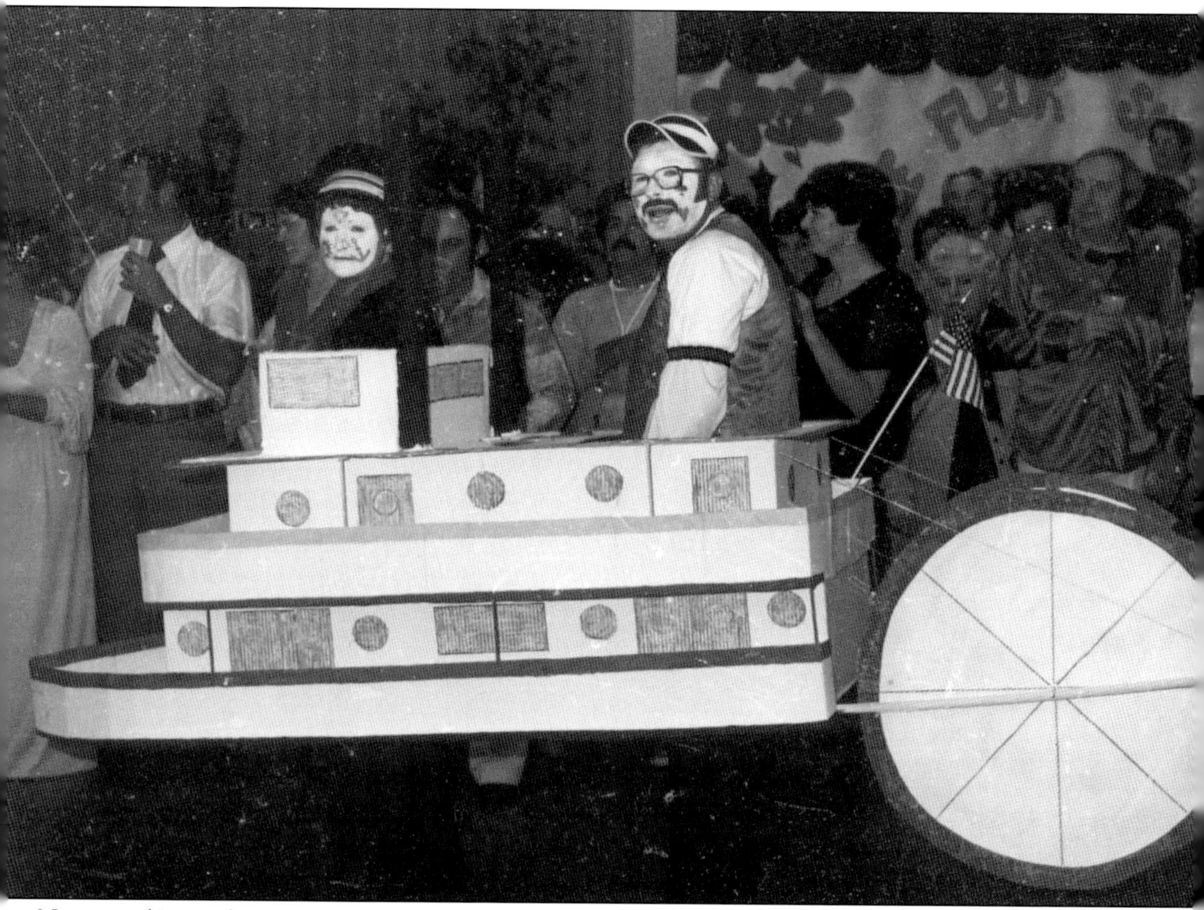

Nancy and Lee Adams are shown on February 5, 1977, at the eighth annual Mardi Gras celebration. St. Mary's Catholic School holds an annual Mardi Gras fund-raiser for the school each February. There are live auctions, games of chance (played with Monopoly money), dinner, and dancing.

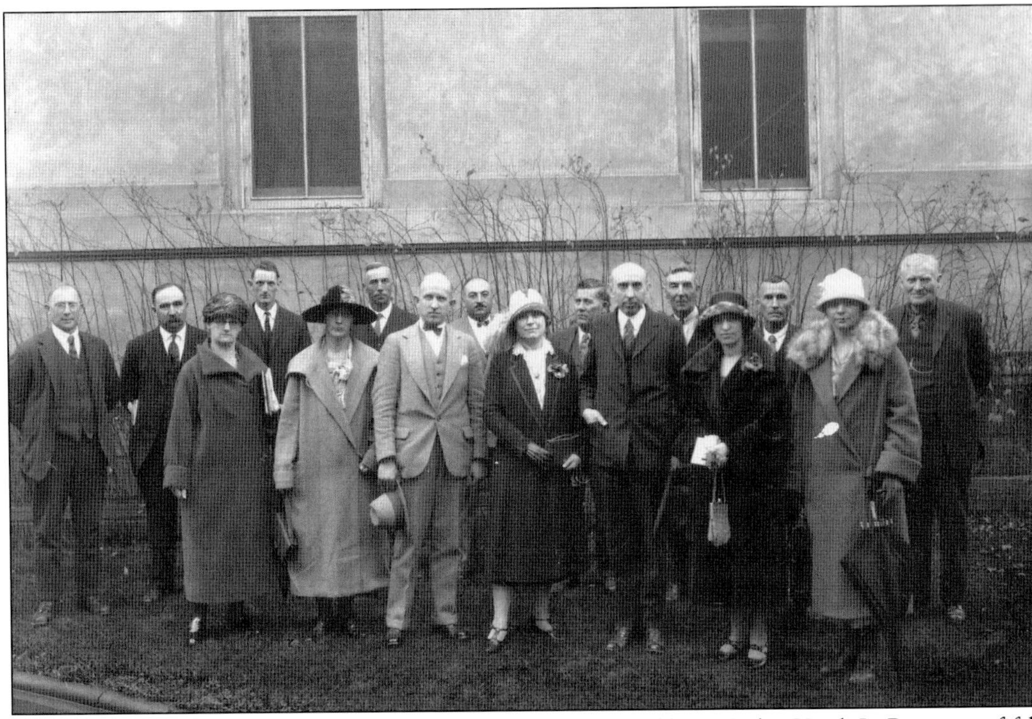

The Mendocino County Grand Jury of 1924–1925 is pictured here. Judge Hugh L. Preston is fifth from the left in the first row.

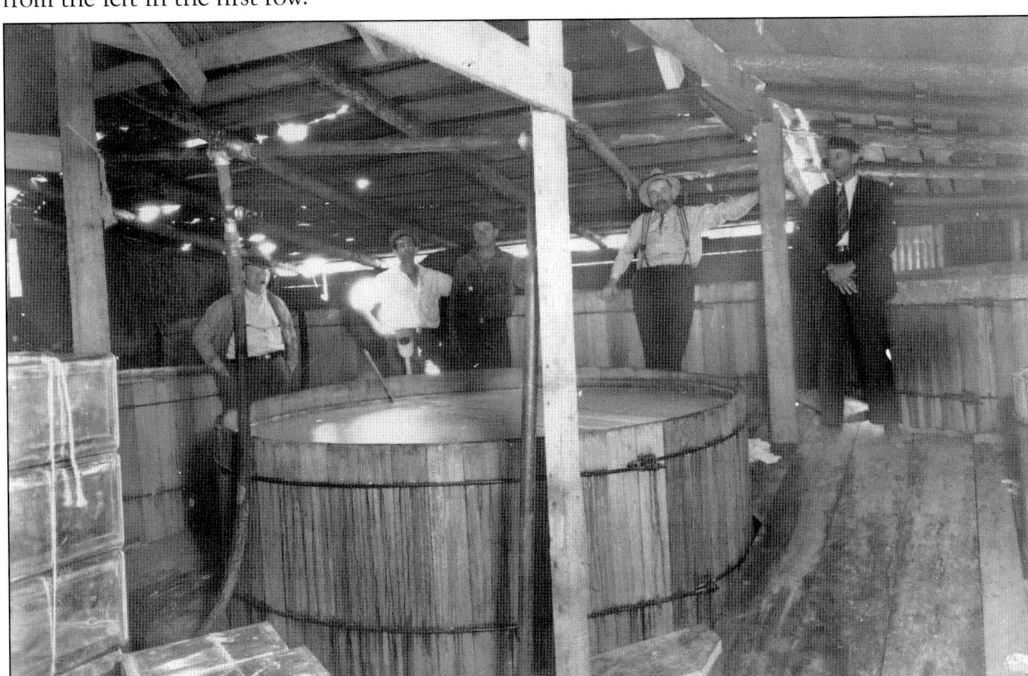

The sheriff and assistant district attorney break up a still, located between Boonville and the coast, in the early 1930s. From left to right are Henry Spurr, assistant district attorney; two unidentified workers; E. L. ("Dick") Williams, sheriff; and Earl Bishop, the deputy sheriff.

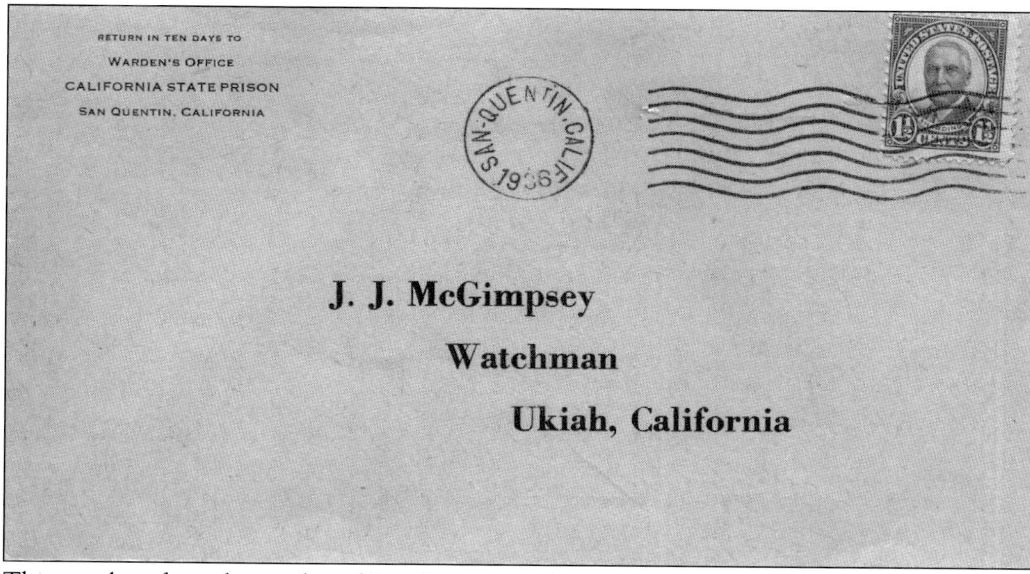

This envelope from the warden of San Quentin to the Ukiah watchman is postmarked 1936. The Ukiah watchman at the time was John J. McGimpsey. (Courtesy of Melody Mack.)

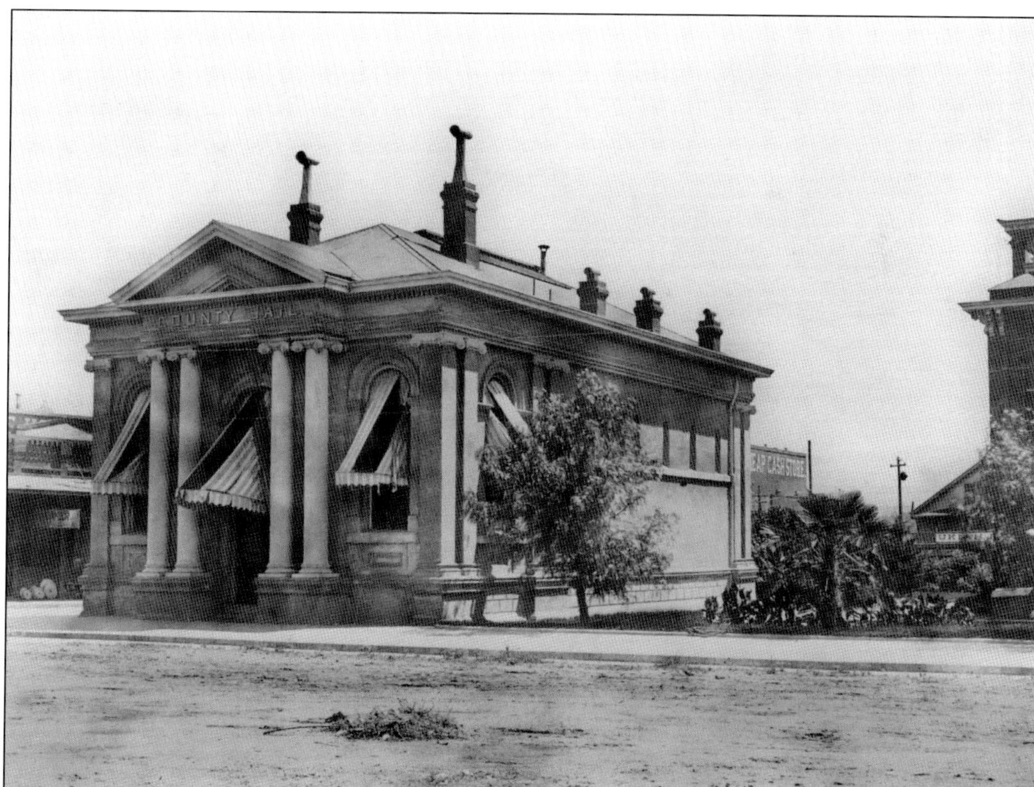

The Mendocino County Jail is shown around 1897. The county jail was built in 1892 and torn down in January 1951. It was located on the southeast corner of School and Standley Streets.

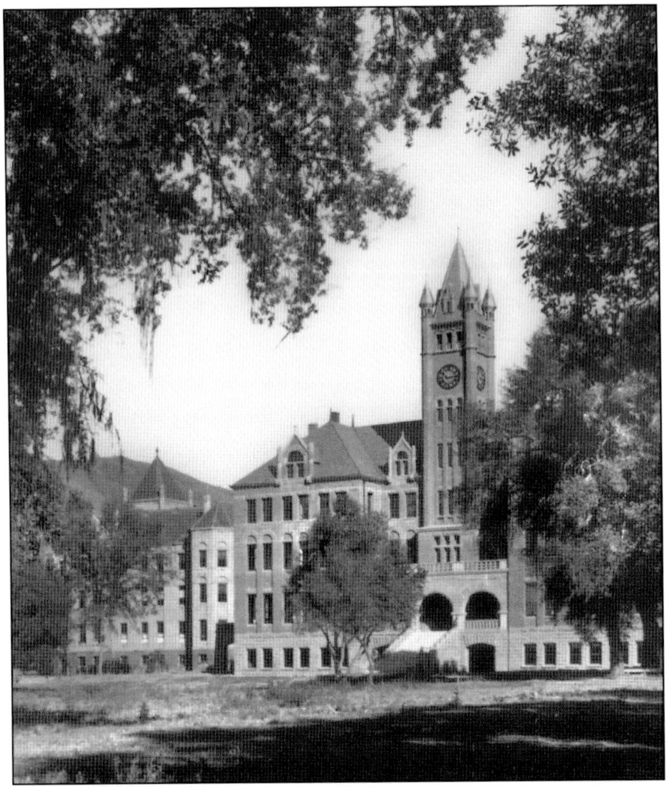

Pictured is the Mendocino State Hospital for the Insane in 1912. The hospital opened in December 1893 and closed in the early 1970s. The property was later sold by the county and became the City of Ten Thousand Buddhas. (Photograph by A. O. Carpenter; courtesy of Grace Hudson Museum.)

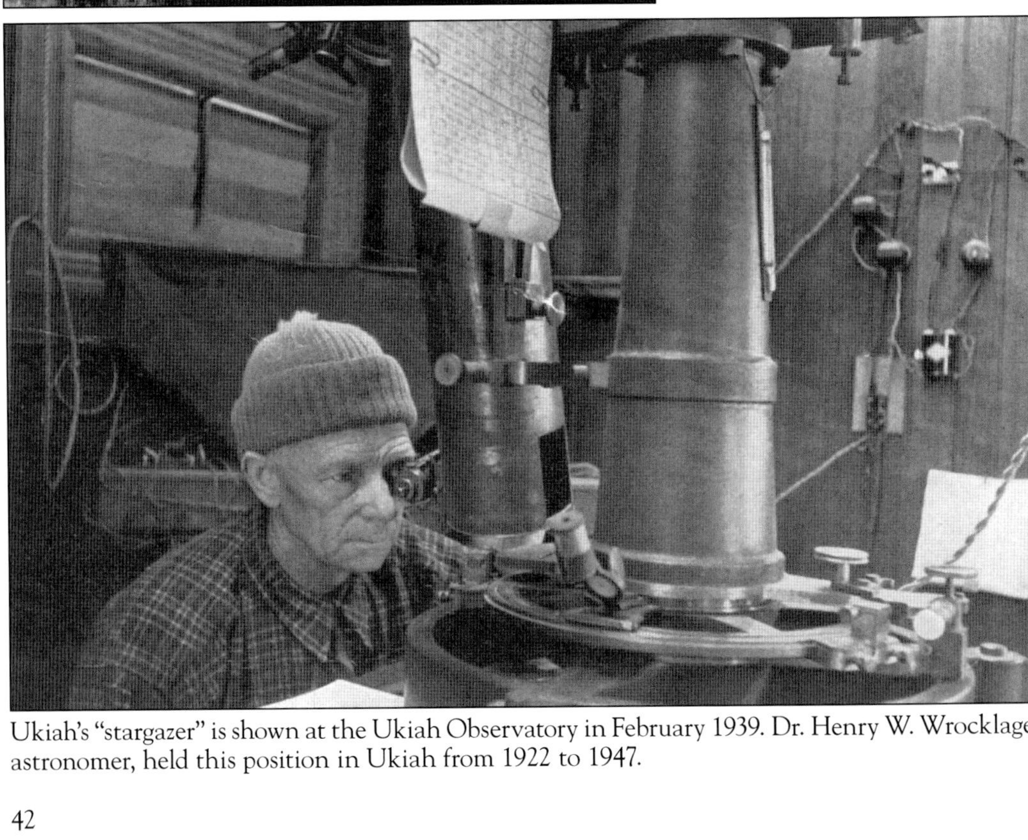

Ukiah's "stargazer" is shown at the Ukiah Observatory in February 1939. Dr. Henry W. Wrocklage, astronomer, held this position in Ukiah from 1922 to 1947.

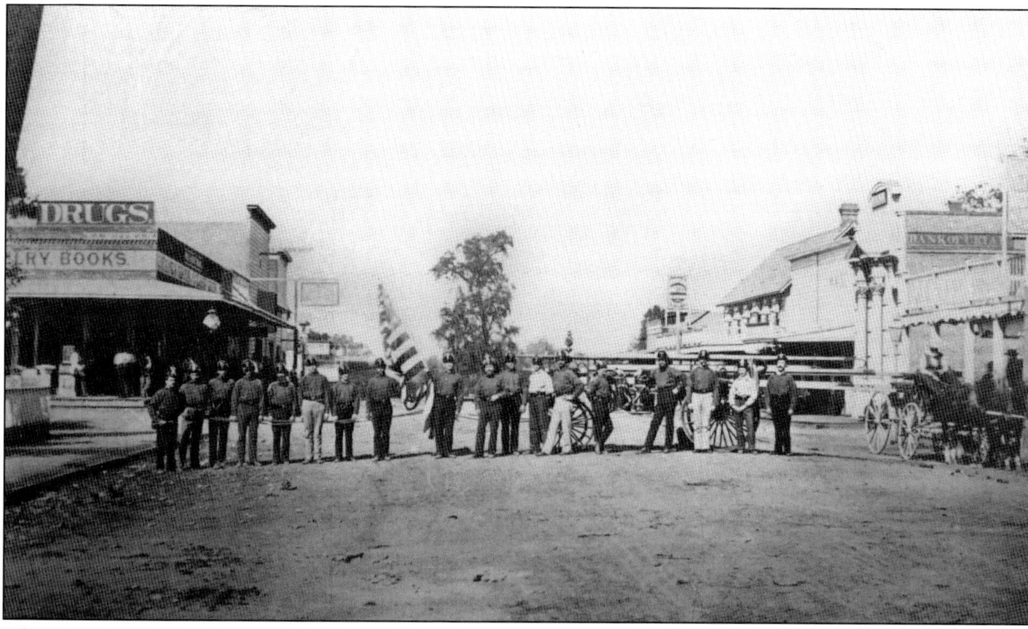

The Eagle Fire Department is assembled in front of the courthouse on State Street in 1878. The Eagle Fire Department was the first organized fire department in Ukiah.

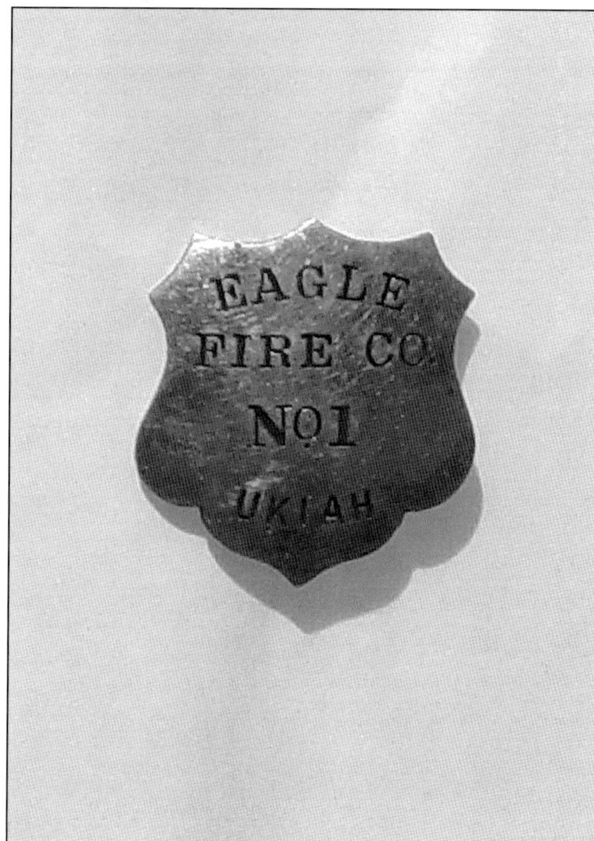

An Eagle Fire Department No. 1 badge is displayed here. (Courtesy of Ed Bold.)

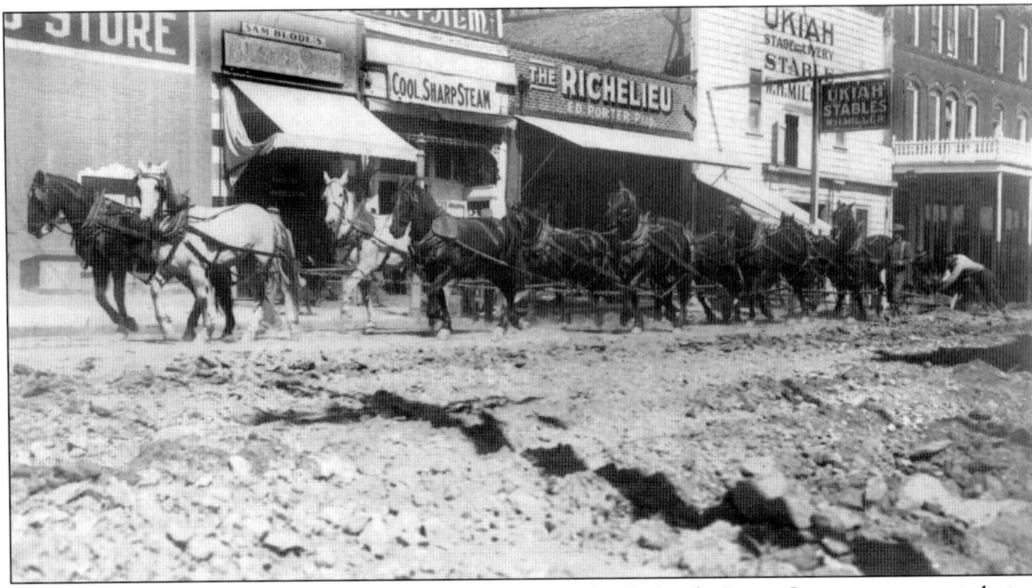

A 10-horse team is shown plowing up the 200 block of North State Street prior to it being paved. The photograph was taken in May 1911. The businesses from left to right are Gibson's Drug Store, Sam Blode's Barber Shop, Palm Saloon, Richelieu Saloon, Ukiah Stables, and the Palace Hotel.

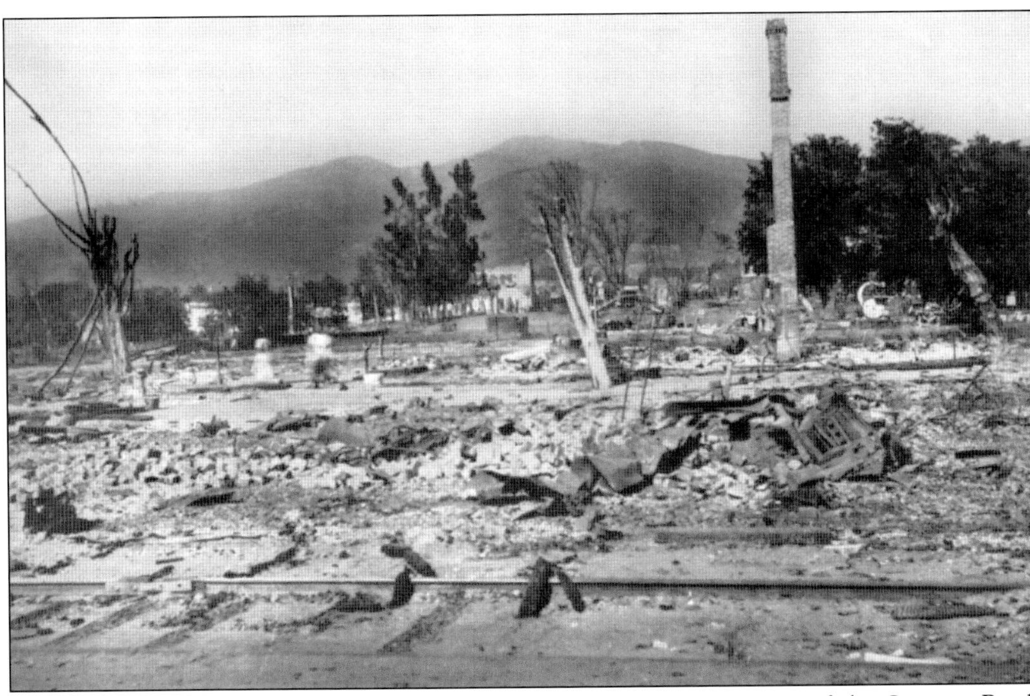

Shown here is a fire in downtown Ukiah on June 18, 1917. (Courtesy of the Savings Bank 1903–1953 anniversary book.)

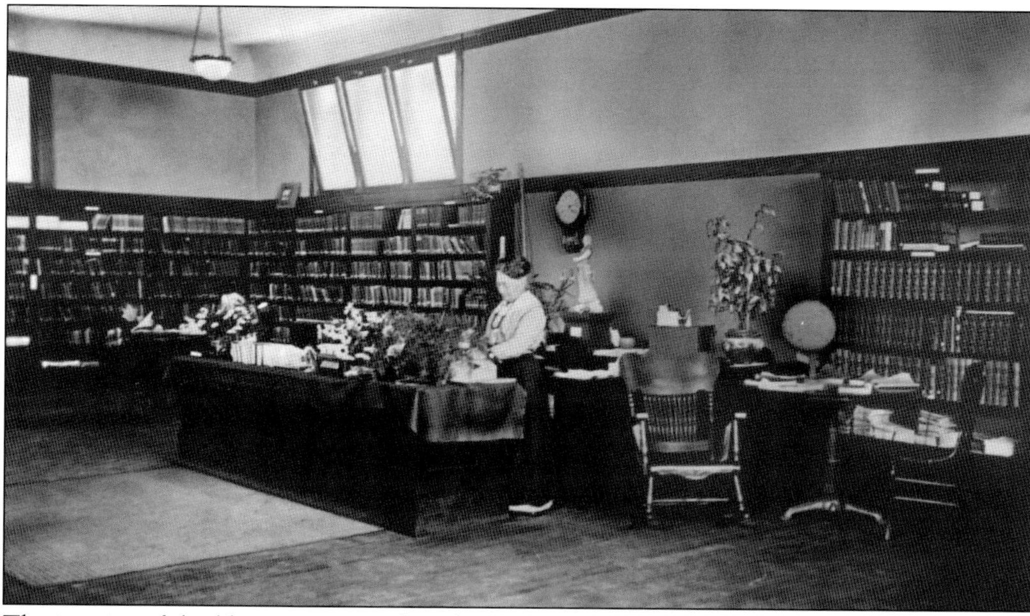

The interior of the library is pictured in the early 1910s. Mary L. Burrey was the librarian. The library was constructed in 1914 and continued to be the city library until 1972. It was located on the northwest corner of State and Clay Streets.

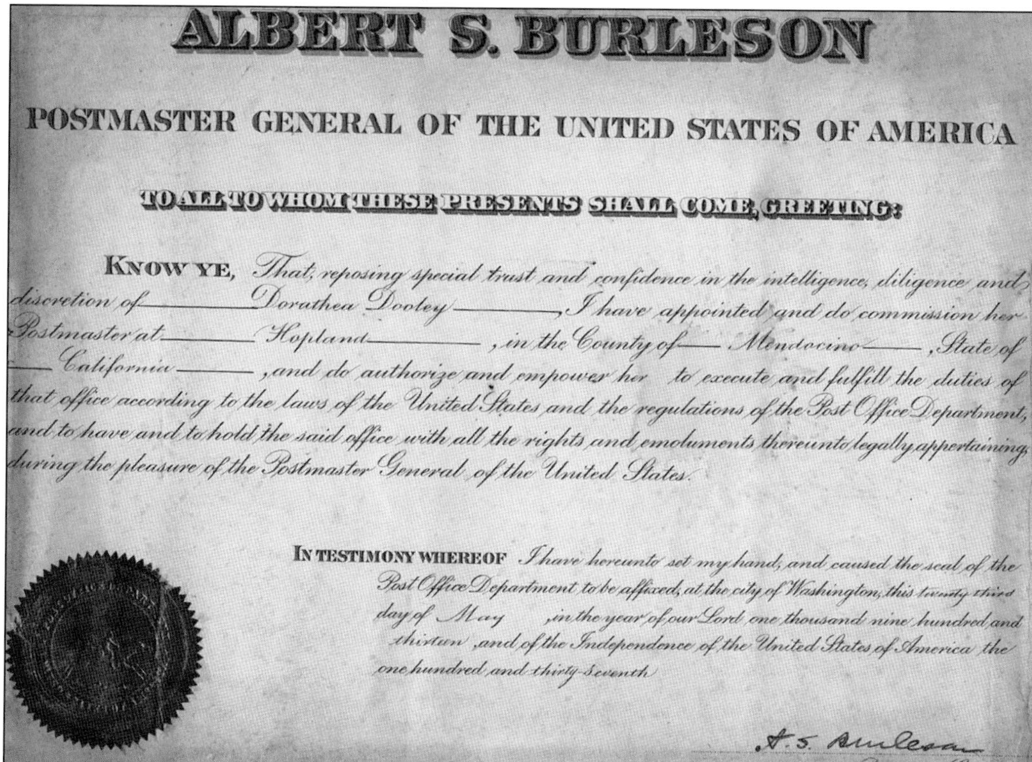

ALBERT S. BURLESON

POSTMASTER GENERAL OF THE UNITED STATES OF AMERICA

TO ALL TO WHOM THESE PRESENTS SHALL COME, GREETING:

KNOW YE, That, reposing special trust and confidence in the intelligence, diligence and discretion of Dorathea Dooley, I have appointed and do commission her Postmaster at Hopland, in the County of Mendocino, State of California, and do authorize and empower her to execute and fulfill the duties of that office according to the laws of the United States and the regulations of the Post Office Department, and to have and to hold the said office with all the rights and emoluments thereunto legally appertaining, during the pleasure of the Postmaster General of the United States.

IN TESTIMONY WHEREOF I have hereunto set my hand, and caused the seal of the Post Office Department to be affixed, at the city of Washington, this twenty third day of May, in the year of our Lord one thousand nine hundred and thirteen, and of the Independence of the United States of America the one hundred and thirty-seventh

A. S. Burleson
Postmaster General.

This certificate names Dorathea Dooley as postmaster of Hopland on May 23, 1913. Dooley was postmaster until October 1921. (Courtesy of Melody Mack.)

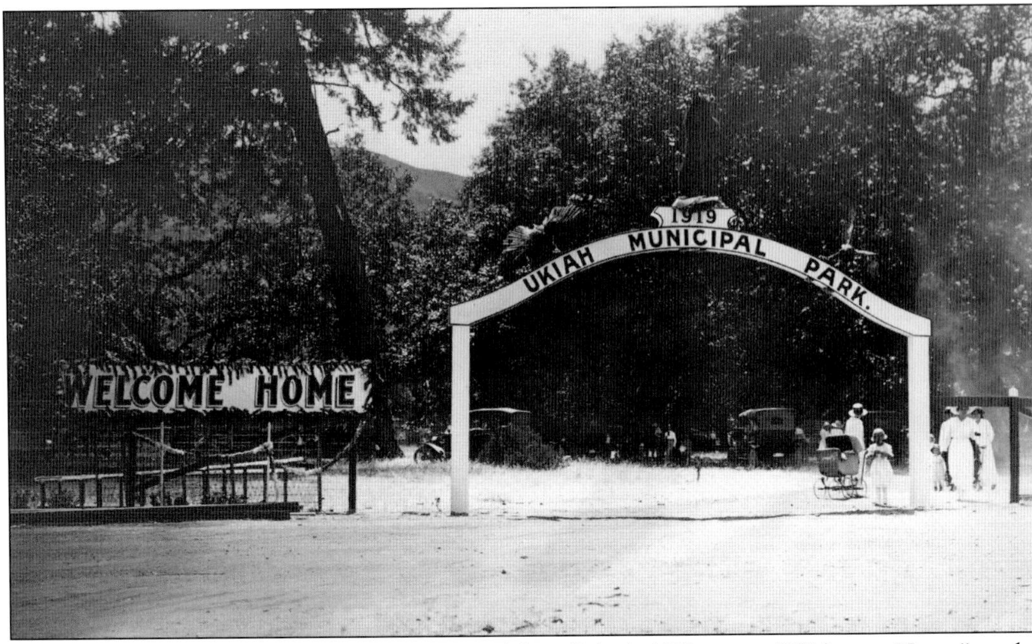

This Ukiah Municipal Park Gateway postcard from July 4, 1919, was a "Welcome Home" to the soldiers from World War I.

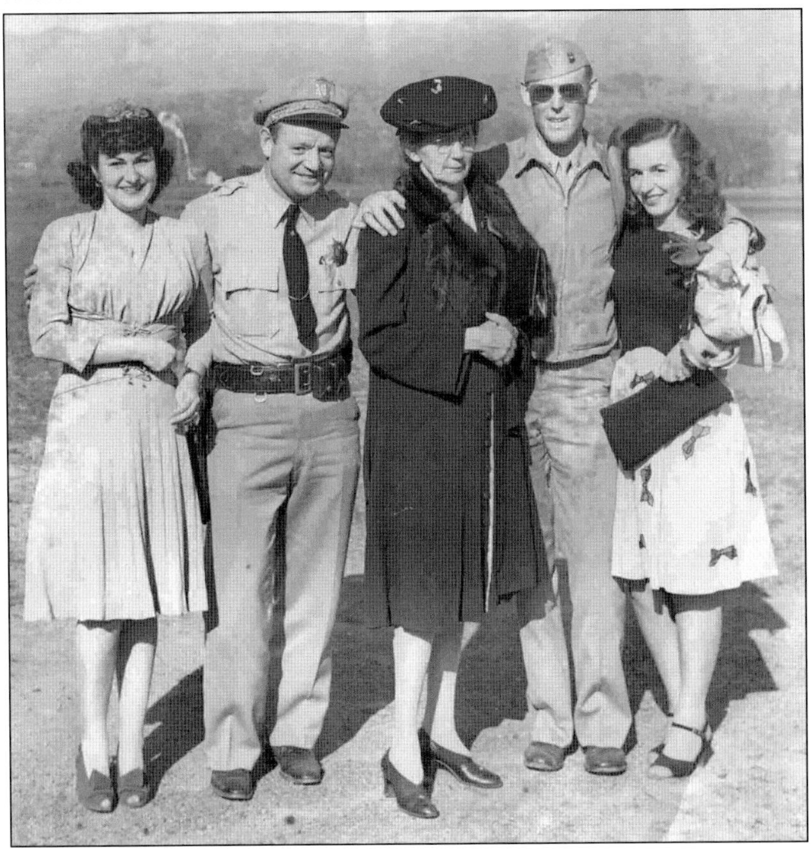

Hero of the South Seas Maj. George F. Dooley is shown with Arif Stultz from the California Highway Patrol, Dorathea Dooley (Major Dooley's mother), and two unidentified women. (Courtesy of Melody Mack.)

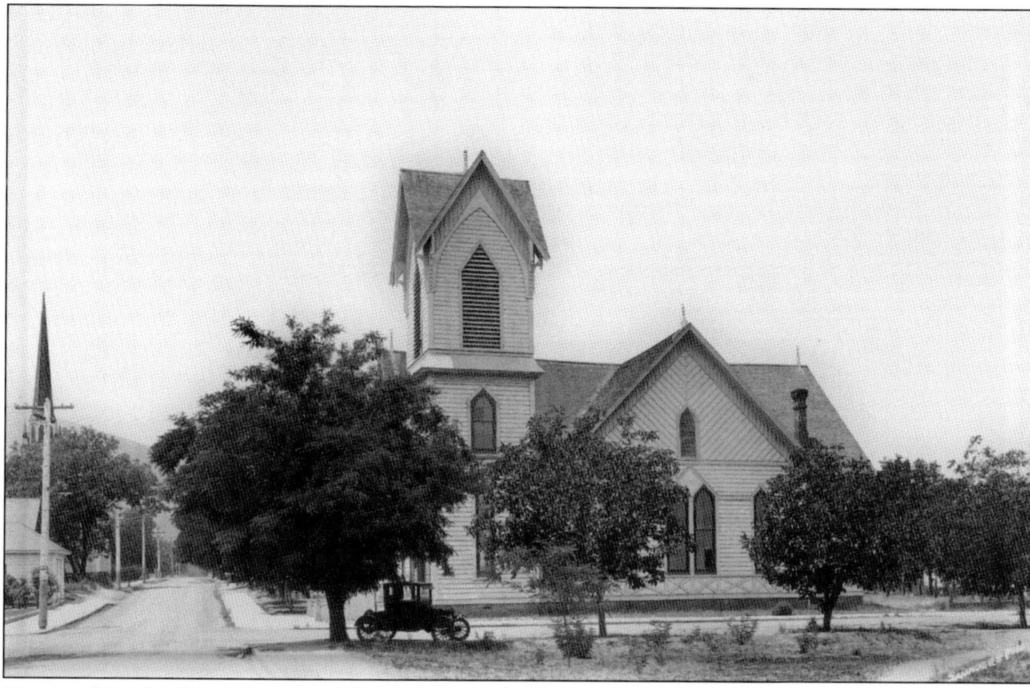

Pictured is the First Baptist Church around 1920. The church was built in 1892 and was located at the northwest corner of Smith and Oak Streets. The church was remodeled in 1924 and modernized.

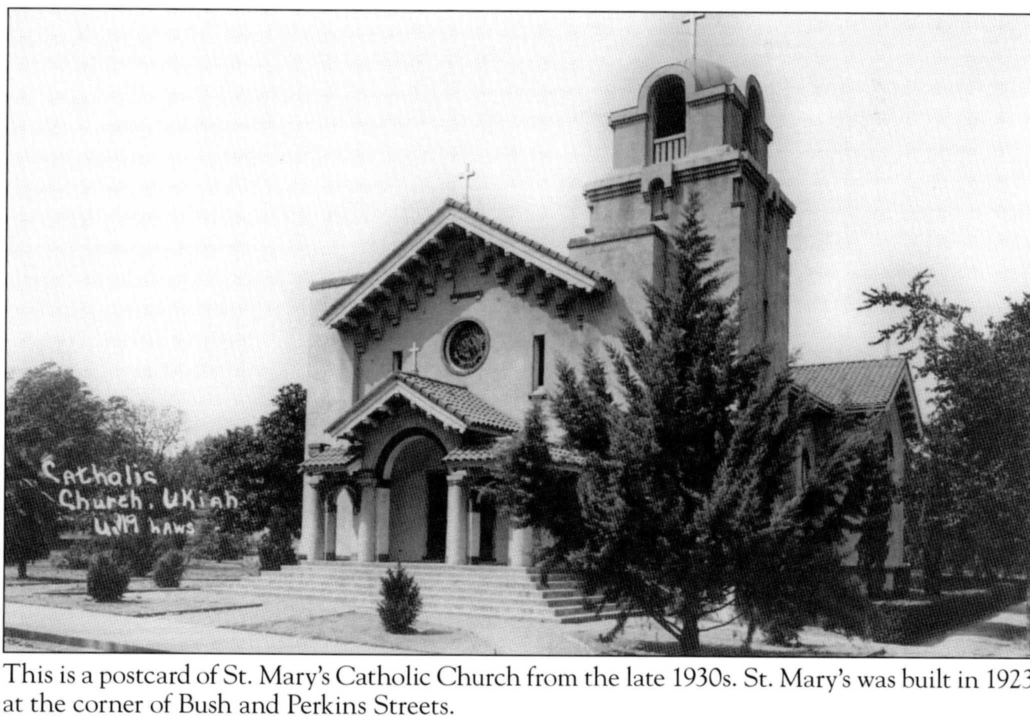

This is a postcard of St. Mary's Catholic Church from the late 1930s. St. Mary's was built in 1923 at the corner of Bush and Perkins Streets.

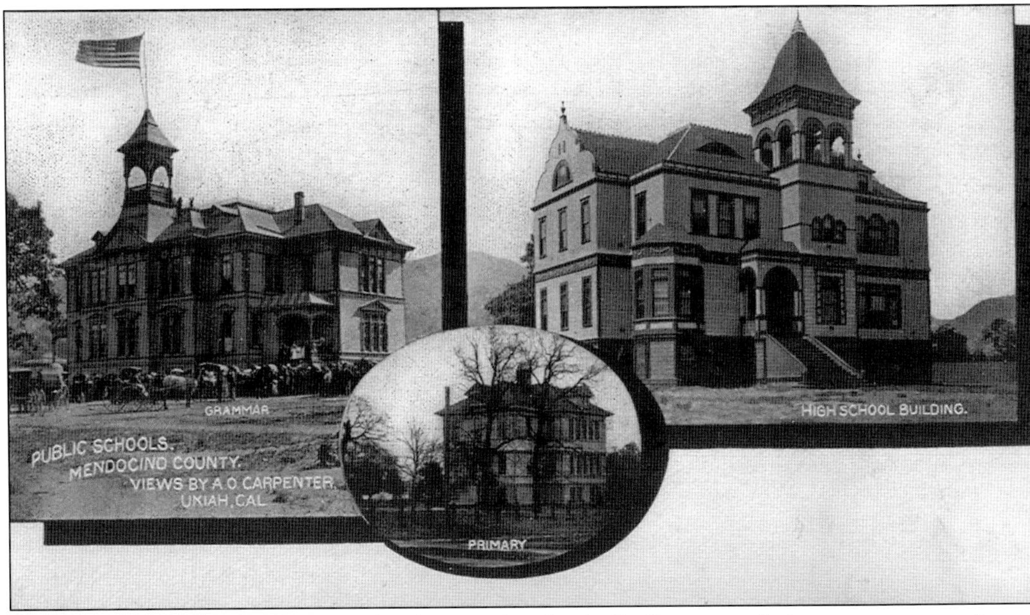

This view of Mendocino County schools was taken by A. O. Carpenter. It shows grammar, primary, and high school buildings in Ukiah. (Courtesy of the Grace Hudson Museum.)

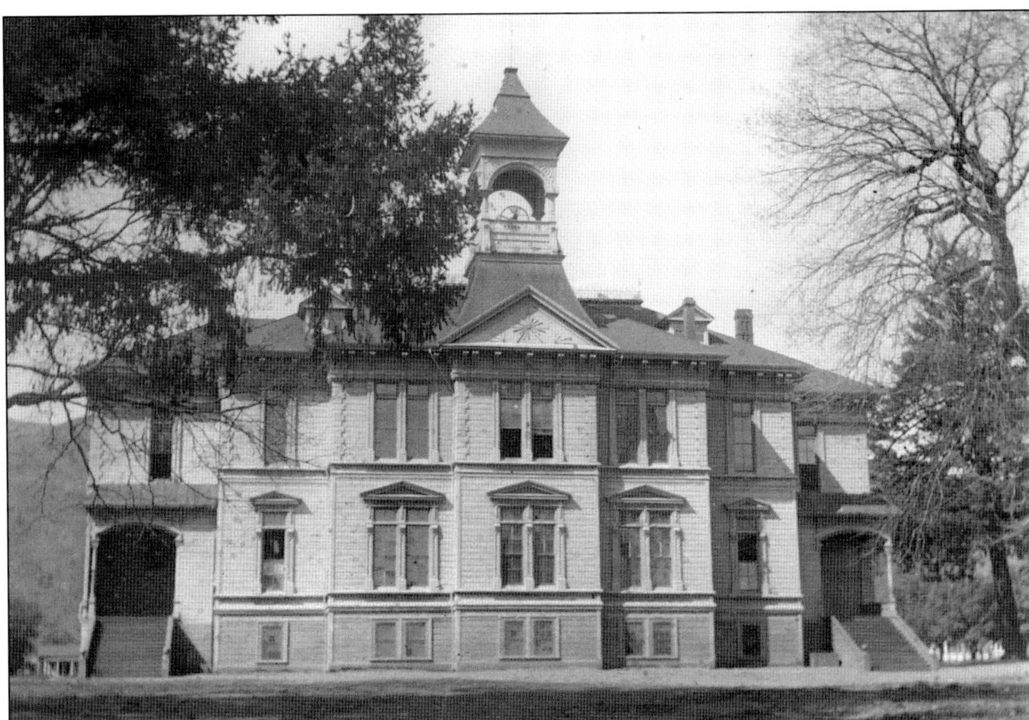

Ukiah Grammar School is shown around 1910. The school was built in 1889. In 1922, the school was moved north two blocks and was torn down in 1929.

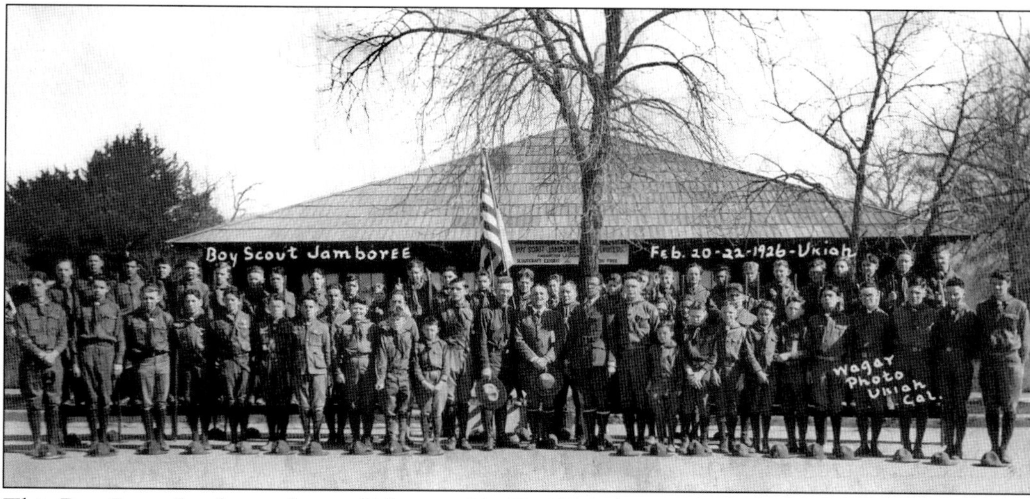

This Boy Scout Jamboree during February 20–22, 1926, drew over 1,500 people into the town of Ukiah. The building shown in the background is the American Legion Hall.

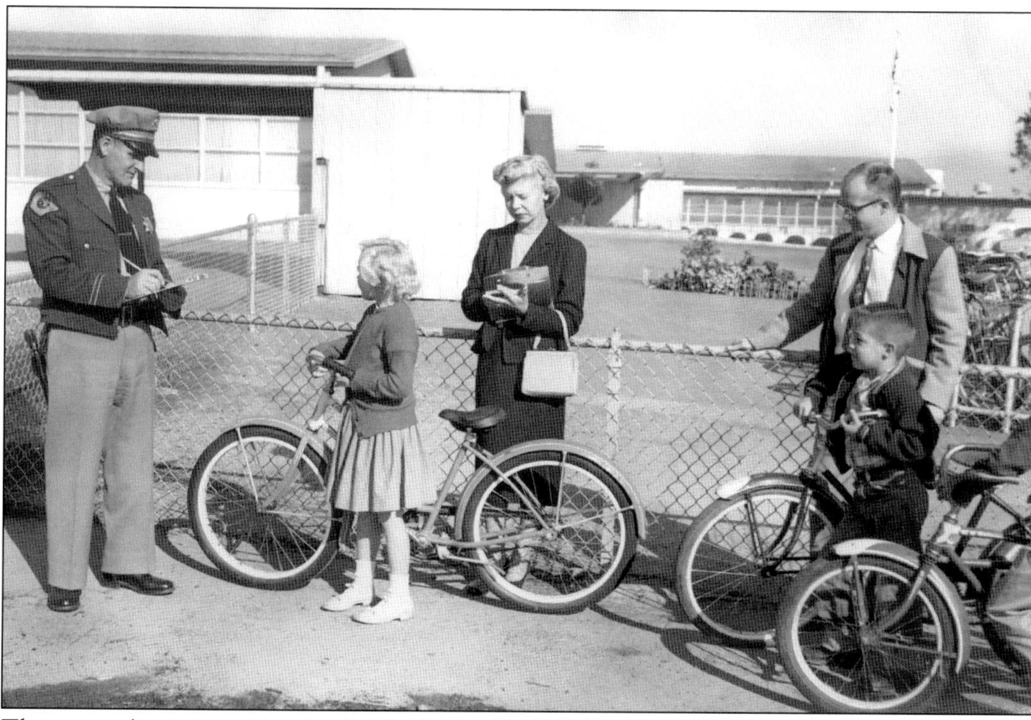

These people are participating in the Frank Zeek School bicycle safety program around 1960. From left to right are police officer Don Scotto; unidentified child and woman; Bob Cannon, the principal; and unidentified boy.

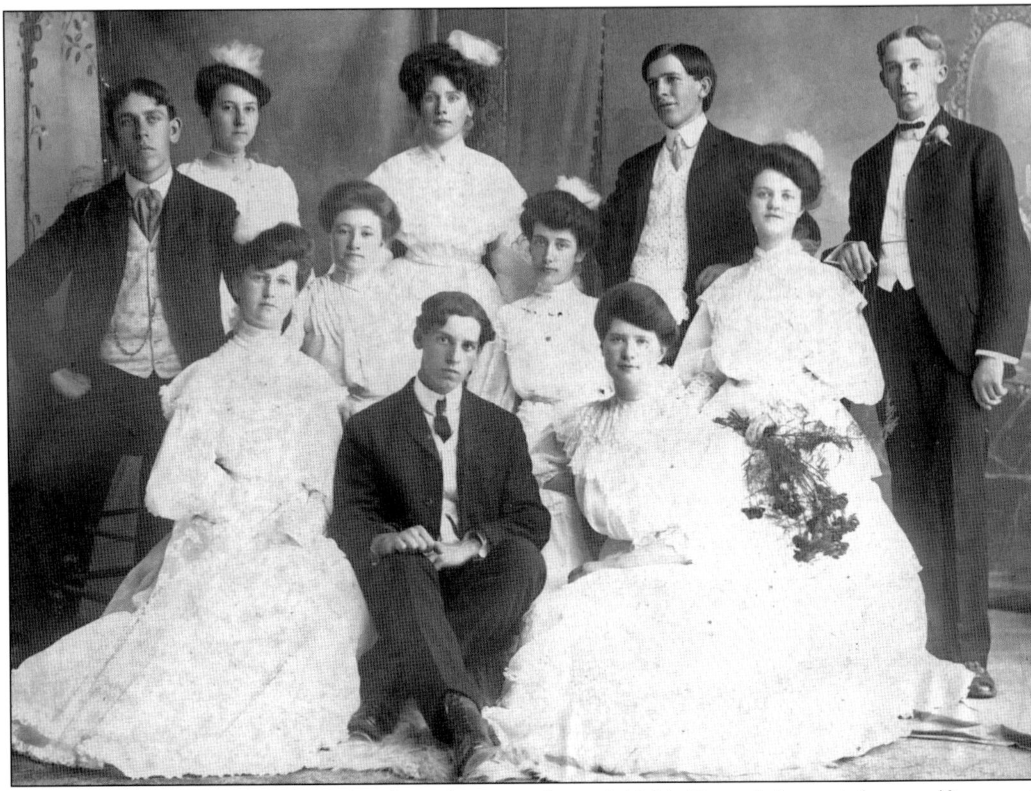

Pictured is the Ukiah High School graduating class of 1904. From left to right are (first row) Elfreda Pierson, Almon E. Roth, and Martha E. Brunner; (second row) E. L. Cunningham, E. Lillian Poor, Alma Atkinson, and Effie May Cooper; (third row) Susie G. Davis, Cecile Clarke, Earle R. Snell, and Carl L. Hoag.

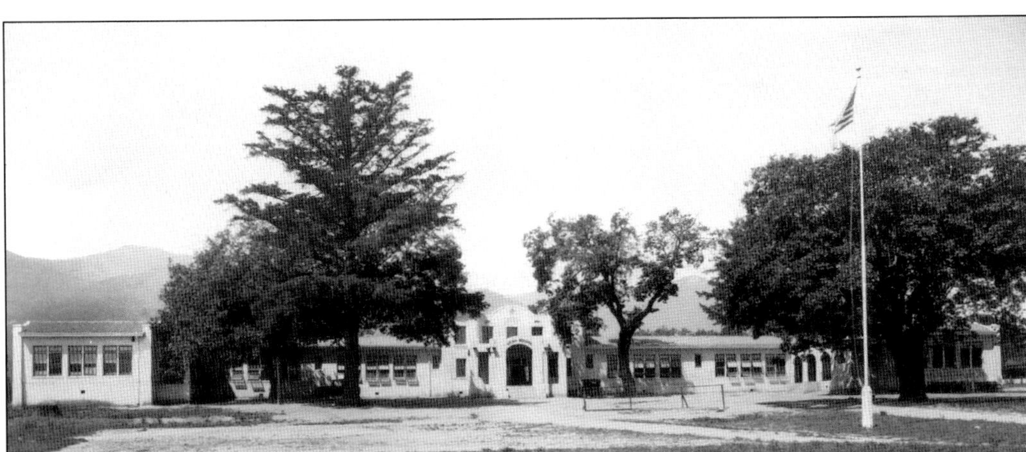

The Ukiah Grammar School is shown in this image from the 1920s. The building was completed in 1923. The Ukiah City Hall is now in the old location of the school.

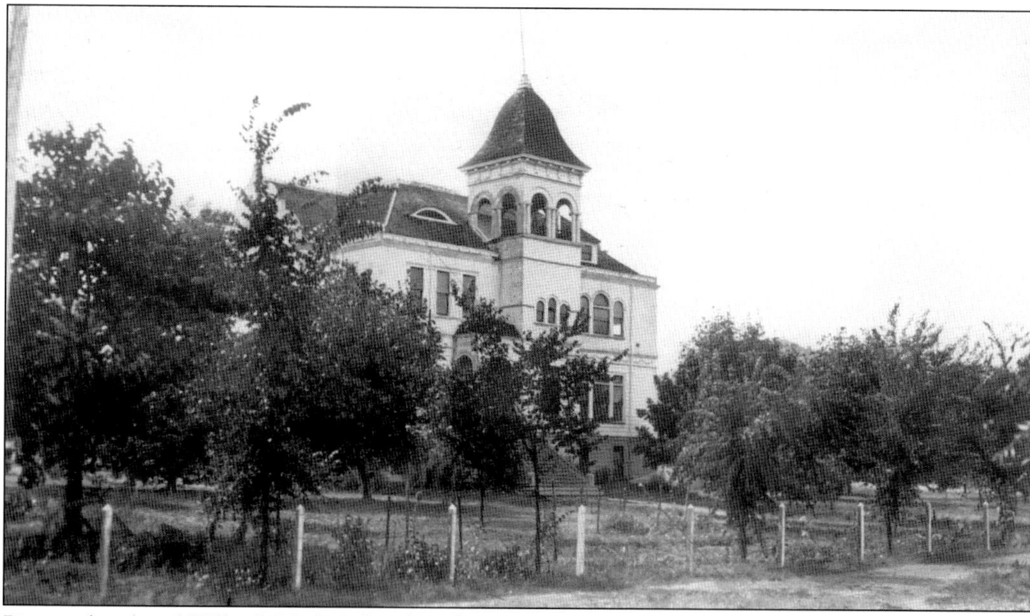

Pictured is the old Ukiah High School in the 1920s. The school was completed in 1894. A firebug torched the building on November 16, 1928. The building burned to the ground in 30 minutes.

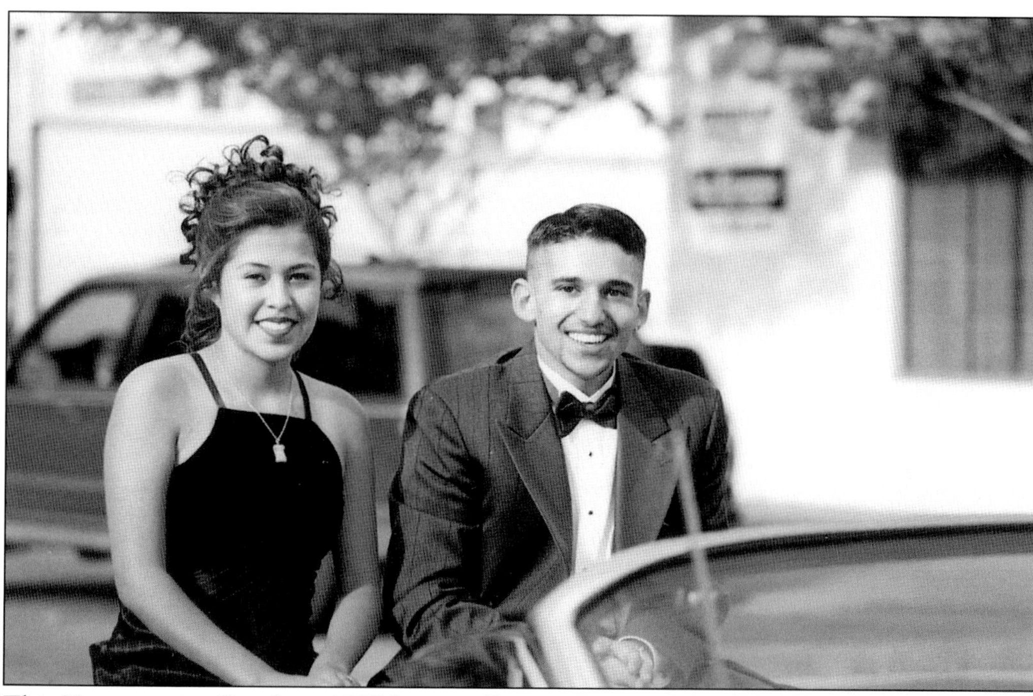

This Homecoming Parade in 1997 features Homecoming King Josh Bergere and Homecoming Queen Estella Alvarez.

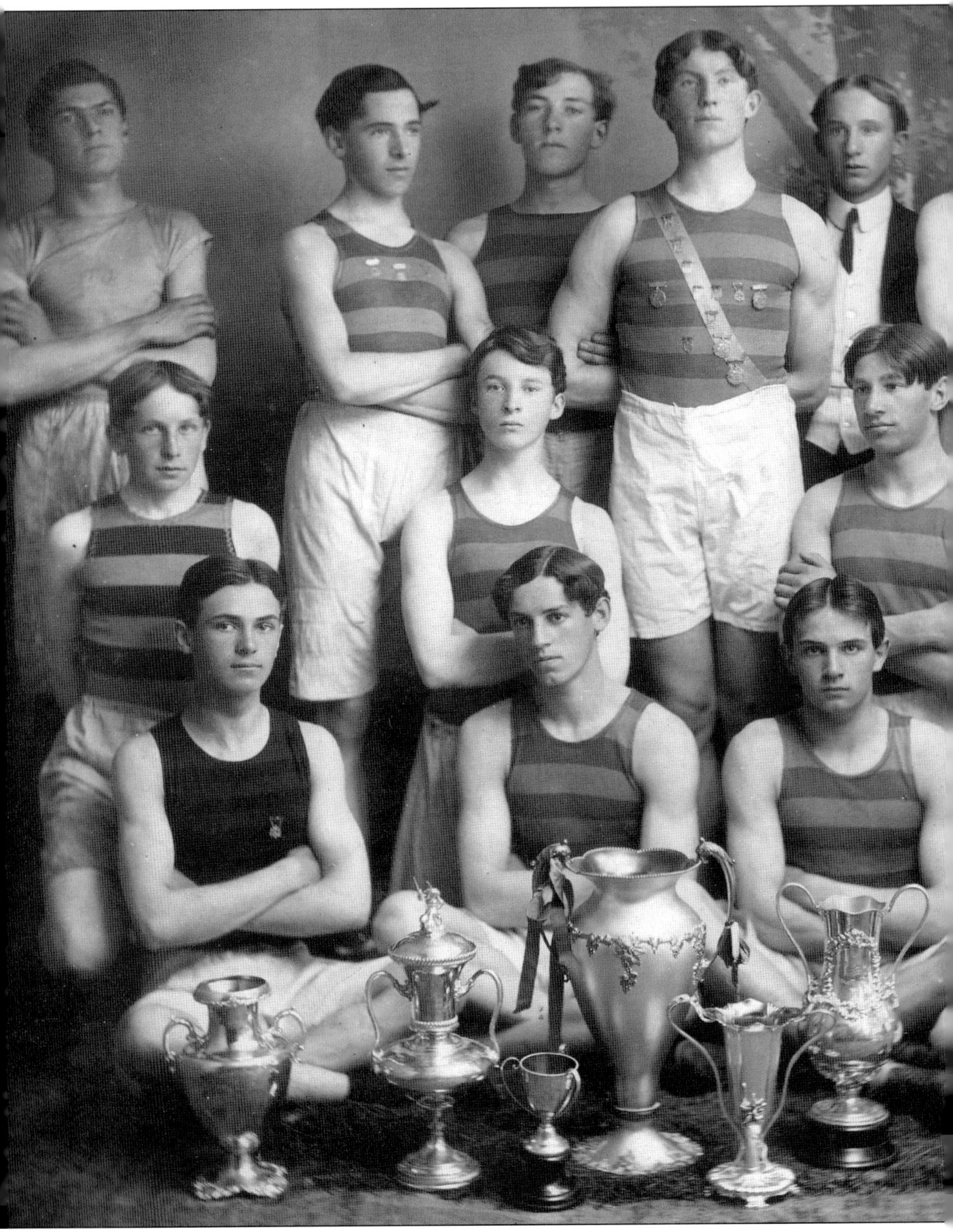

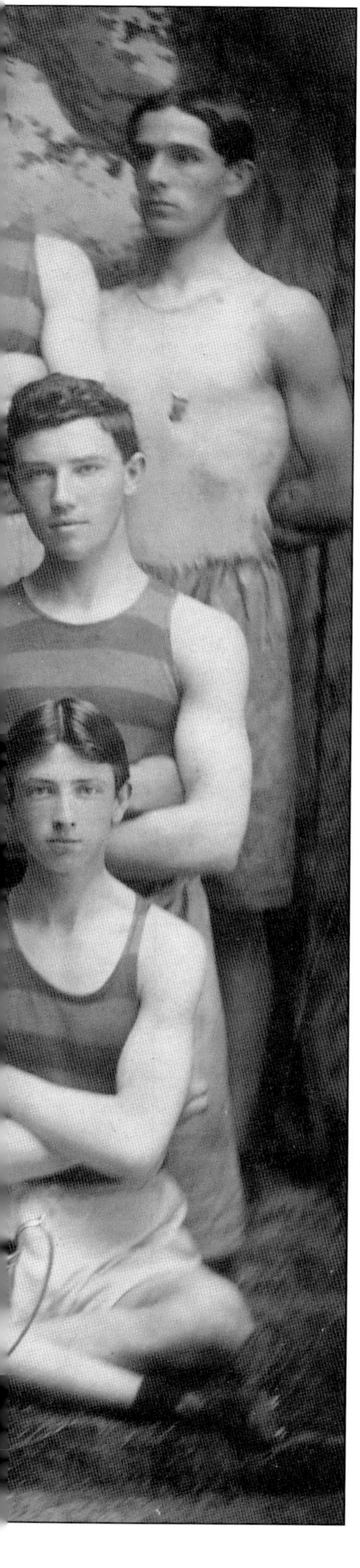

Pictured is the Ukiah High School track team in 1904. From left to right are (first row) H. L. Fallas, Almon E. Roth, Wesley M. Rawies, and Mervin Perkins; (second row) Mark Carpenter, Fred Moore, Victor Henley, and Sam Phillips; (third row) Tom Jameson, B. G. Pemberton, W. K. Ford, Harry L. Horton, Carl Hoag, E. L. Cunningham, and George Dillingham. (Photograph by A. O. Carpenter; courtesy of the Grace Hudson Museum.)

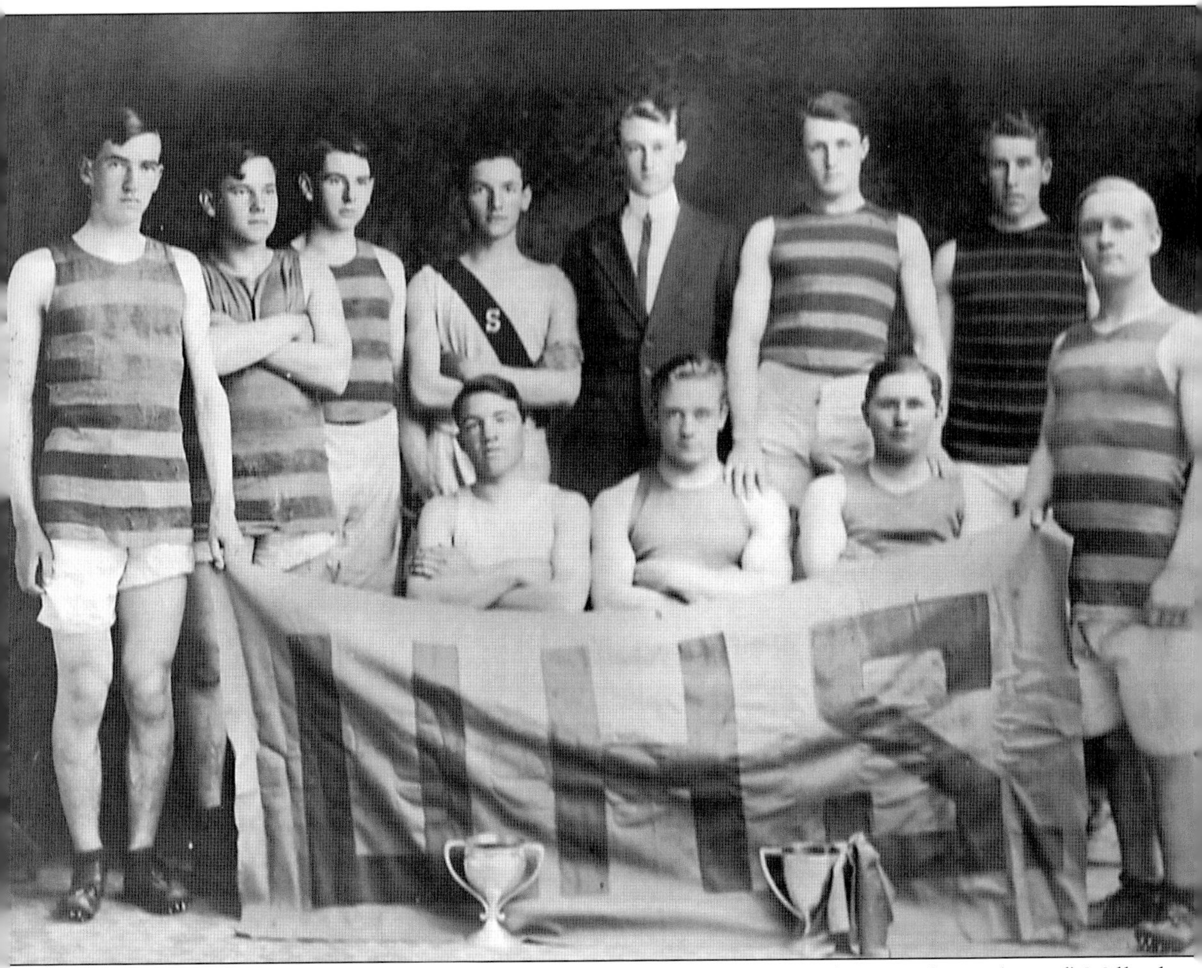

The Ukiah High School track team is pictured here in 1912. From left to right are (seated) Millard Lawson, Reginald Caughey, and Russell Ford; (standing) Roy Clay, Willis Prather, William Connolly, Lester Thornton, Alvin Hufft, Lawrence Waugh, L. Allensby, and Lilburn Gibson.

Three

Business and Industry

From a sleepy little inland community to becoming the county seat, Ukiah grew by leaps and bounds. Businesses that sprung up ranged from the hop industry to logging and pear farms. Along Highway 101 in the springtime, both sides of the road would be covered with blooming pear trees. During World War II, local businesses got together and formed the Harvest Service Program to help harvest the pear crop. In the late 1800s, one might stop by A. O. Carpenter's Home Gallery to have a photograph taken of the family.

During the same time period, Ukiah merchants sponsored a Trades Carnival. Young ladies competed in the festivities wearing costumes representing the local businesses. Ukiah was home to several stagecoach companies and saloons to "wet the whistle" of thirsty travelers stopping in the town. Vichy Hot Springs opened to the east of downtown and boasted of providing rejuvenating mineral baths to such visitors as Mark Twain and Jack London. The elegant Palace Hotel opened along with the Ukiah House. A lady visiting Ukiah might stop in the Emery Millinery shop for a new hat while gentlemen had a drink at the Palm Saloon. Banks, department stores, and other businesses were opened in the small downtown area, sometimes side by side with the local livery stable. A person could find anything they wanted or needed within a few short blocks.

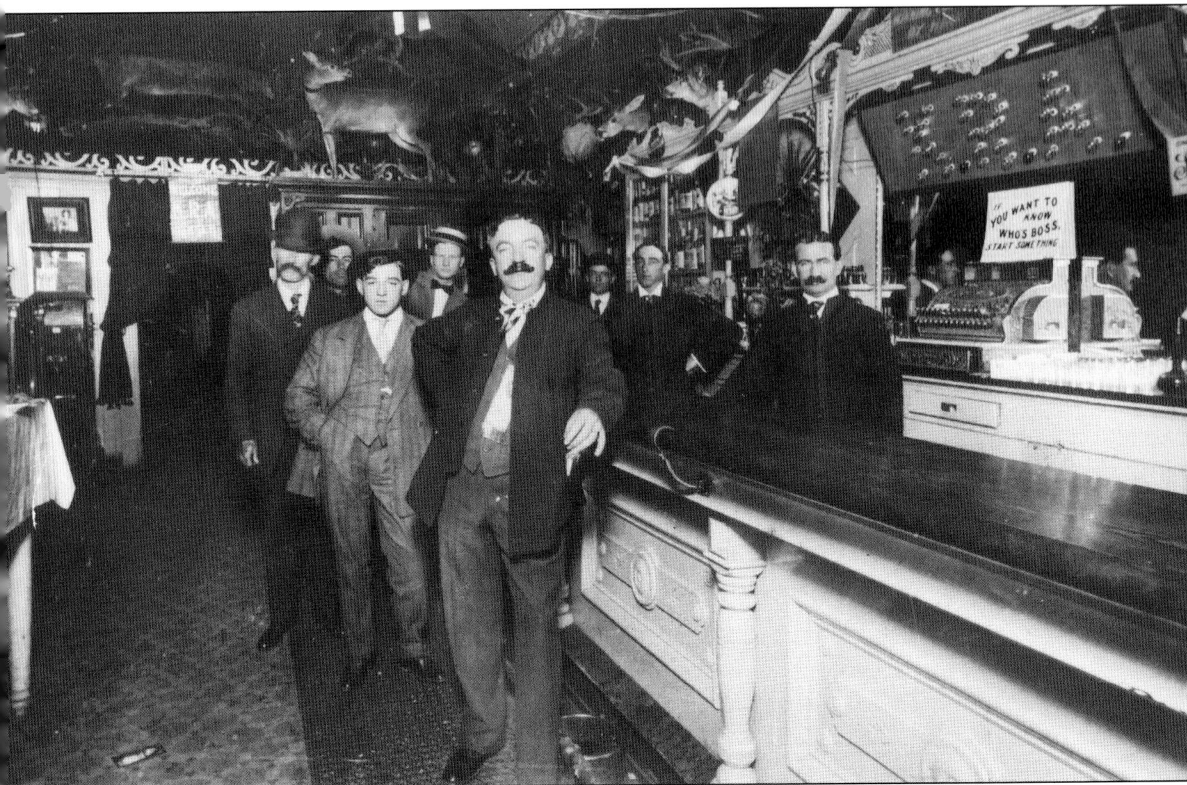

Pictured is the interior of the Palm Saloon in May 1909. The sign with the letters K. R. A. stands for the Knights of the Royal Arch, an organization of liquor dealers and saloon keepers. Their 1909 convention was held in Ukiah. The gentleman pictured in the center is Harry P. Siems, who was the owner of the Palm Saloon, an upscale bar in downtown Ukiah.

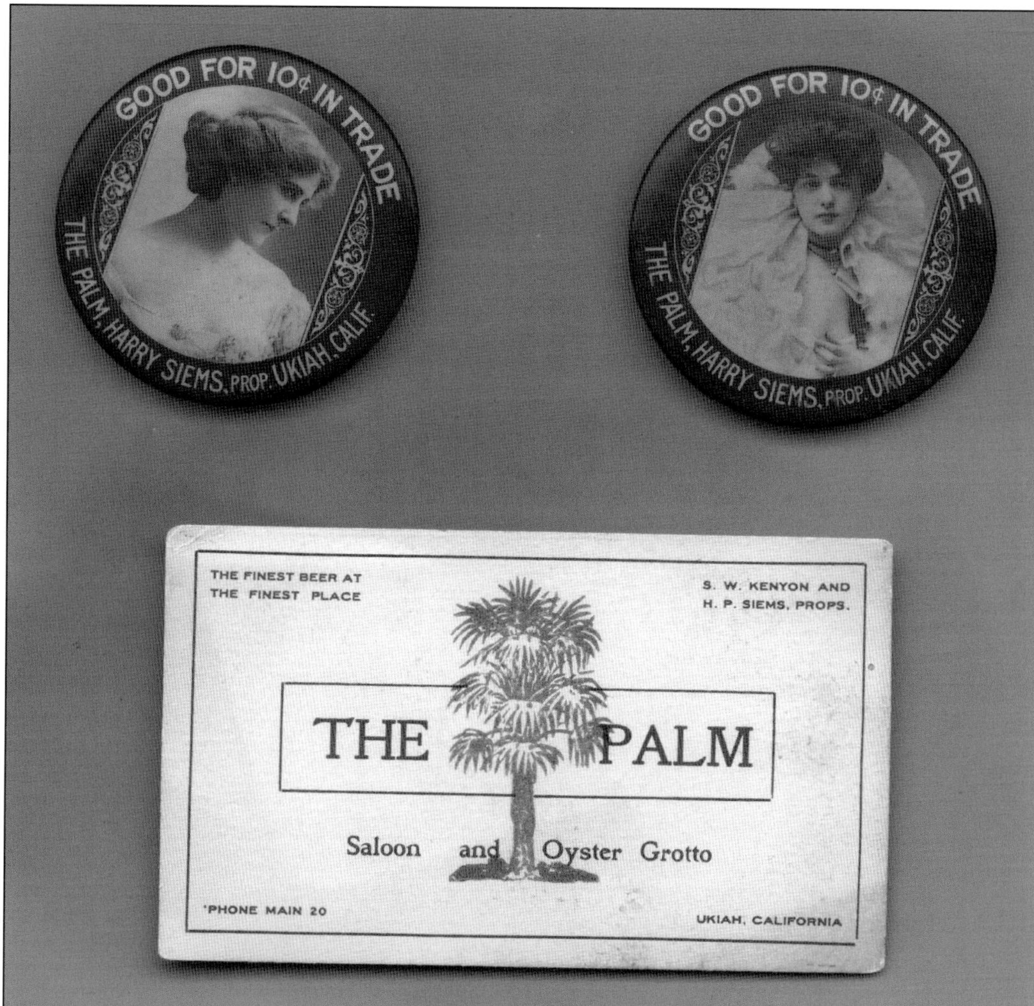

This business card is prior to 1902. Mr. Kenyon and Harry P. Siems were business partners in the Palm Saloon from October 1901 to October 1902. The token pictured was good for 10¢ off on the customer's next visit to the bar. On the opposite side of the token was a mirror. There were several different tokens with beautiful ladies on them. These tokens were discovered in an old toolbox in the 1990s. Siems kept the Palm Saloon open until 1912. (Courtesy of Ed Bold.)

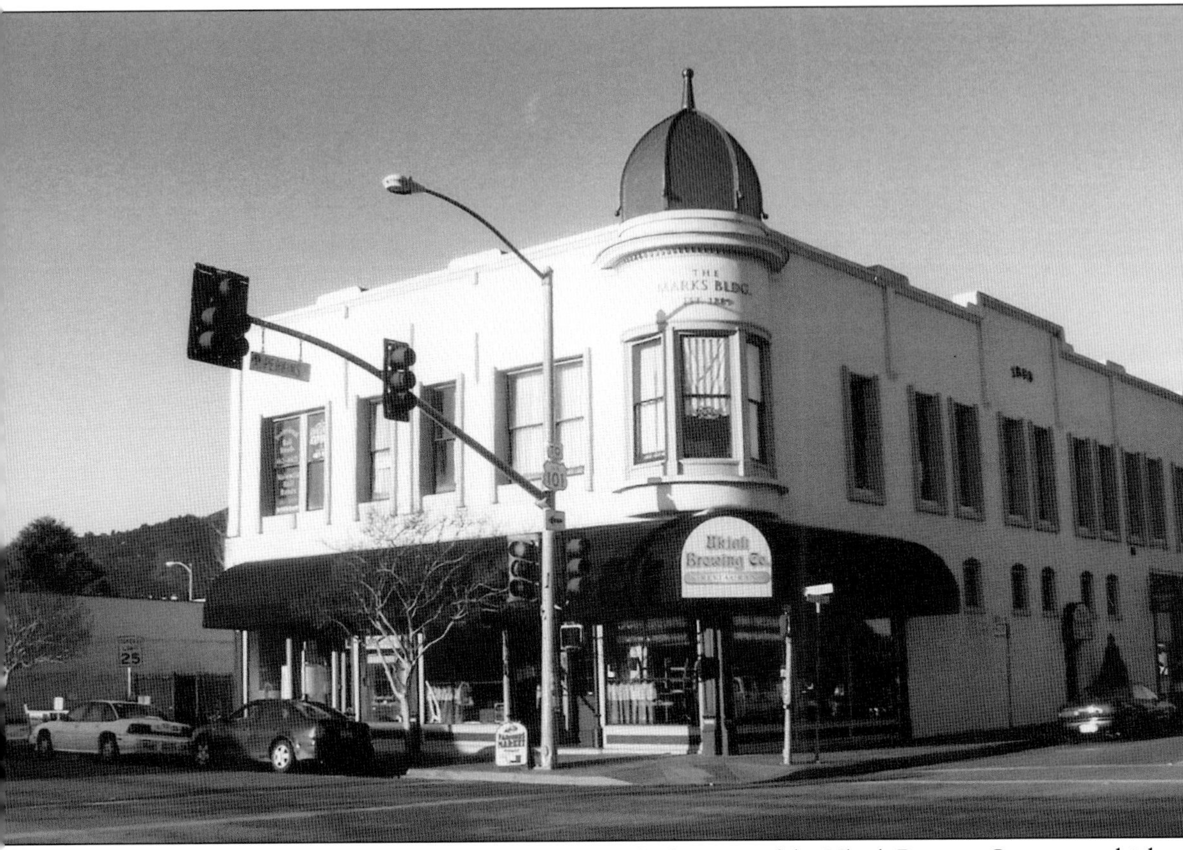

The Marks Building, constructed in 1890, is now the location of the Ukiah Brewing Company, which opened in May 2000. The brewing company is the first organic brewery in Mendocino County.

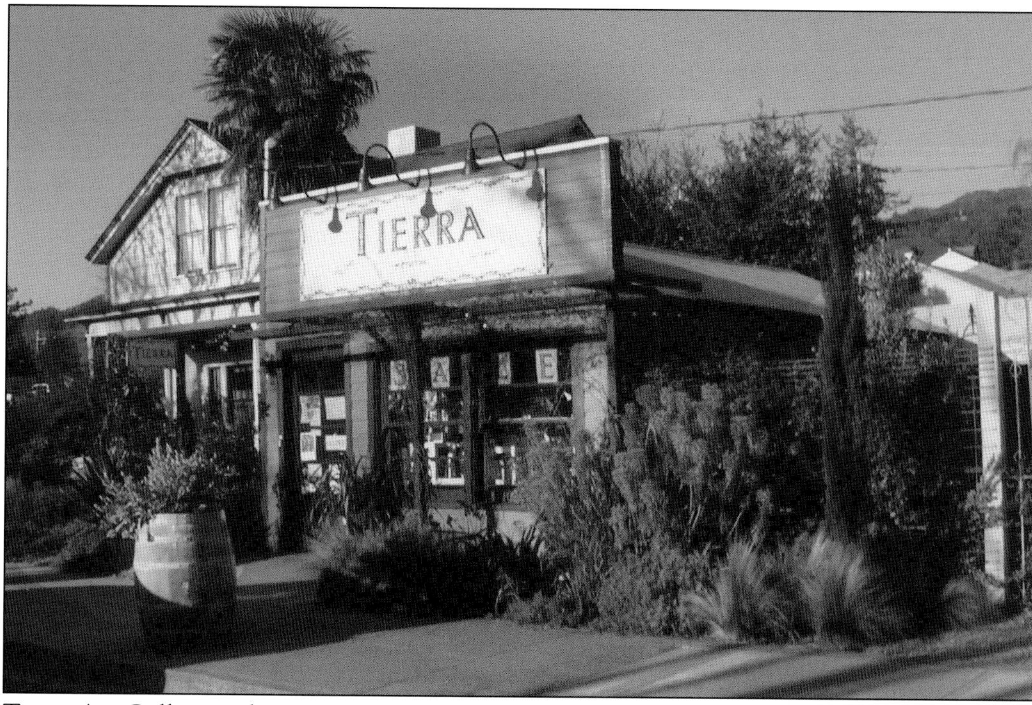

Tierra Art Gallery and Tasting Room is pictured in 2006 across the street from the old Ukiah Opera House.

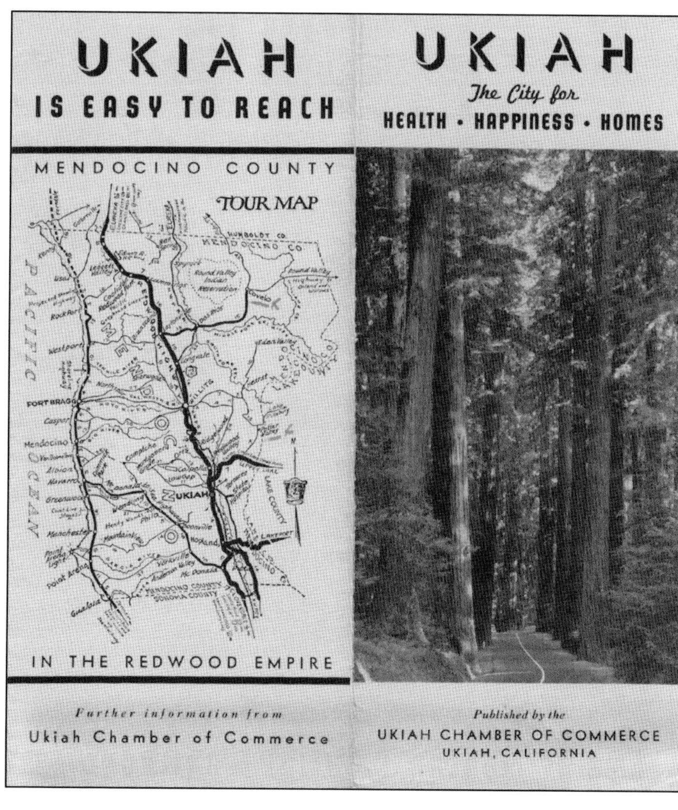

This Ukiah Chamber of Commerce brochure promoted "Health, Happiness, Homes" in the 1930s.

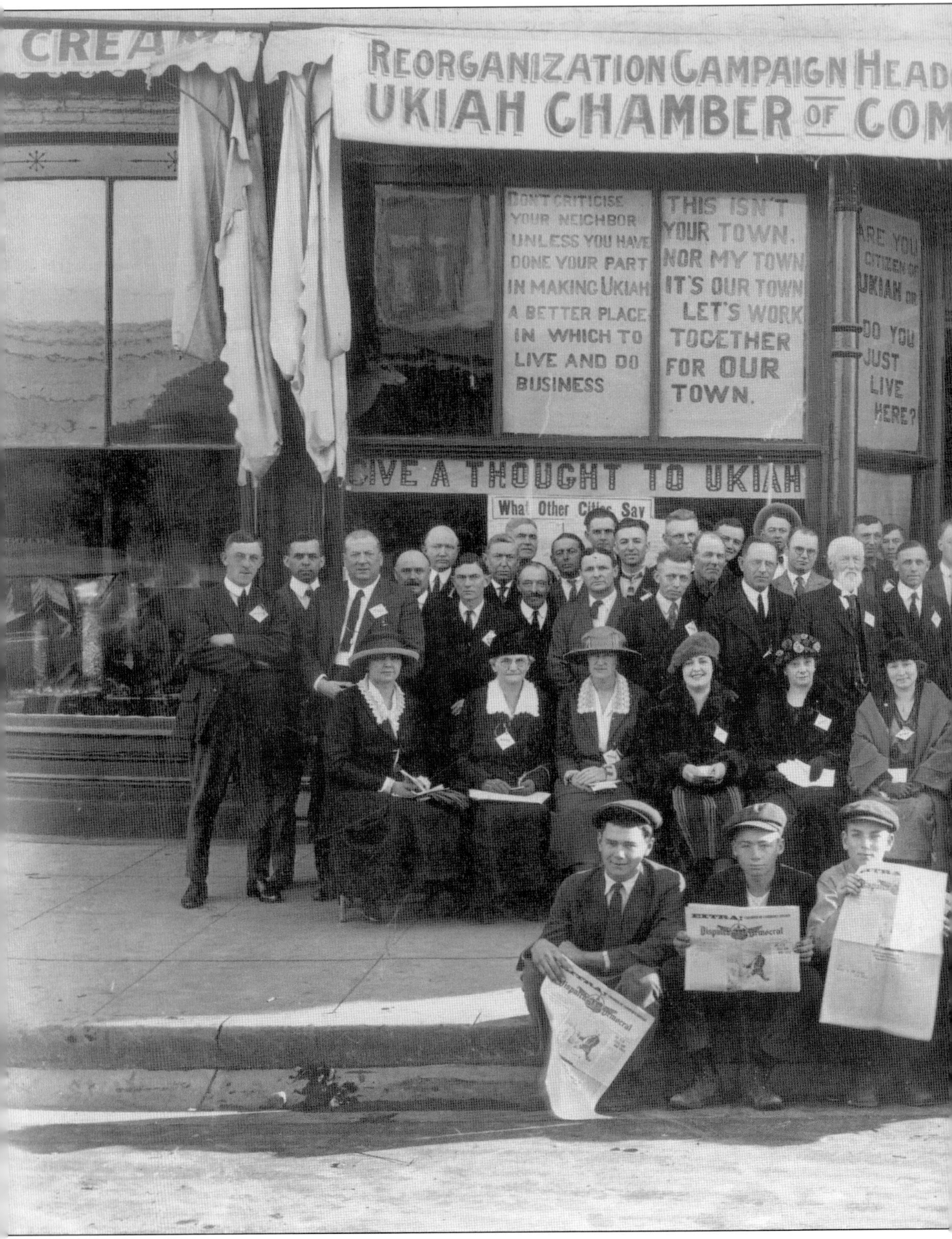
REORGANIZATION CAMPAIGN HEAD
UKIAH CHAMBER OF COM
DON'T CRITICISE YOUR NEIGHBOR UNLESS YOU HAVE DONE YOUR PART IN MAKING UKIAH A BETTER PLACE IN WHICH TO LIVE AND DO BUSINESS
THIS ISN'T YOUR TOWN, NOR MY TOWN IT'S OUR TOWN LET'S WORK TOGETHER FOR OUR TOWN.
ARE YOU CITIZEN OF UKIAH OR DO YOU JUST LIVE HERE?
IVE A THOUGHT TO UKIAH
What Other Cities Say
EXTRA!

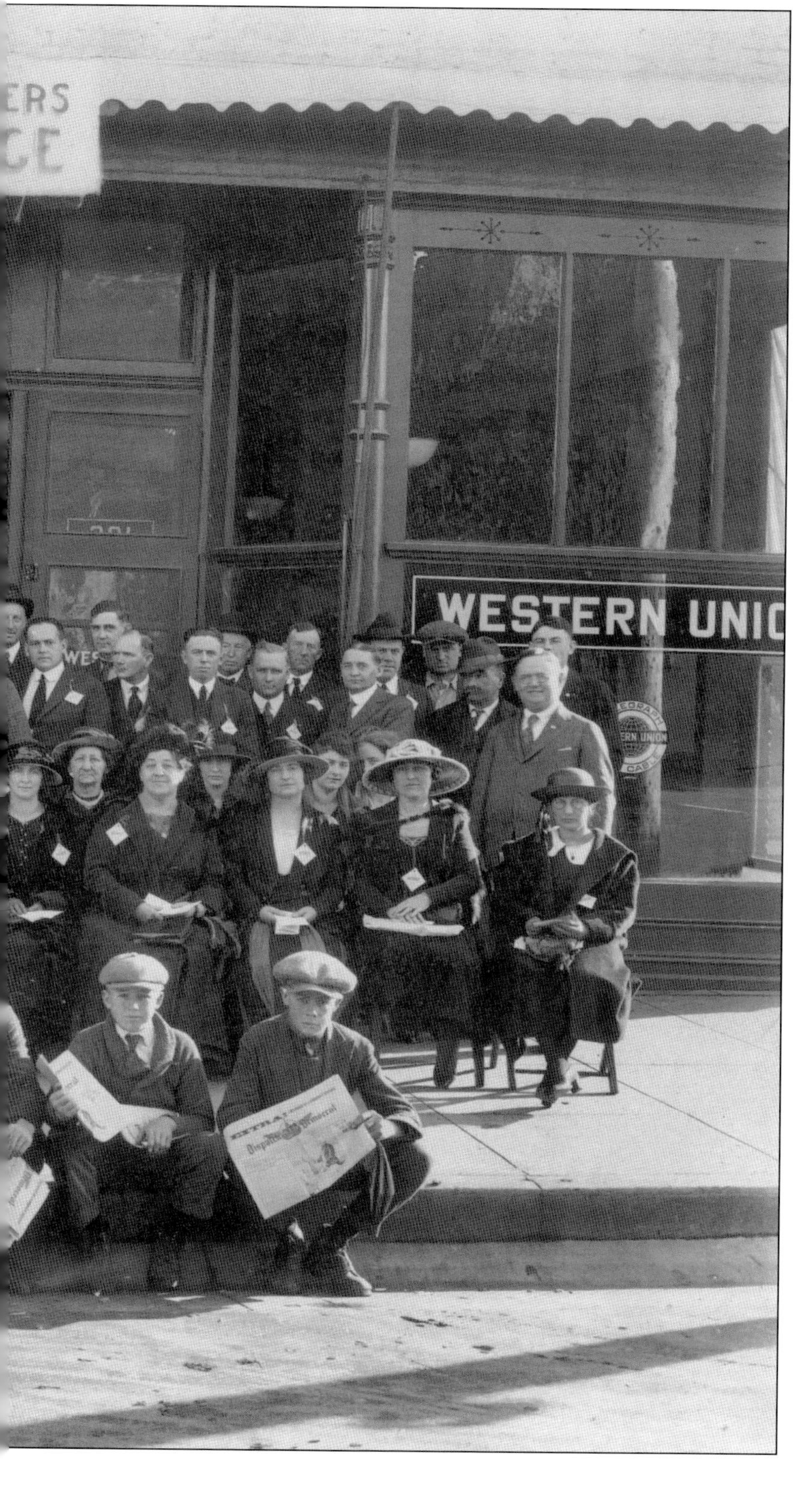

Reorganization of Ukiah Chamber of Commerce took place in November 1921. Young newspaper carriers from the *Dispatch Democrat* are shown sitting on the curb. This picture was taken on the northeast corner of Smith and State Streets.

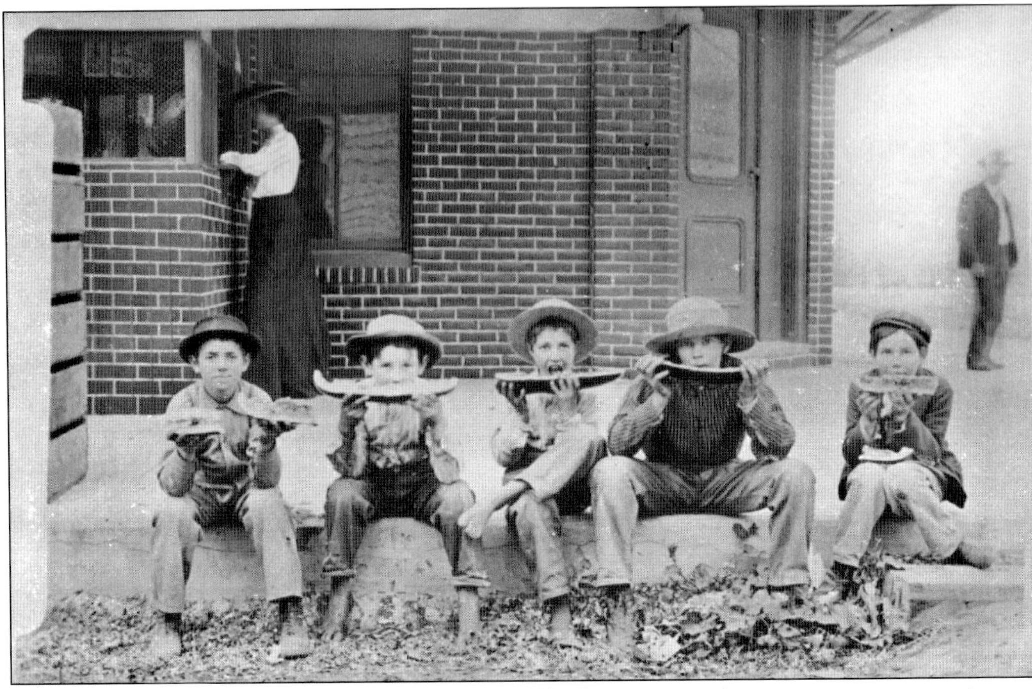

Champion watermelon eaters are shown in 1902. The best watermelon eaters in town are pictured in front of the Hale Brothers Fruit and Vegetable Stand. This is a great advertisement for fresh fruit. The site is now the location of the Savings Bank.

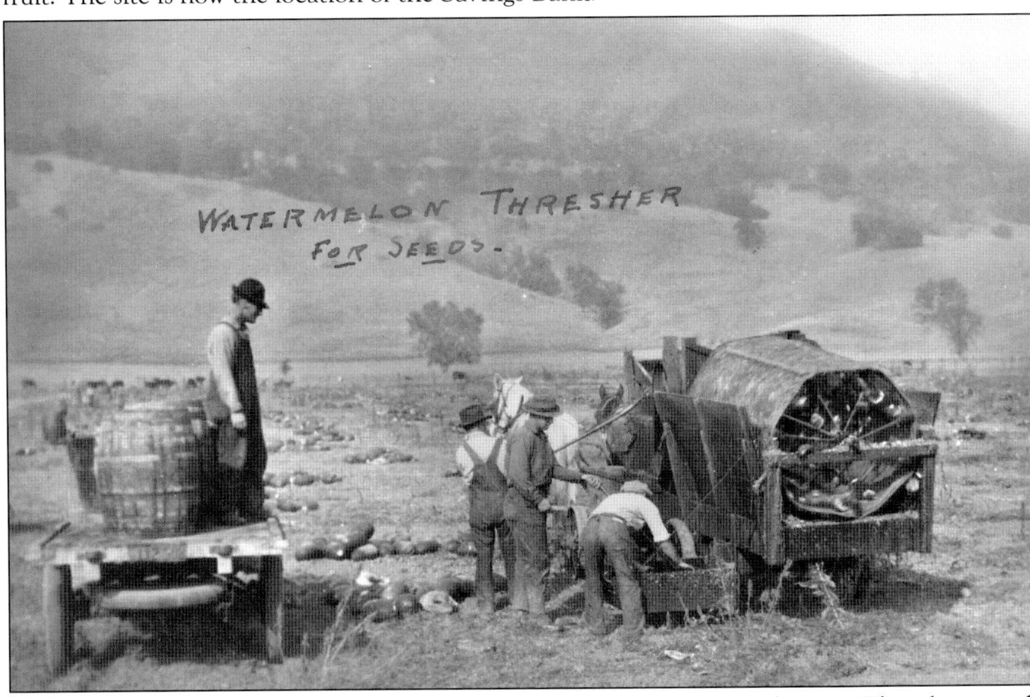

This watermelon thresher was used to extract the watermelon seeds for planting. This photograph was taken in the 1920s at the Carner Ranch in Potter Valley, a few short miles from the center of Ukiah.

Jennie Luce is shown with a banner representing the Grand Hotel at the Trades Carnival in May 1894. Young ladies of Ukiah dressed in costumes representing local businesses.

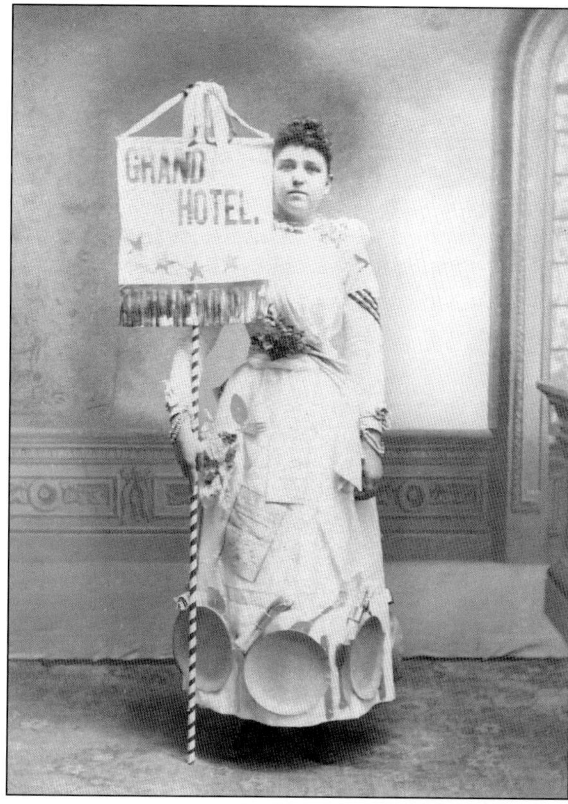

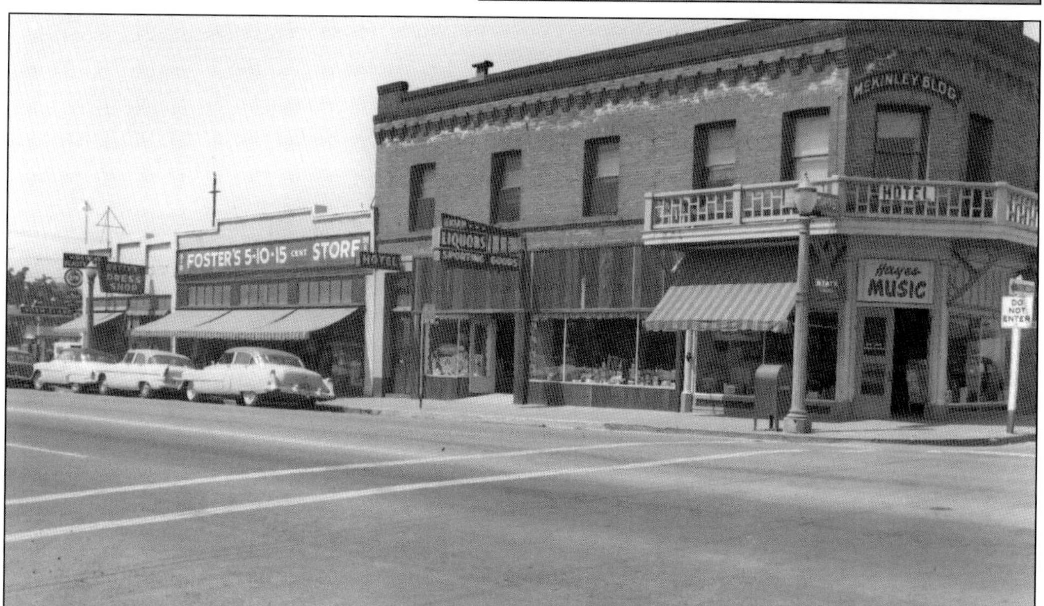

Hayes Music was located on the southwest corner of State and Church Streets. This image is from July 1, 1956.

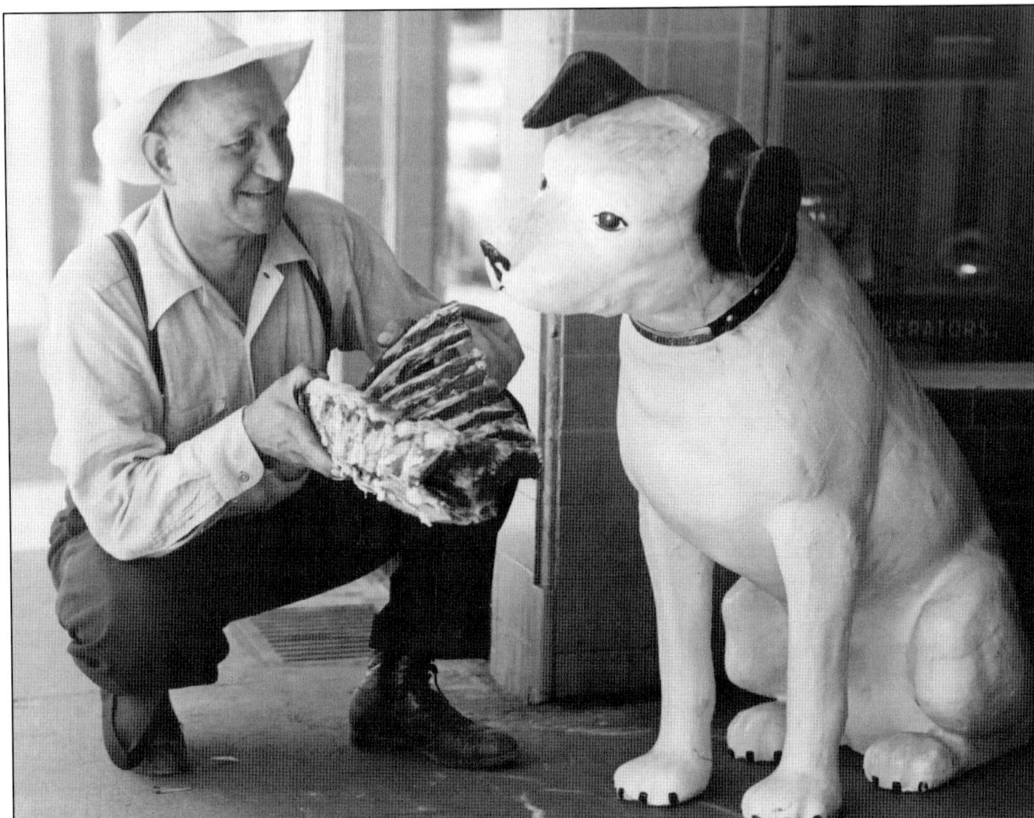

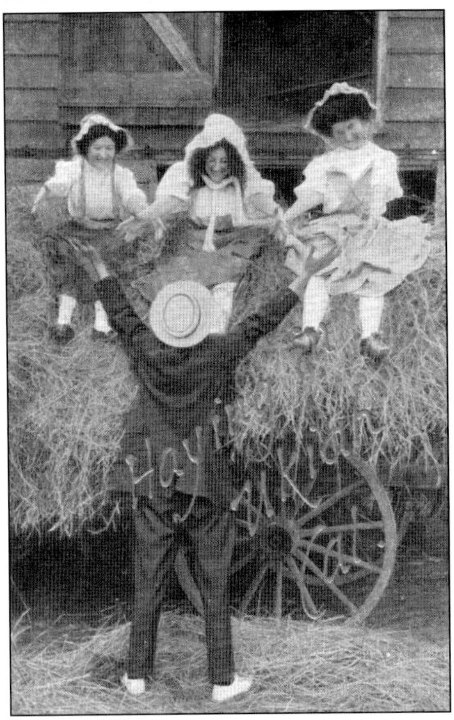

George Vevoda is pictured with the RCA dog in July 1948. George Vevoda was a local Chevrolet dealer who was also president of the Ukiah Humane Society. The picture was a spoof. Someone reported a dog tied up outside a local business with no food or water on a hot day. George dropped everything and went over with a big water dish and a huge roast. It was a great publicity stunt for his business and for the Ukiah Humane Society.

This is a "Haying in Ukiah" comic postcard. This card was from a series of comic postcards made for small towns throughout the state.

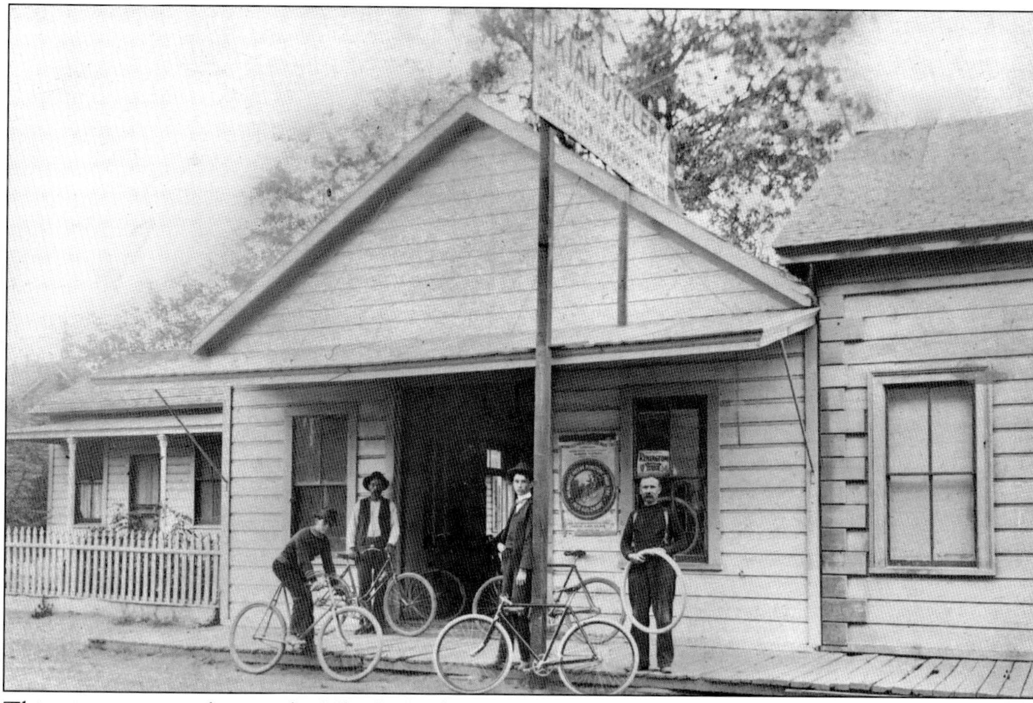

This picture was taken at the Ukiah Cyclery around 1899 at 208 West Perkins Street, its original location. Pictured from left to right are Myrus McKesson, unidentified, Eldred McKesson, and Samuel D. McKesson.

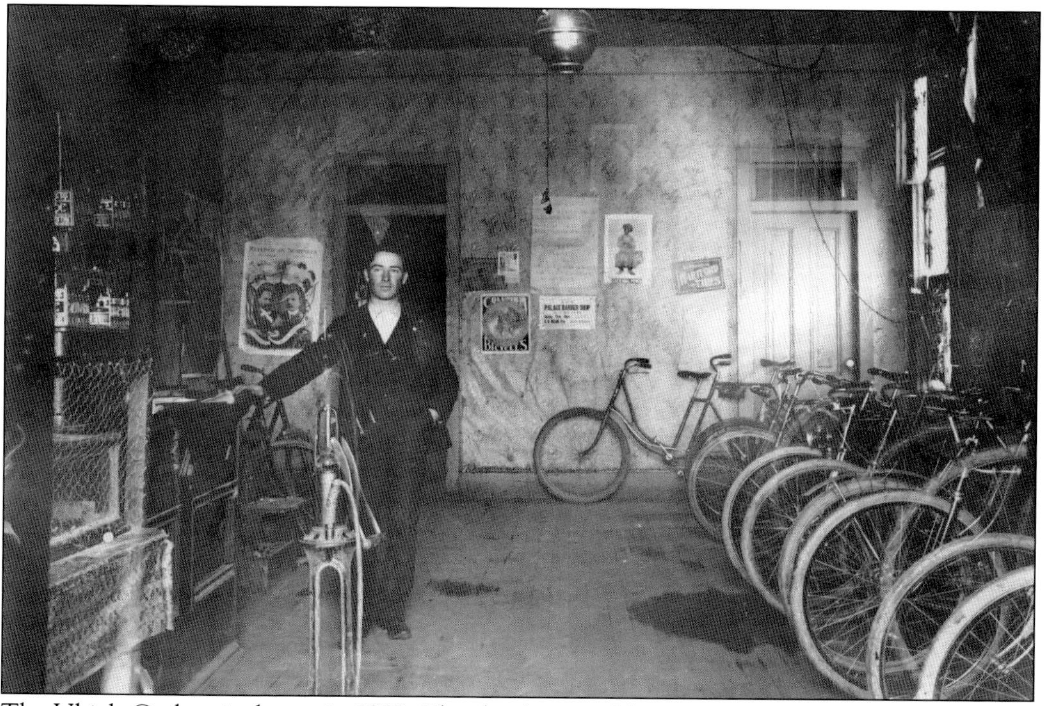

The Ukiah Cyclery is shown in 1902. The shop's second location was on the southwest corner of School and Standley Streets. Myrus McKesson is pictured in the shop.

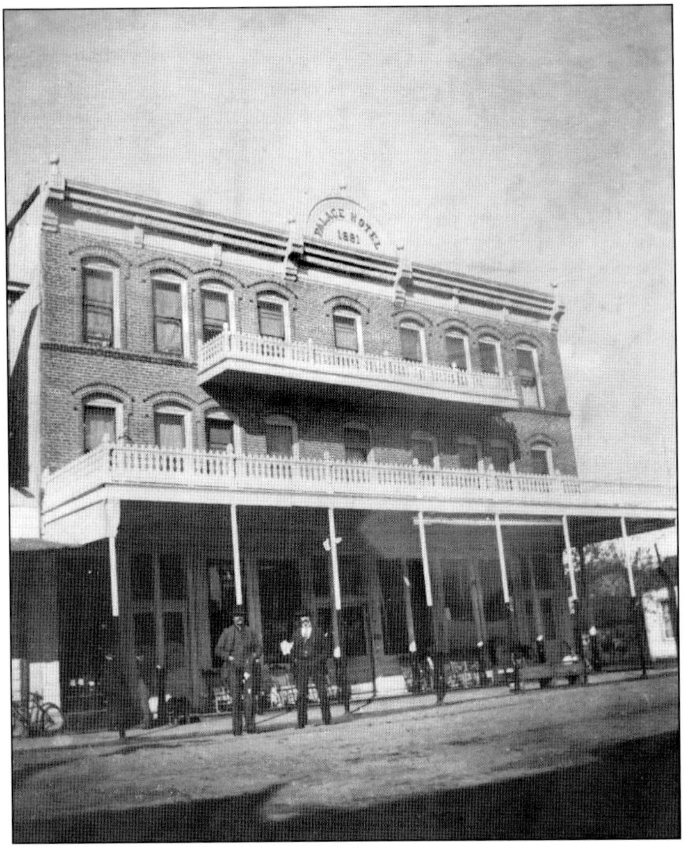

Two unidentified gentlemen are shown in front of the Palace Hotel around 1892.

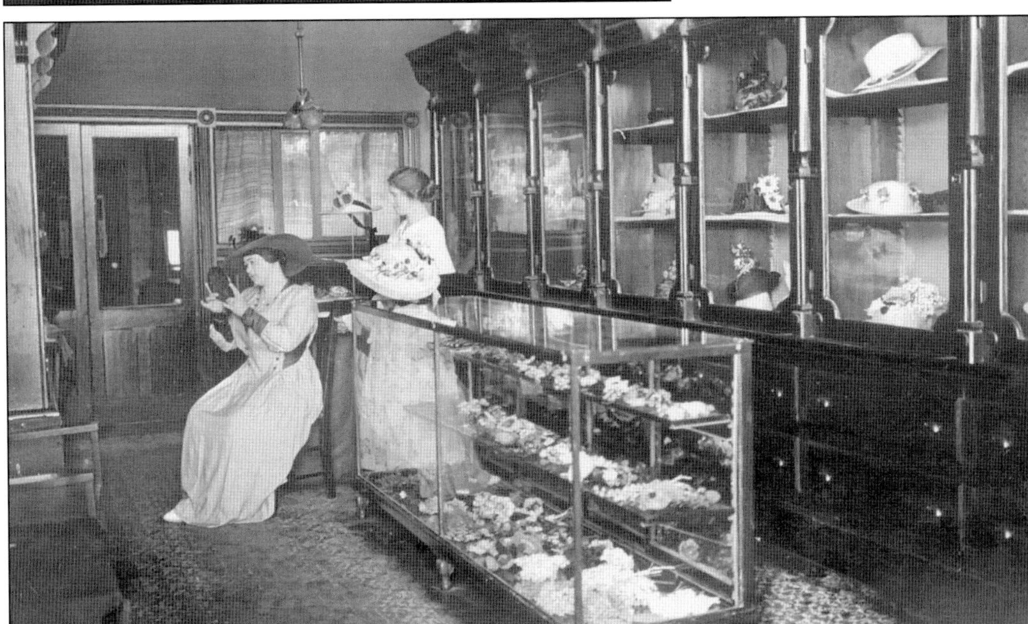

At the Emery Millinery Shop around 1916, owner Grace Emery is waiting on customer Elizabeth Moore Cox.

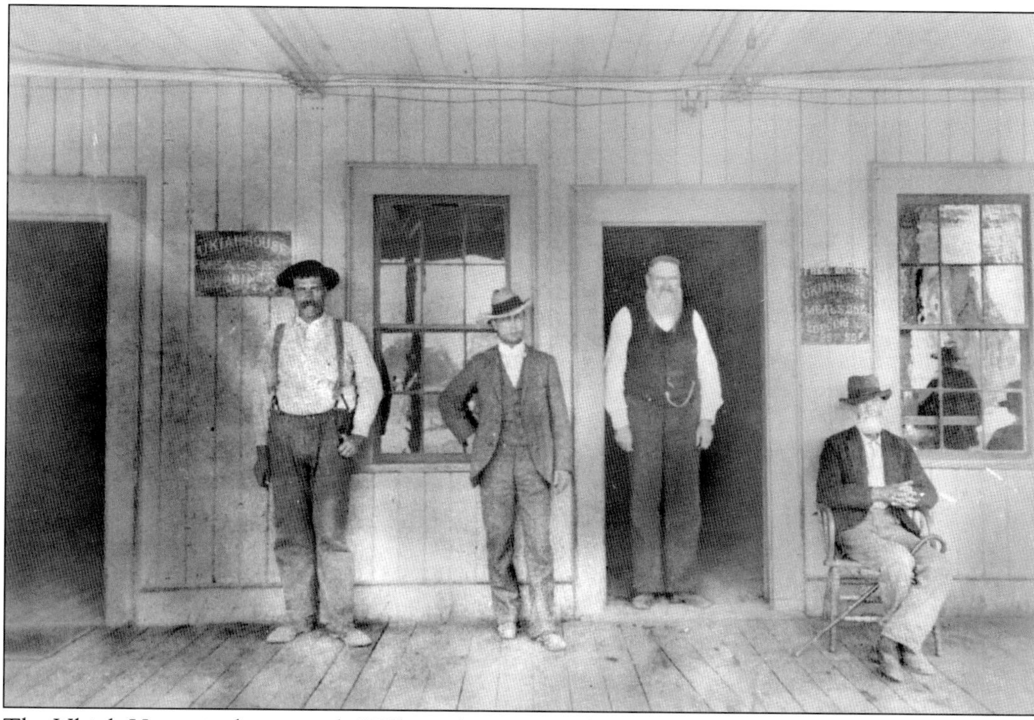

The Ukiah House is shown with William A. Hagans, the proprietor, in the doorway. Hagans was considered a giant in his time at 6 feet, 6 inches tall. This photograph was taken in 1897.

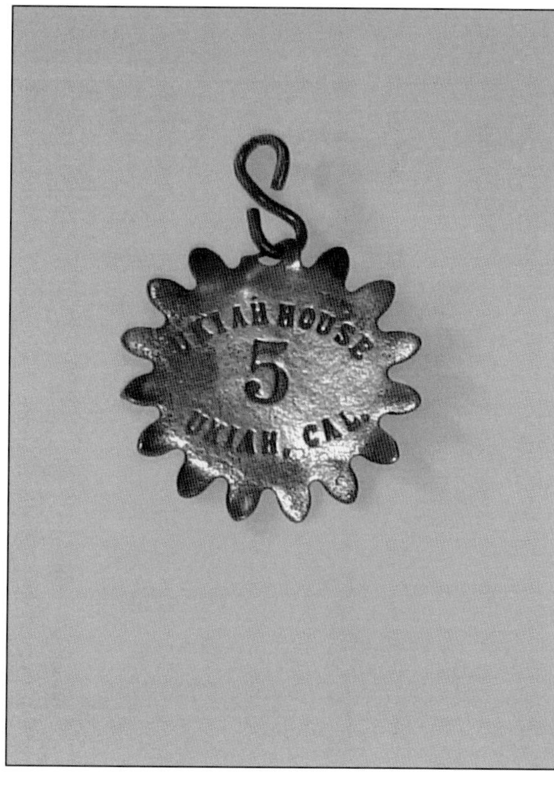

Pictured is a room key fob from the Ukiah House Hotel. The key and fob were found along the Russian River in the 1980s. Unfortunately the key was lost many years ago. (Courtesy of Ed Bold.)

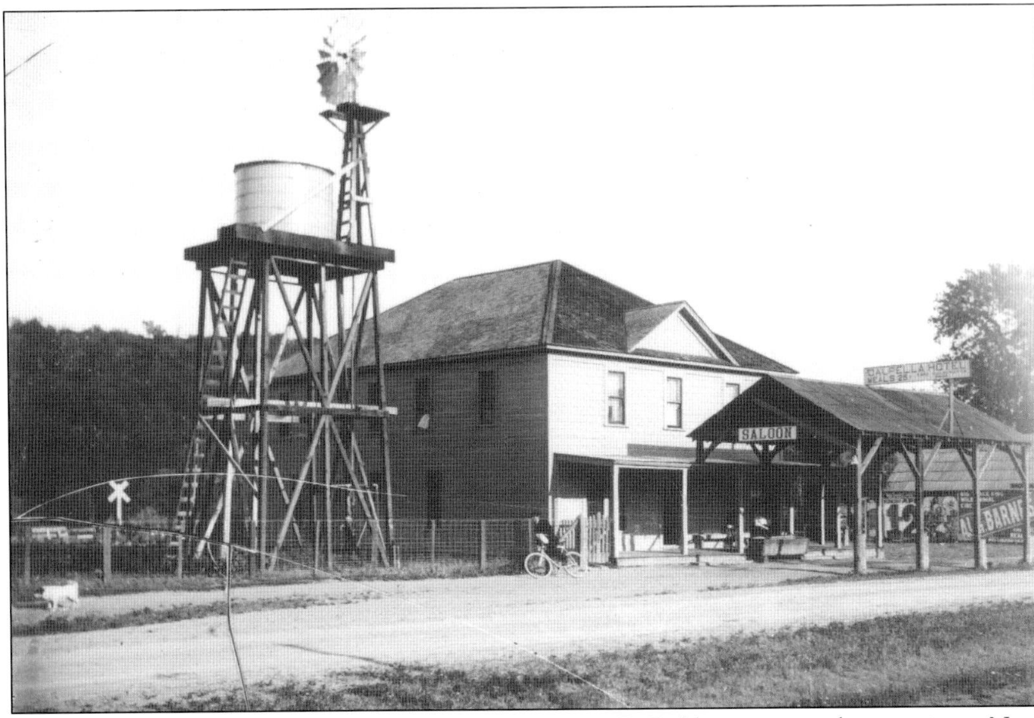

The Calpella Hotel and Saloon is pictured in 1911. Tom D. Balderstron was the proprietor. Note the sign that indicates meals are 25¢.

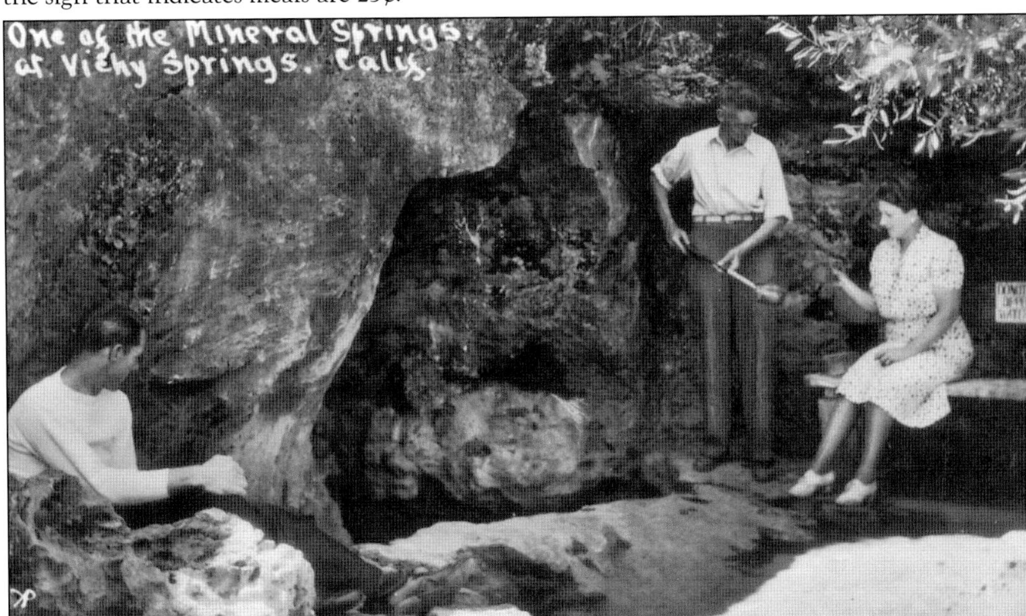

This 1936 postcard shows Vichy Springs, one of the many natural mineral springs around Ukiah. The springs were started in 1854. The name was changed to Vichy Springs about 1865. Many luminaries stayed at Vichy Springs through the years. It has been said that Mark Twain and Jack London, as well as presidents of the United States, enjoyed the healing waters at Vichy Springs. John L. Sullivan, the famous pugilist, had a sparring camp at this location.

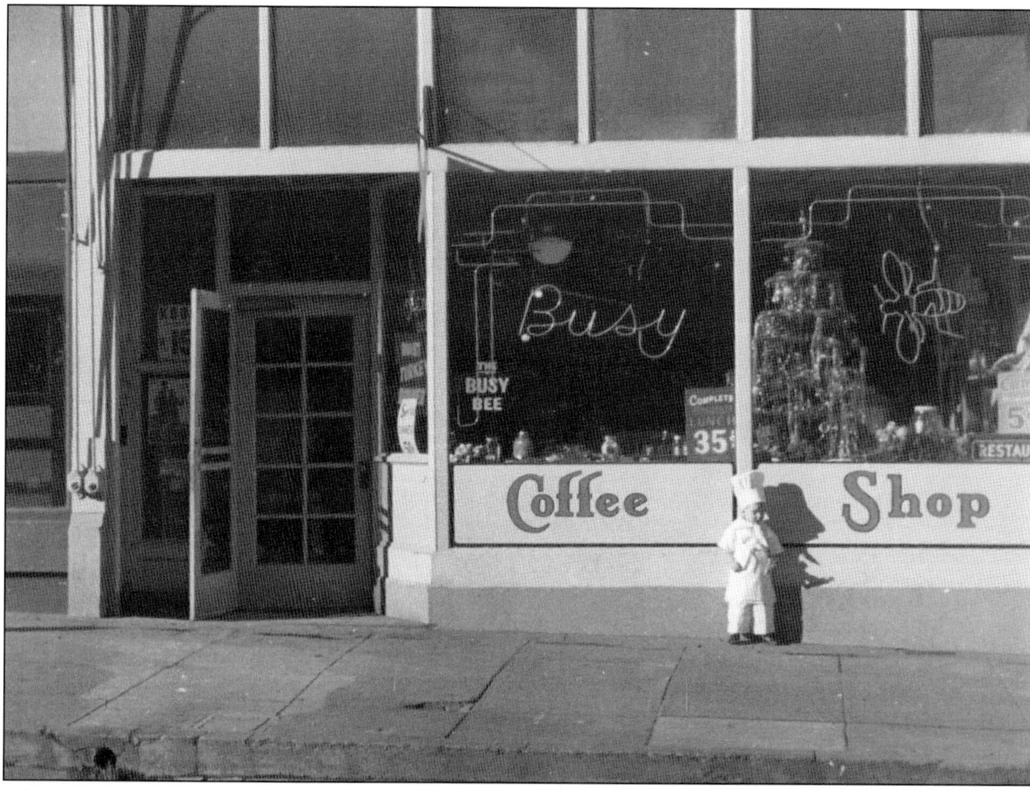

The Busy Bee Café at 372 North State Street is shown here in December 1937.

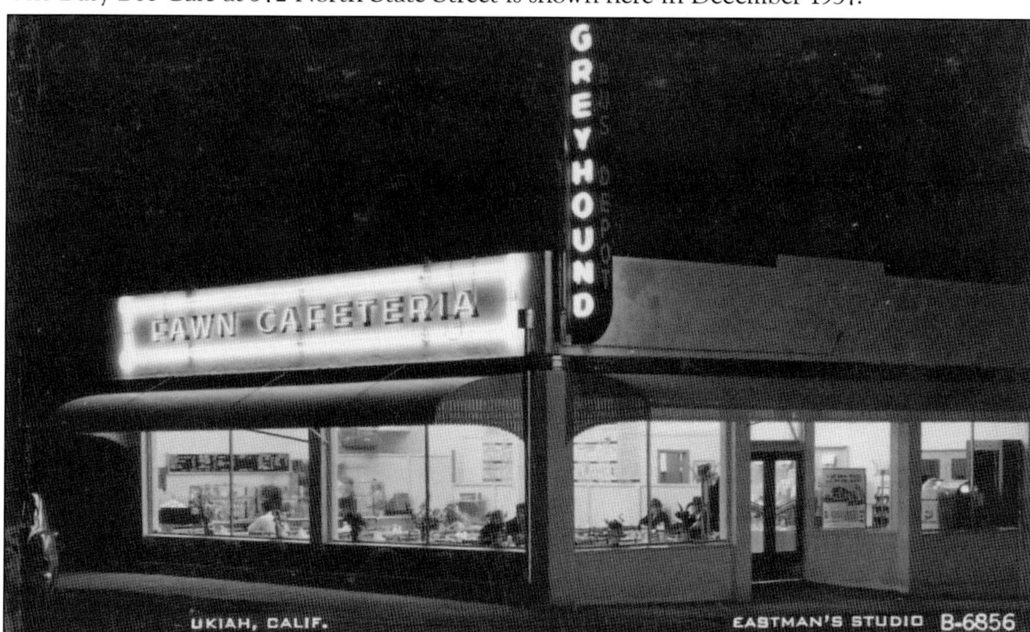

This image shows the Fawn Cafeteria and Greyhound bus stop around 1949. The café was located at the northeast corner of Main and Perkins Streets and was torn down in August and September 1967. It is now the location of the Mendocino County Library.

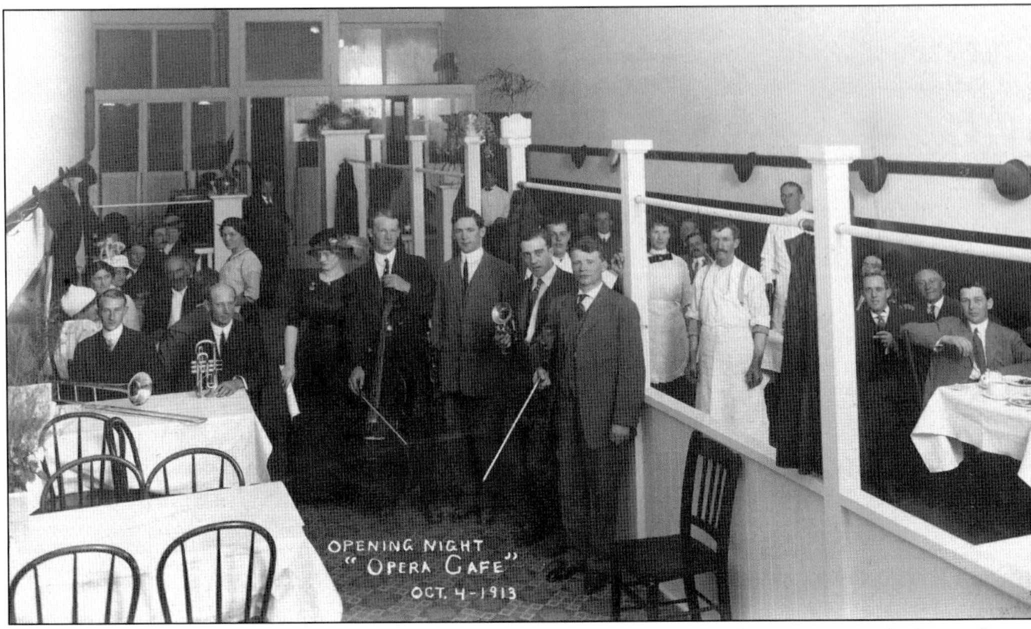

Keller's Orchestra performs at the opening night of the Opera Café at 372 North State Street on October 13, 1914.

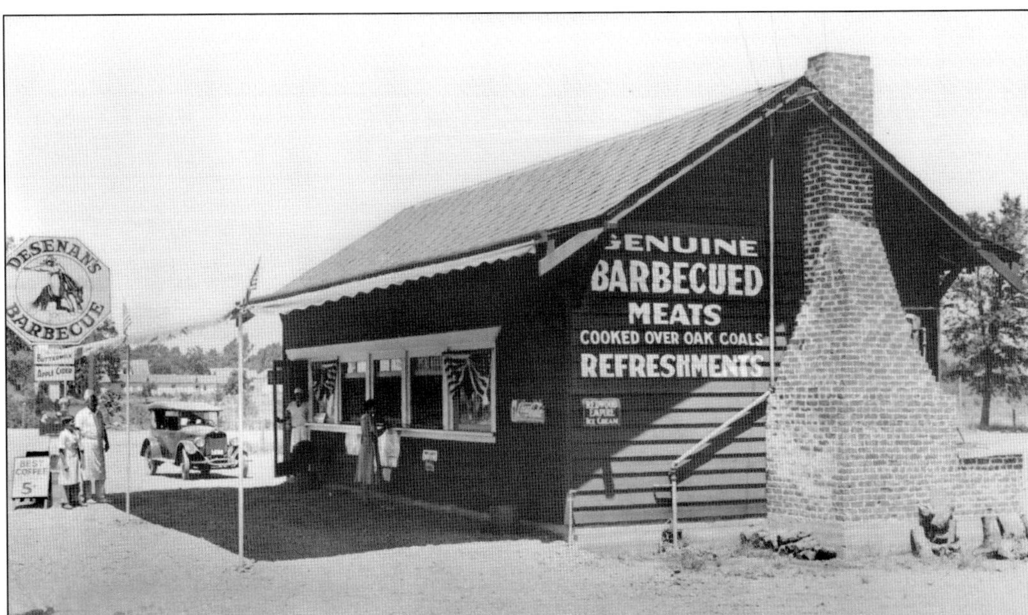

Desenan's Barbecue was located on the southeast corner of State and Gobbi Streets. Edgar Desenan is pictured in 1930 in a white apron with his wife, Mary Desenan, by the window of the restaurant.

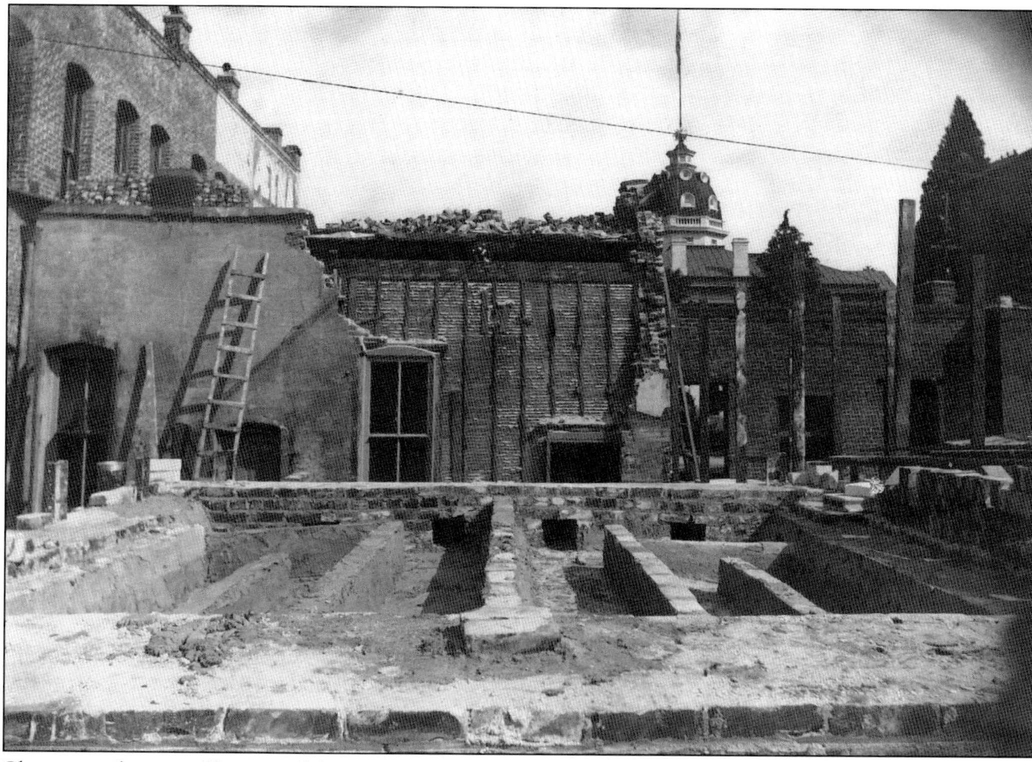

Shown is the installation of the new oven at the Model Bakery in August 1917. This is now the location of Schat's Bakery.

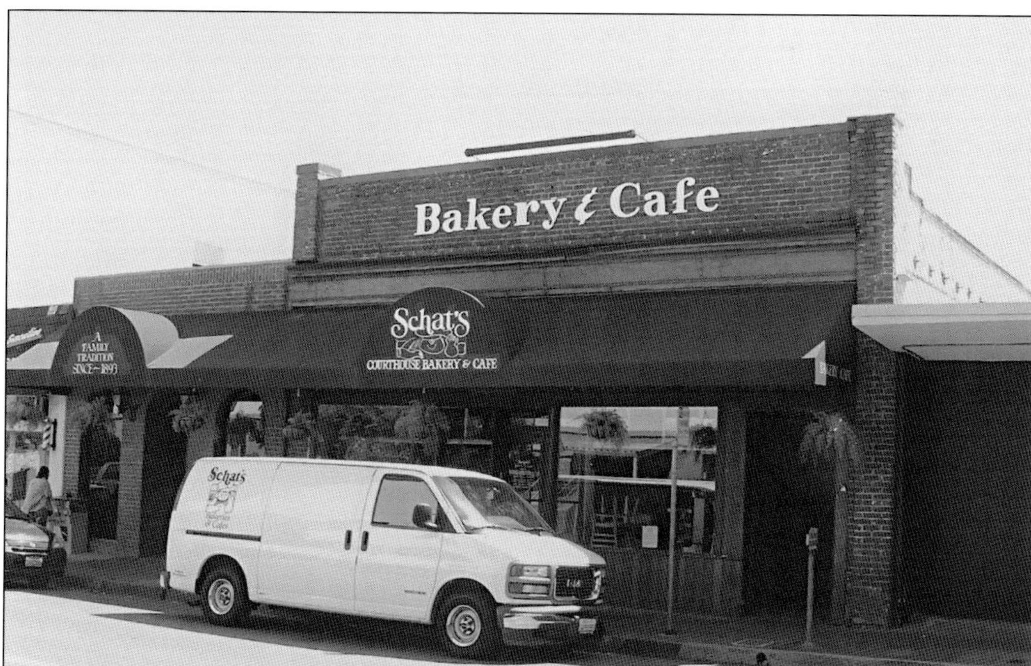

Schat's Bakery and Café, formerly the site of the Model Bakery, is seen in the image above.

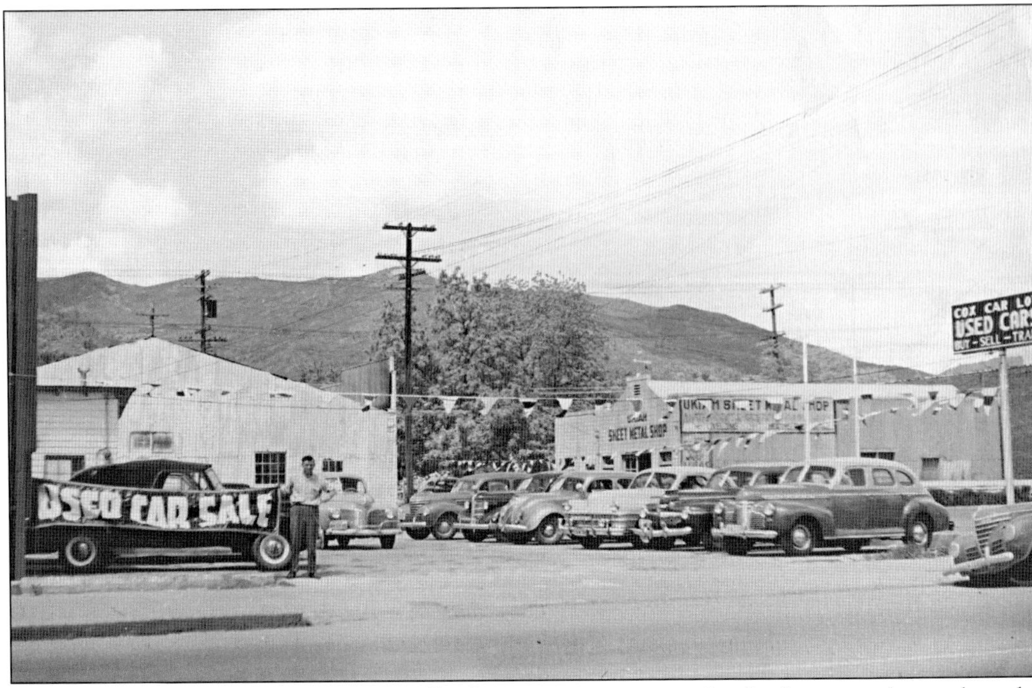

Cox Car Lot is shown around 1948. Kelly Cox, owner, is pictured at his business, located on the corner of South State and Stephenson Streets. This location is now the site of the Alex Thomas Plaza. (Courtesy of Janis Cox.)

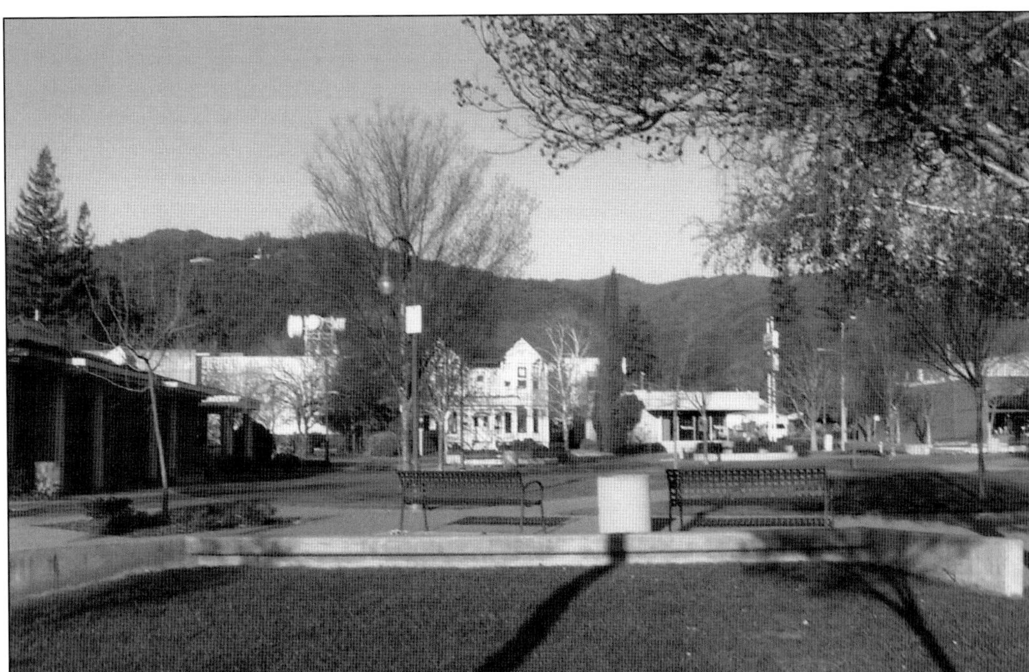

Alex Thomas Plaza, formerly the site of Cox Car Lot, is pictured here in a current photograph.

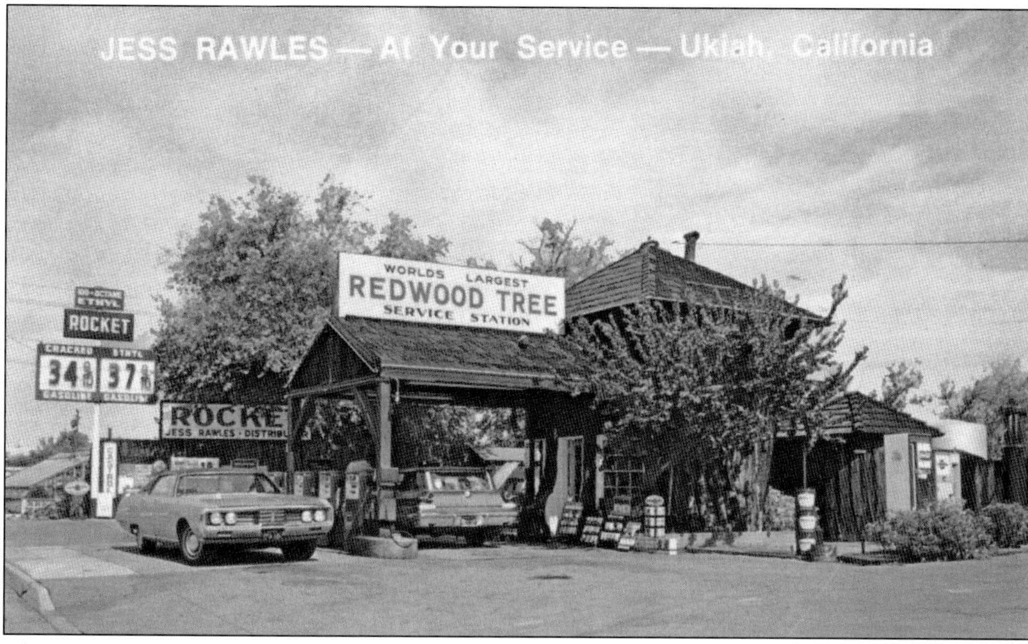

This Redwood Tree Service Station postcard is from the 1960s. The 1,500-year-old redwood tree was transported from the woods 17 miles west of Ukiah and made into a service station. The station was built in 1936. (Courtesy of Ed Bold.)

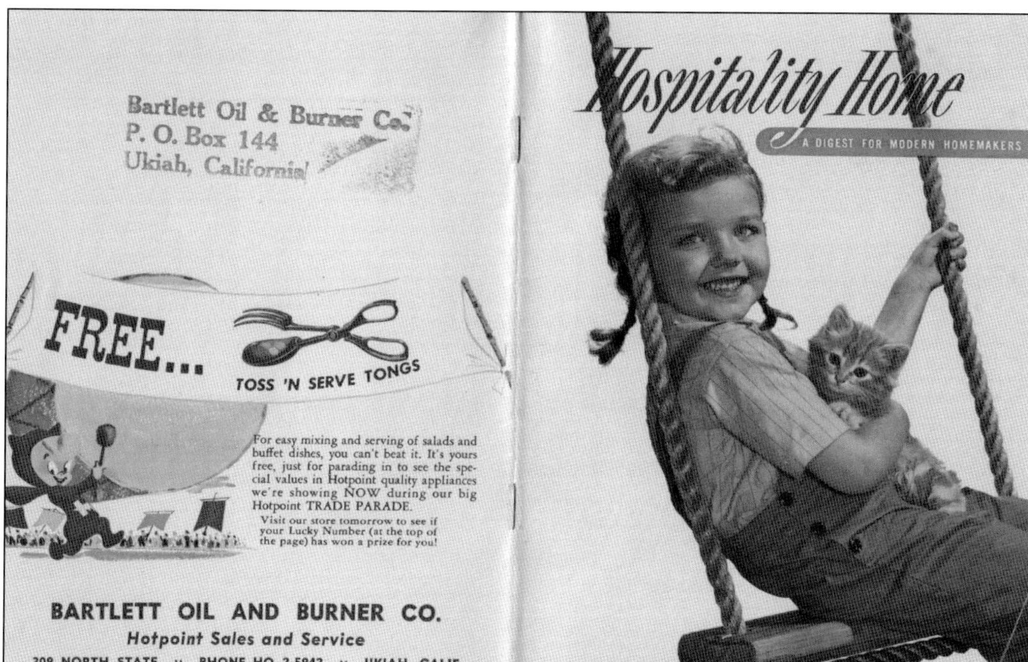

The Bartlett Oil and Burner Company released this 1950s appliance store handout brochure that advertised "Get Your Free Salad Tongs." (Courtesy of Ed Bold.)

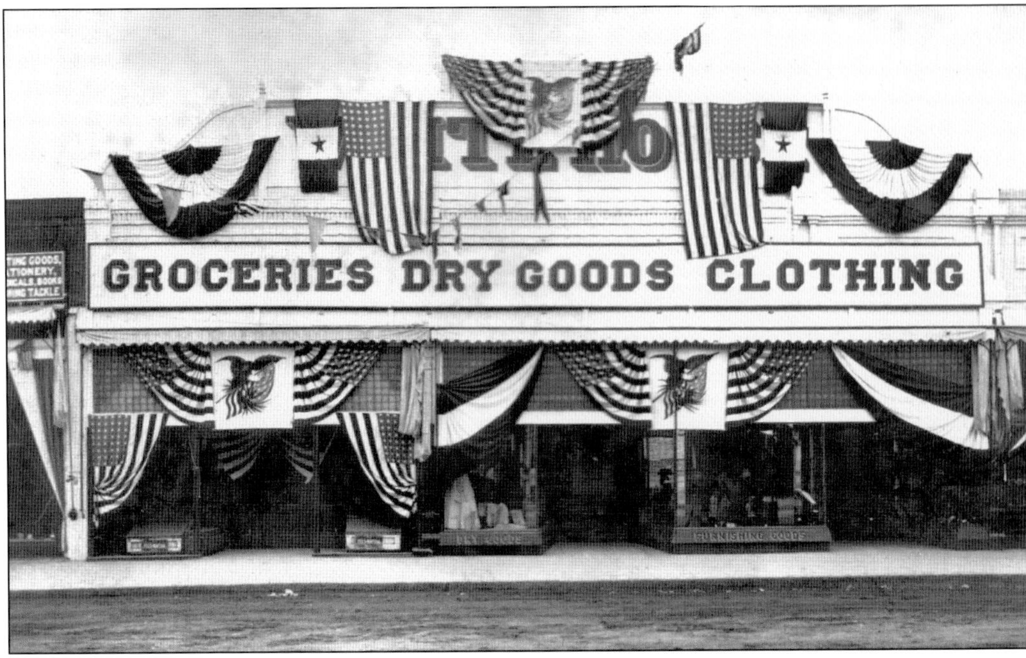

The White House Store on North State Street in May 1910 is decorated for the FOE (the Fraternal Order of Eagles) convention.

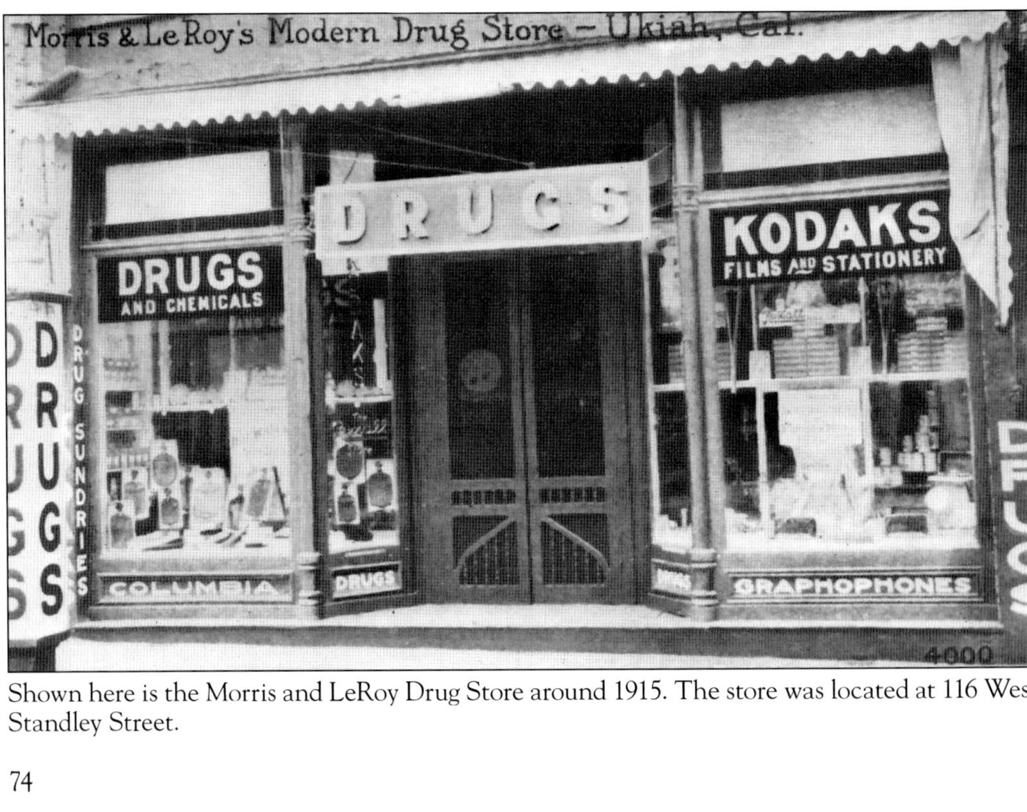

Shown here is the Morris and LeRoy Drug Store around 1915. The store was located at 116 West Standley Street.

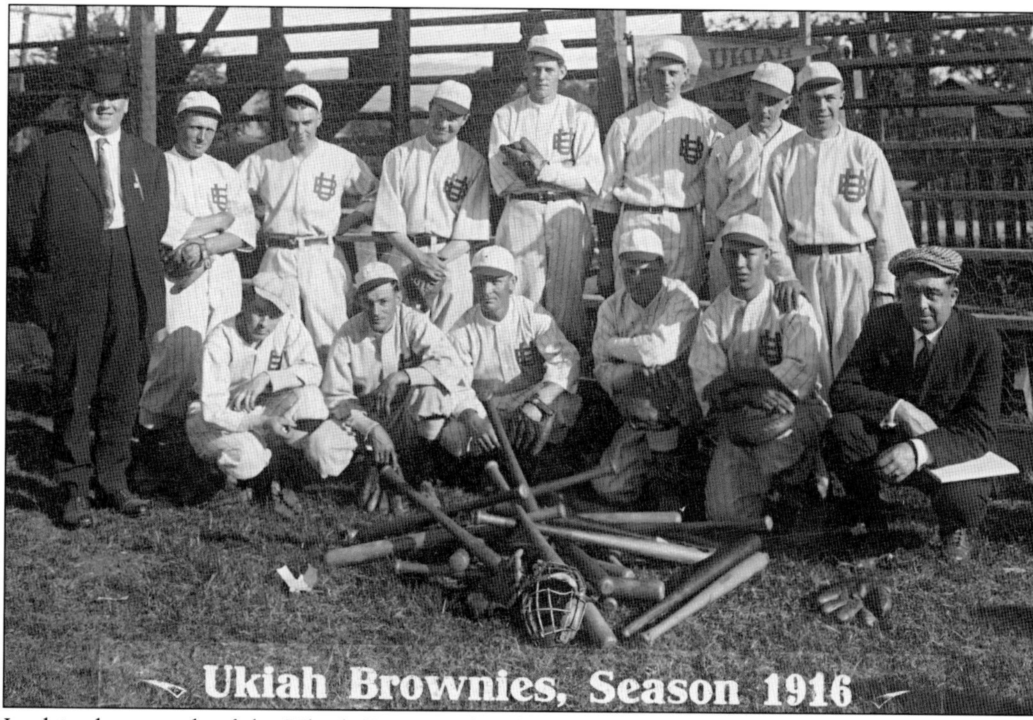

In this photograph of the Ukiah Brownies baseball team in 1916, Donald Brown, the manager, is at the far left. In 1916, the Brownies won 12 games, lost 6, and tied 1.

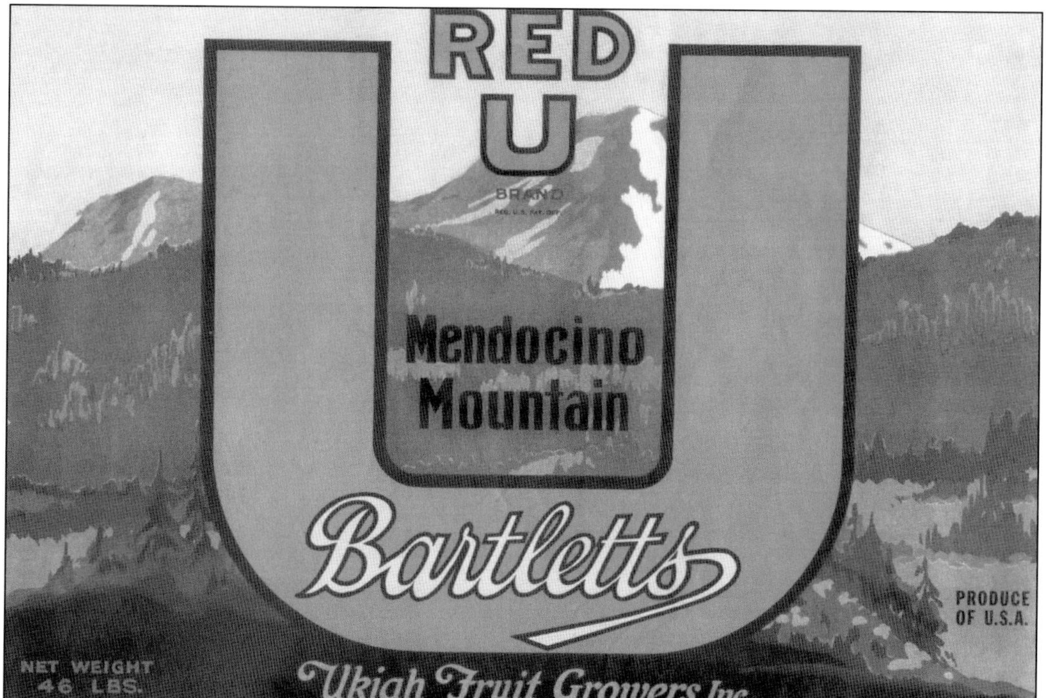

This fruit label for Mendocino Mountain Bartlett Pears was used by Ukiah Fruit Growers, Inc. The company was in business from 1927 to 1977. (Courtesy of Ed Bold.)

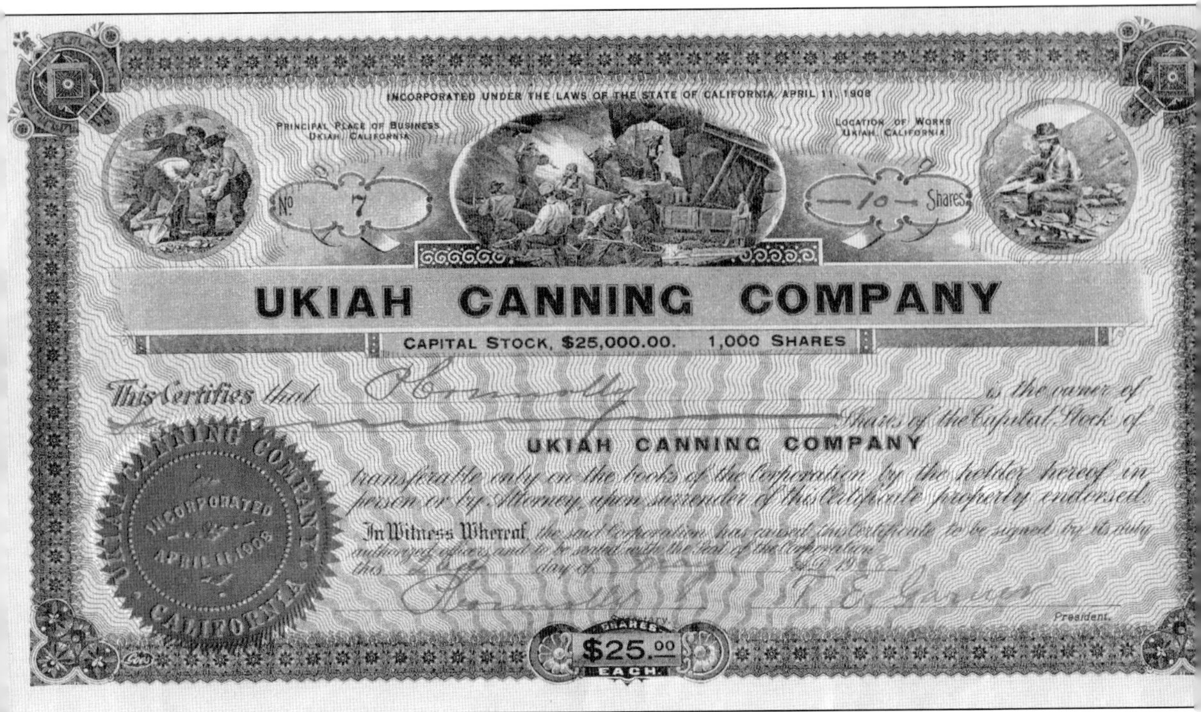

This Ukiah Canning Company stock certificate is from 1908. The company was incorporated in April 1908 and was in business for two seasons, starting in September 1908. After the September 1909 season, the company closed because of indebtedness. (Courtesy of Ed Bold.)

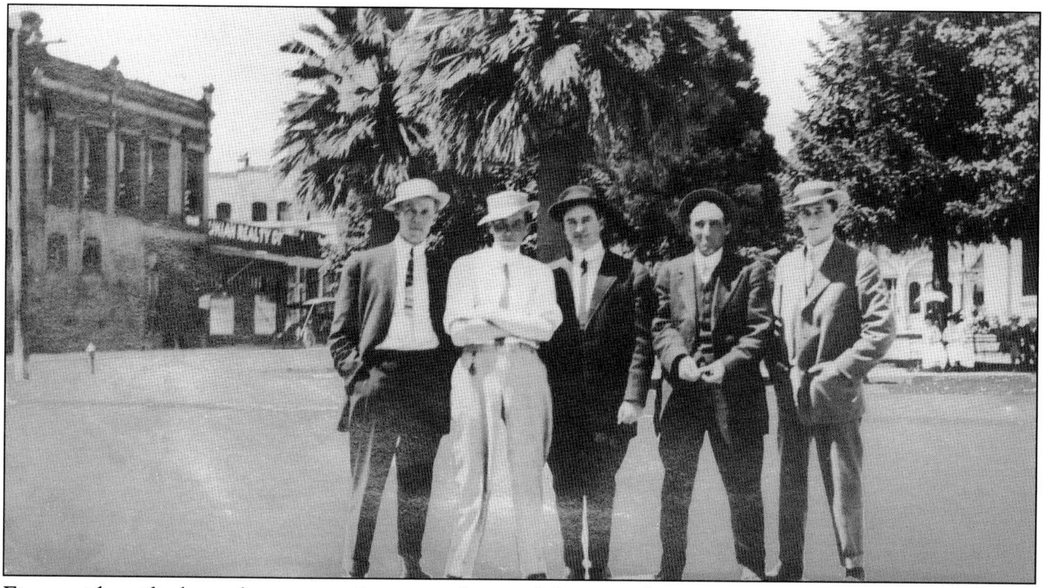

Five unidentified gentlemen are shown in front of the courthouse in 1911 or 1912. Ukiah Realty Company is shown in the background at 109 West Perkins Street.

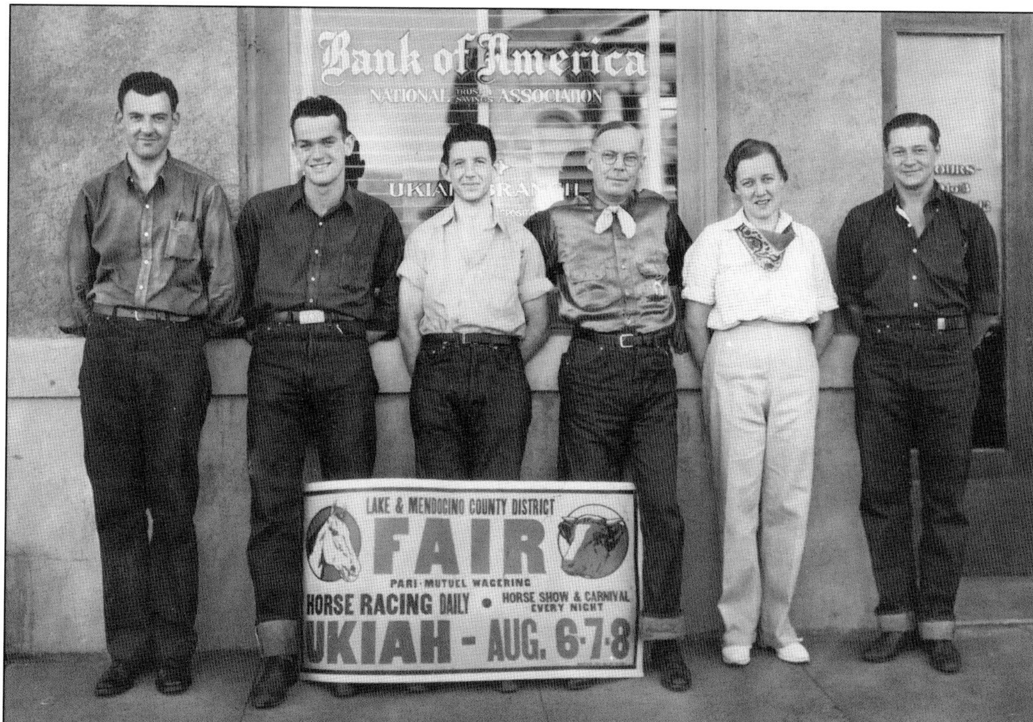

Bank of America employees on August 1937 are posing for the district fair. From left to right are Wayne Goodwin, Andrew Stanton, George Kroetz, Fred Dickey, Mildred Smith, and John Yasaitis.

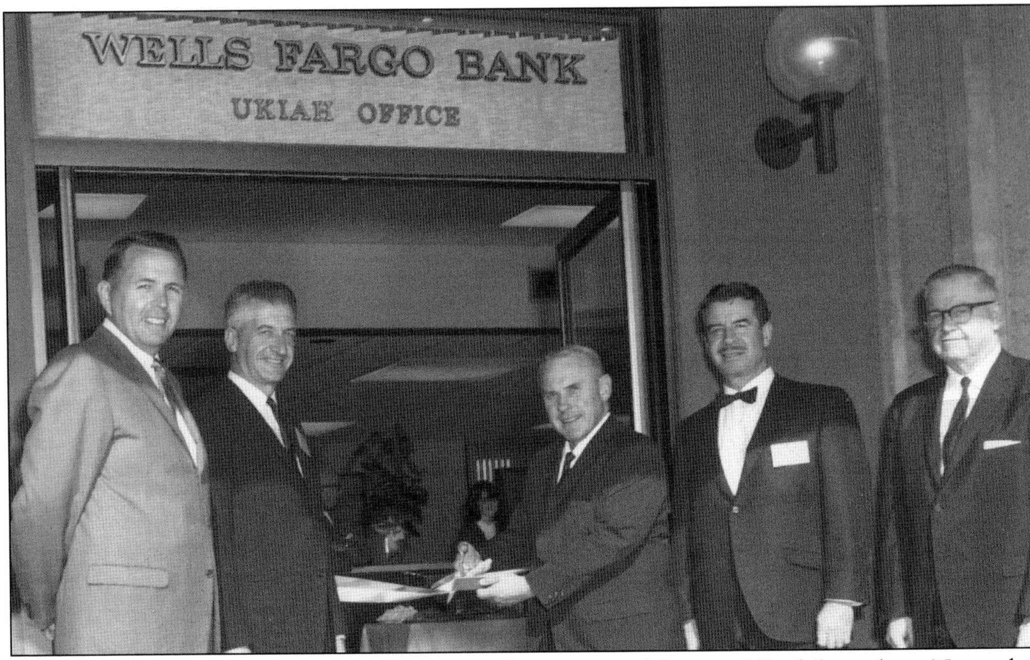

A Wells Fargo Bank ribbon-cutting celebrates the opening of the new Ukiah branch on November 20, 1965. From left to right are Jack Kummert, manager; Ralph Crawford Jr.; Meredith ("Buzz") Harlowe, Ukiah City councilman and ribbon cutter; Jim Keegan; and Harold Trenholm, president of the Ukiah Chamber of Commerce.

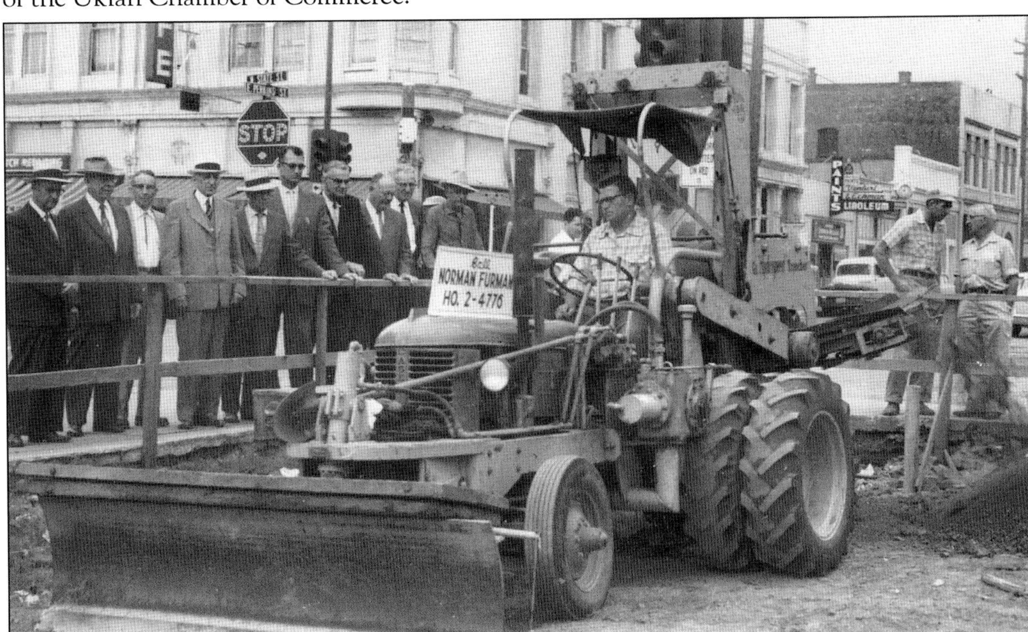

This picture shows the ground-breaking for Mendocino Title on August 28, 1958. Norman Furman is on the equipment. The location of the building was the northeast corner of State and Perkins Streets.

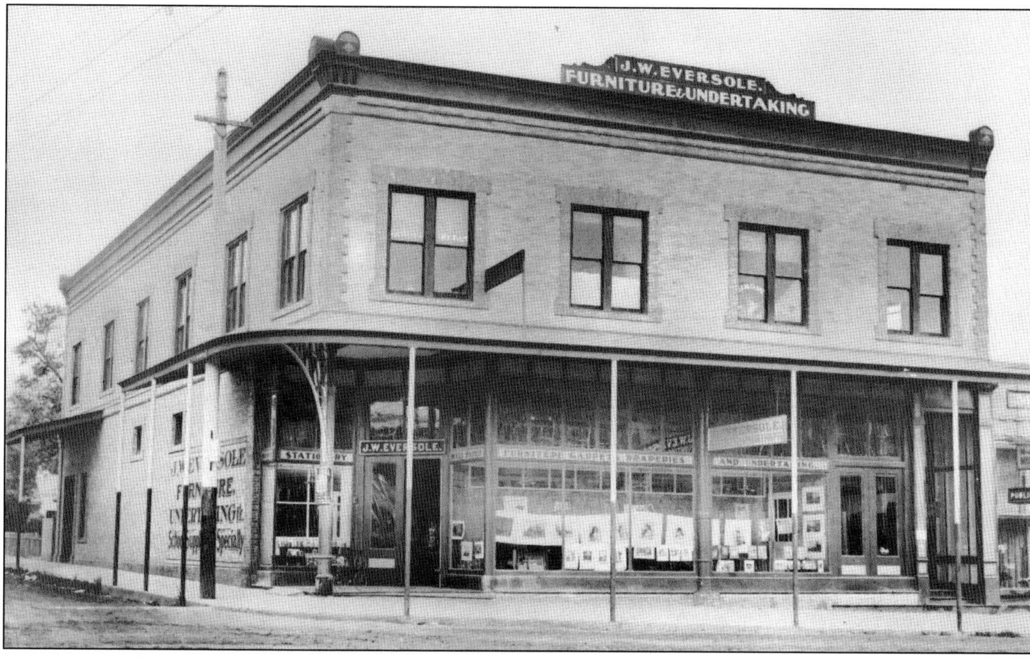

J. W. Eversole Furniture and Undertaking, shown in 1906, was located at the corner of Smith and State Streets.

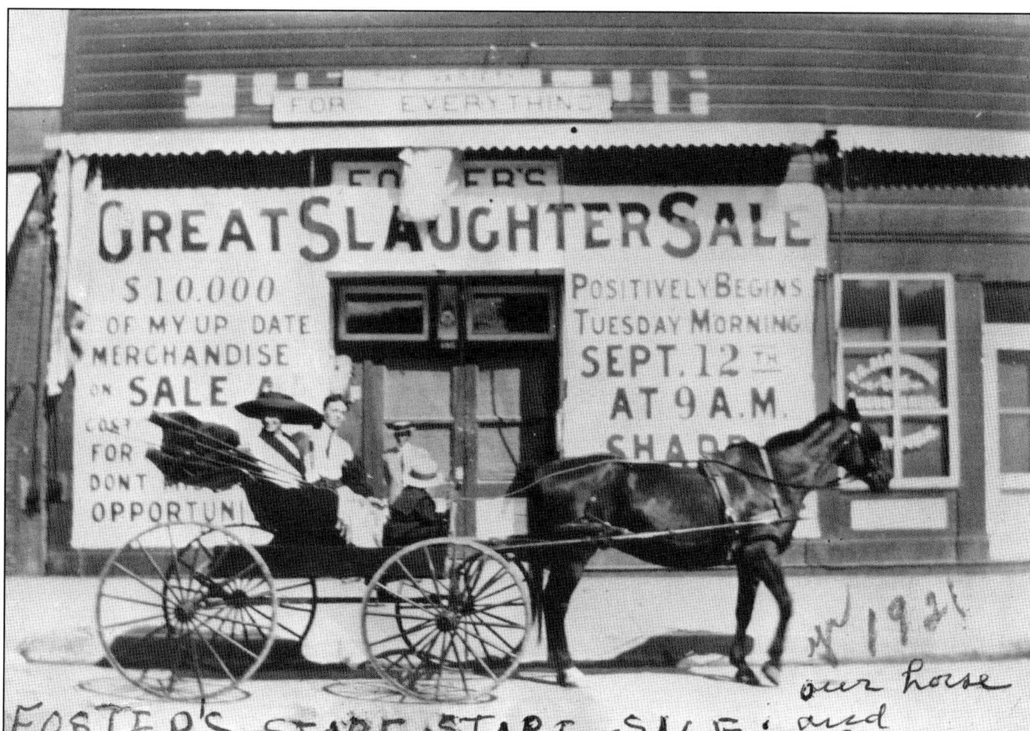

Foster's Variety Store was located at 115 South State Street. Lyndell and Katherine Foster are pictured here in September 1921. F. C. Albertson Insurance is on the right of the picture. Foster used many unique ideas to promote his business, including a balloon ascension shown on page 94.

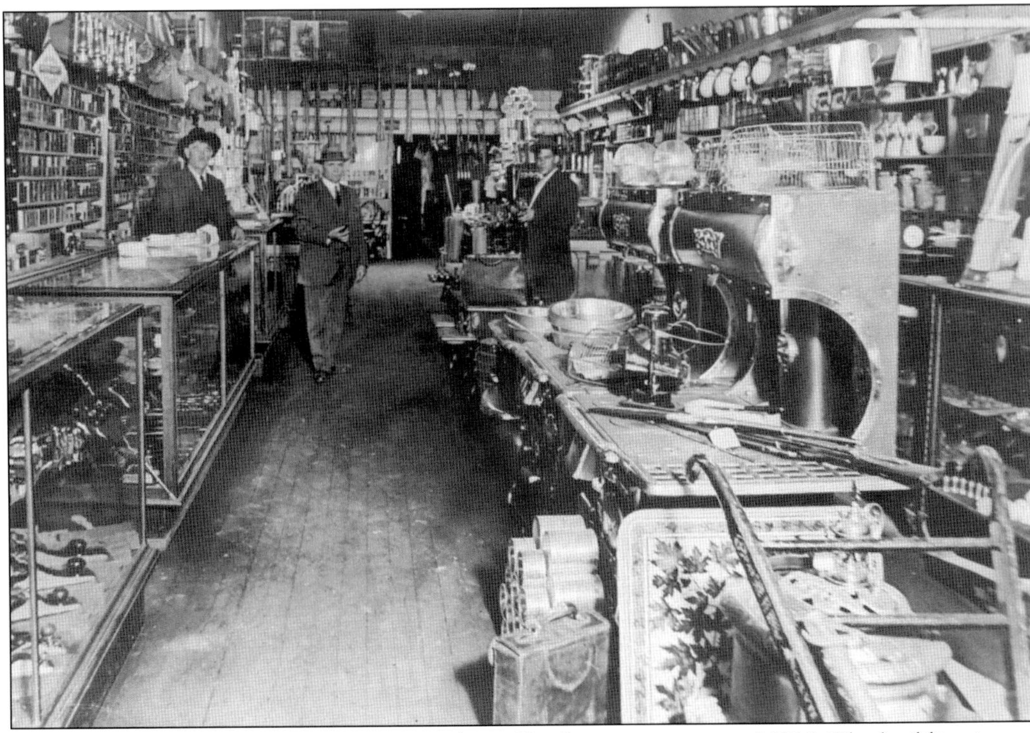

This is an interior view of the James A. Gibson Hardware store around 1910. The building is now the home of the China Chef restaurant at 255 North State Street.

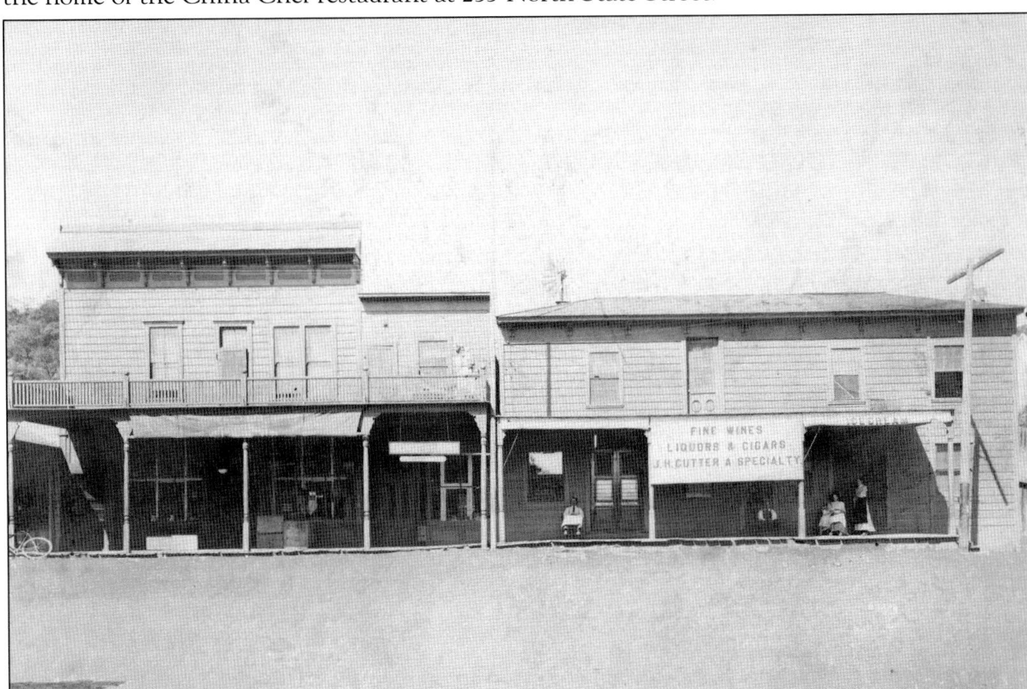

The Frank Dooley Store and Independent Saloon are shown in this 1905 photograph. This is now the location of the Bluebird Café in Hopland.

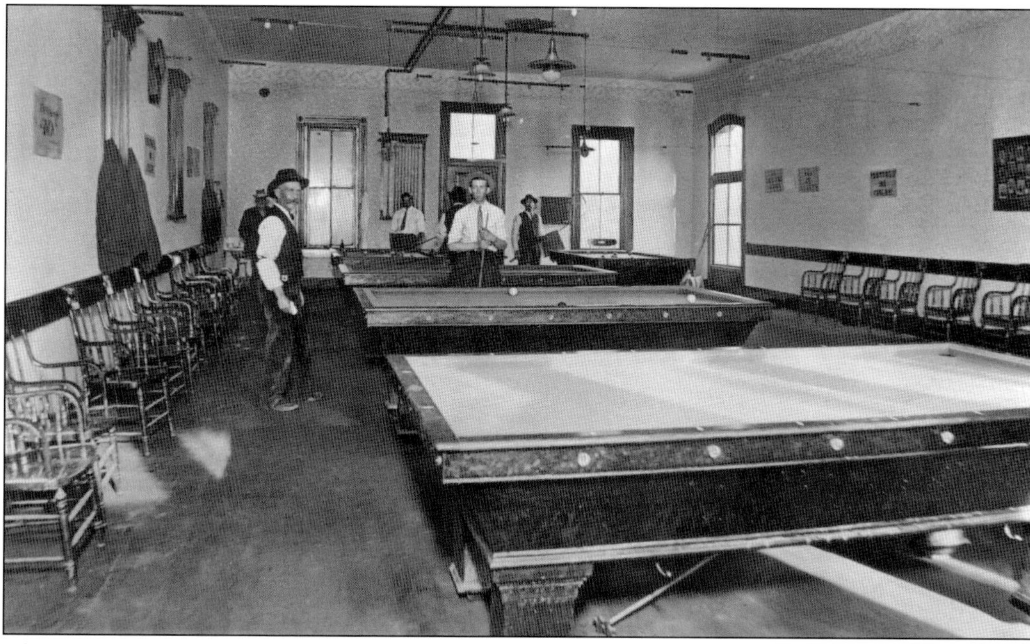

This picture is of the McKesson Pool Hall in 1911. Samuel D. McKesson, the proprietor, is shown on the left. The pool hall was located in the Dowling Building, which was on the northeast corner of North State and Smith Streets.

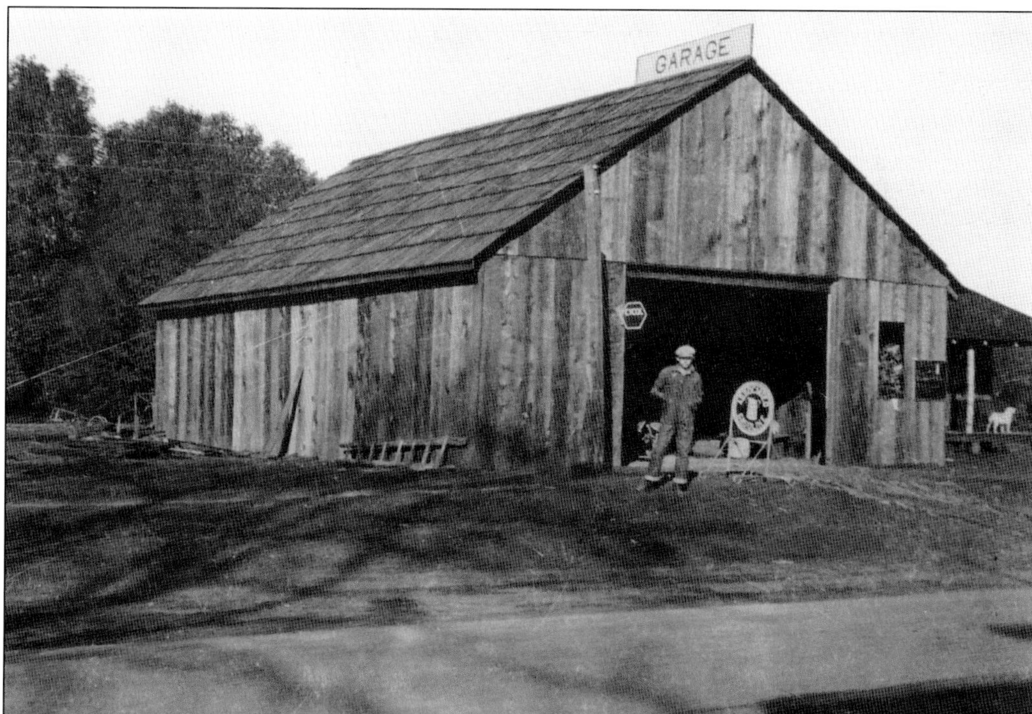

The Sam Newell Garage is shown in this 1923 picture. Sam Newell's garage was located in Calpella, which is 5 miles north of Ukiah.

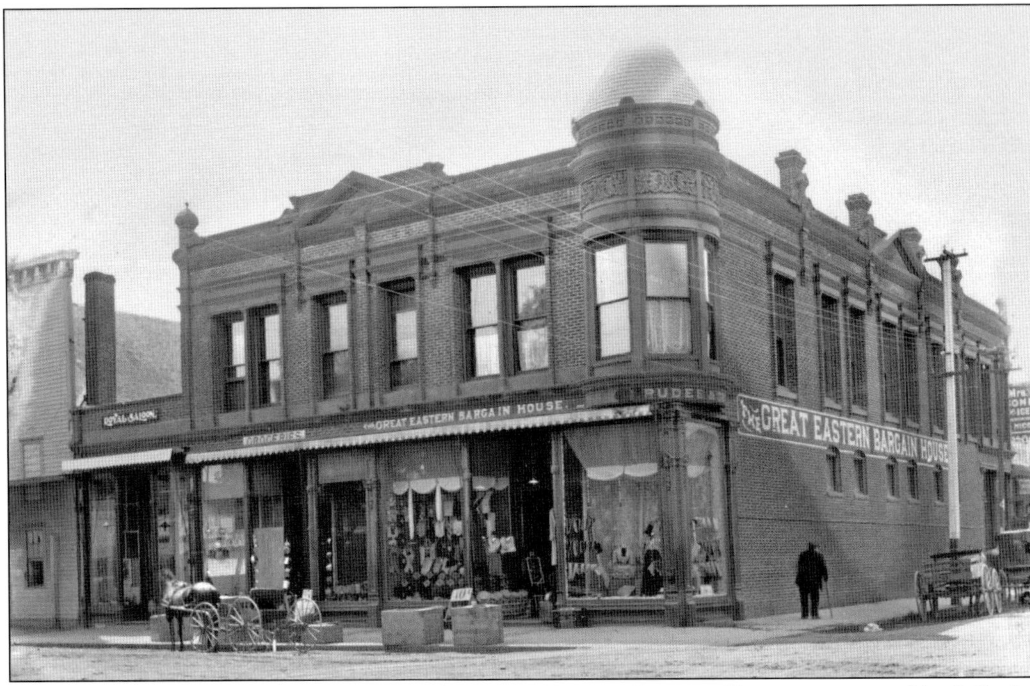

The Marks Building is shown in 1898. The Great Eastern Bargain House was owned by I. Rudee from 1896 to 1899. It is now the location of the Ukiah Brewery at the southwest corner of Perkins and State Streets.

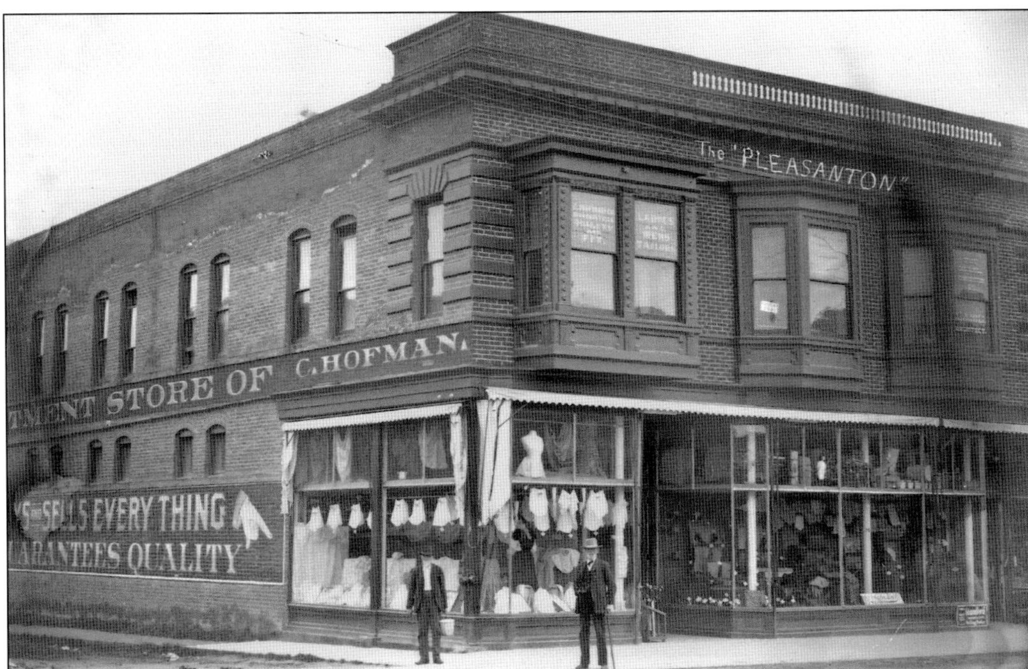

The C. Hofman Department Store is shown in 1907. The Hotel Pleasanton was located above the department store. The building was constructed in 1899 and stands on the southeast corner of State and Standley Streets.

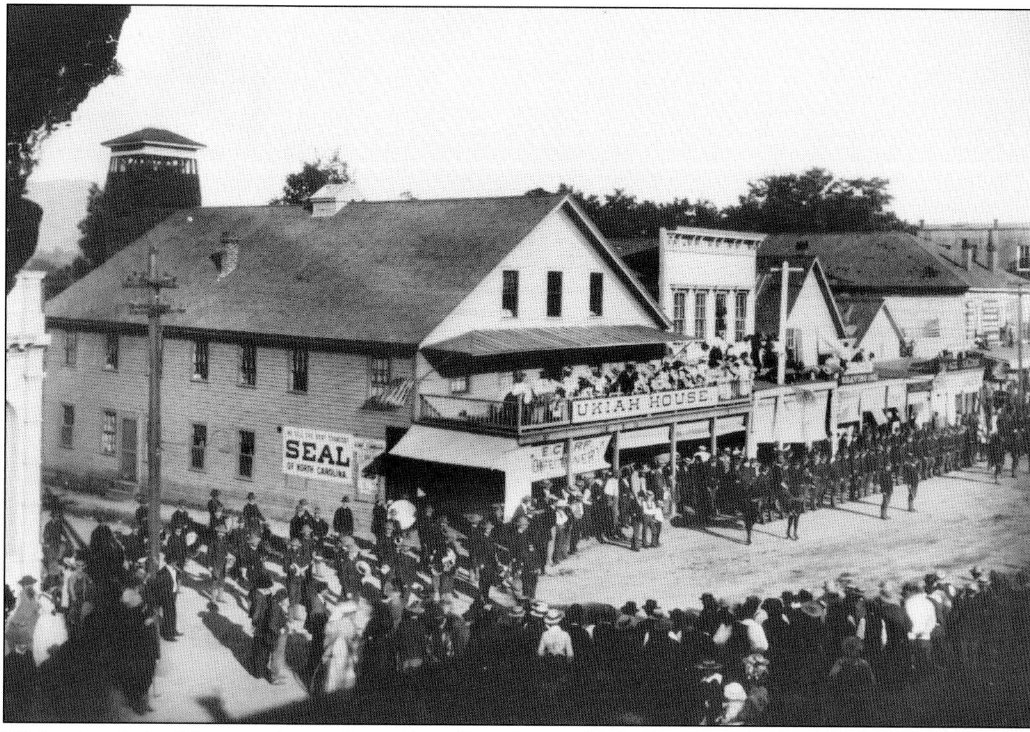

This view is looking southeast from Standley Street. It shows the Ukiah House with the water tower in the background. The water tower was erected in 1892 and is pictured here on June 28, 1895. This is the only known photograph of the water tower.

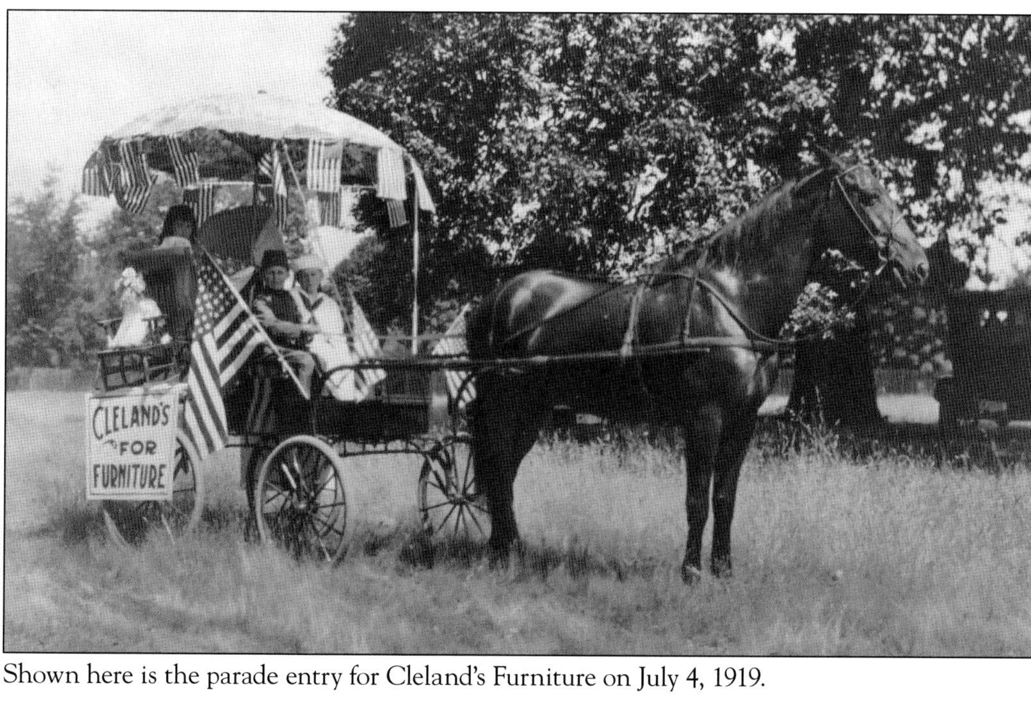

Shown here is the parade entry for Cleland's Furniture on July 4, 1919.

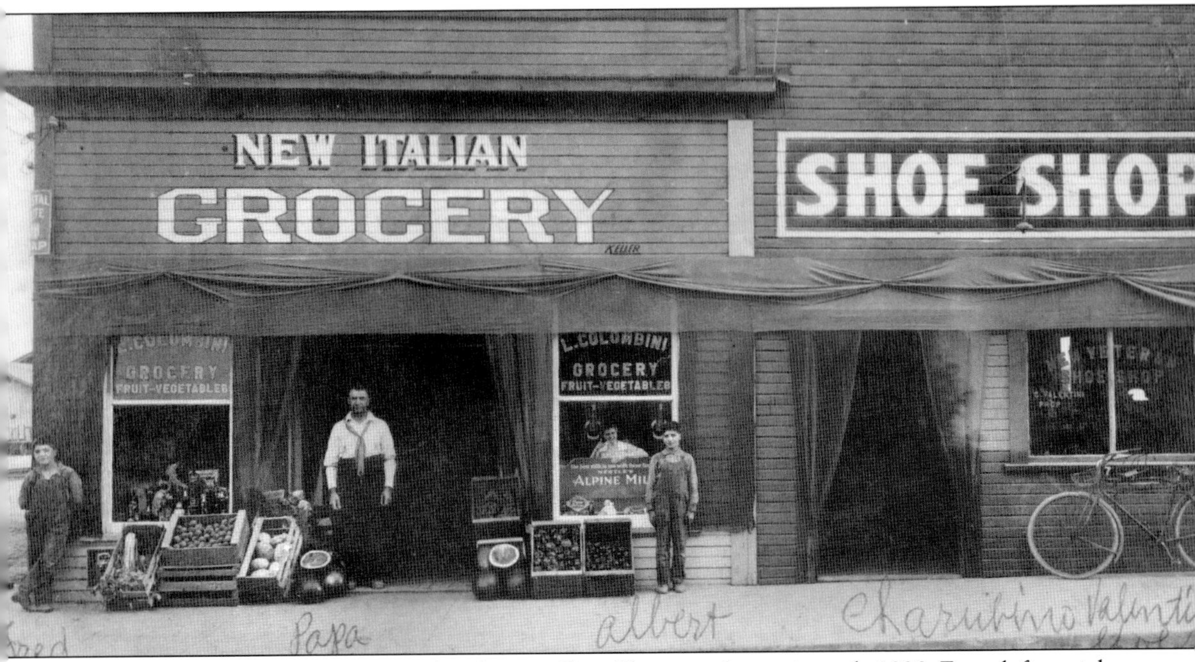

The New Italian Grocery and Valentini Shoe Shop are shown in early 1920. From left to right are Fred, Louis ("Papa"), and Albert Colombini. The bicycle shown in front of the shop was ridden to work every day by Cherubino Valentini.

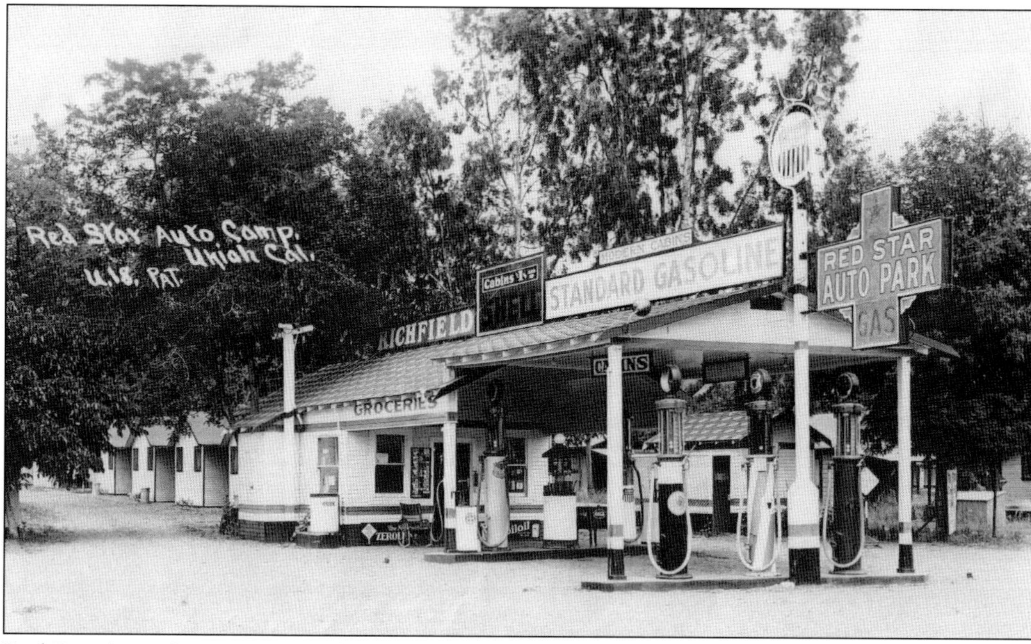

Red Star Auto Camp is pictured around 1930. The automobile camp was located on the southwest corner of Gobbi and State Streets.

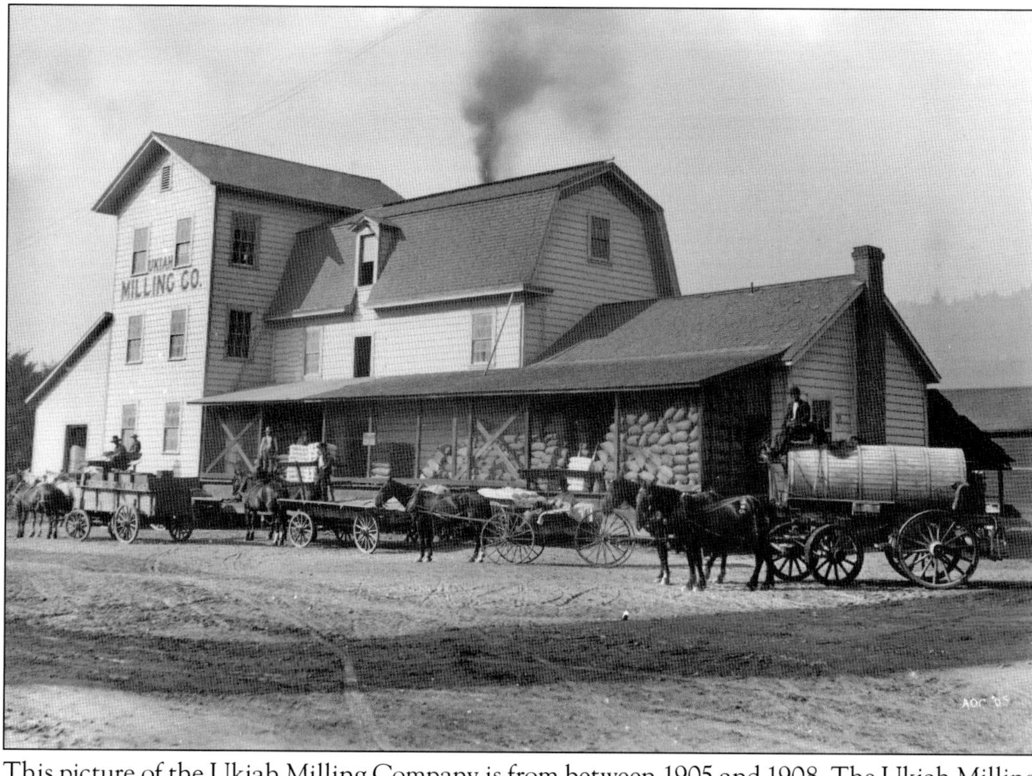

This picture of the Ukiah Milling Company is from between 1905 and 1908. The Ukiah Milling Company was owned by Ludwig Holzhauser. The company was located at the southwest corner of State and Mill Streets. The building was torn down in April 1932.

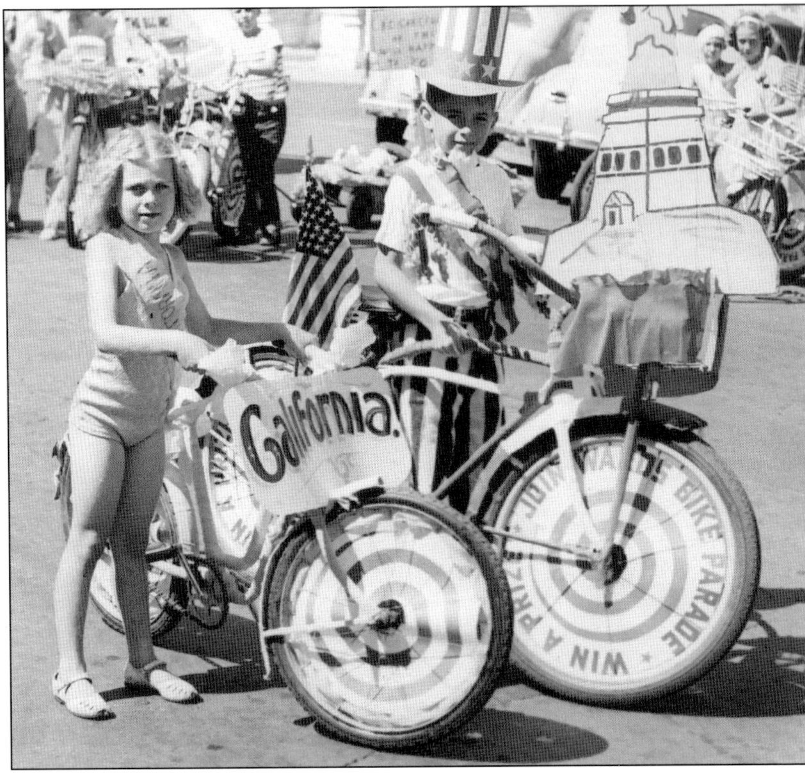

The Montgomery Ward "Win-A-Bike" Parade is shown on June 26, 1948. Marva Lou Romer is dressed as Miss California and Dean Richardson as Uncle Sam.

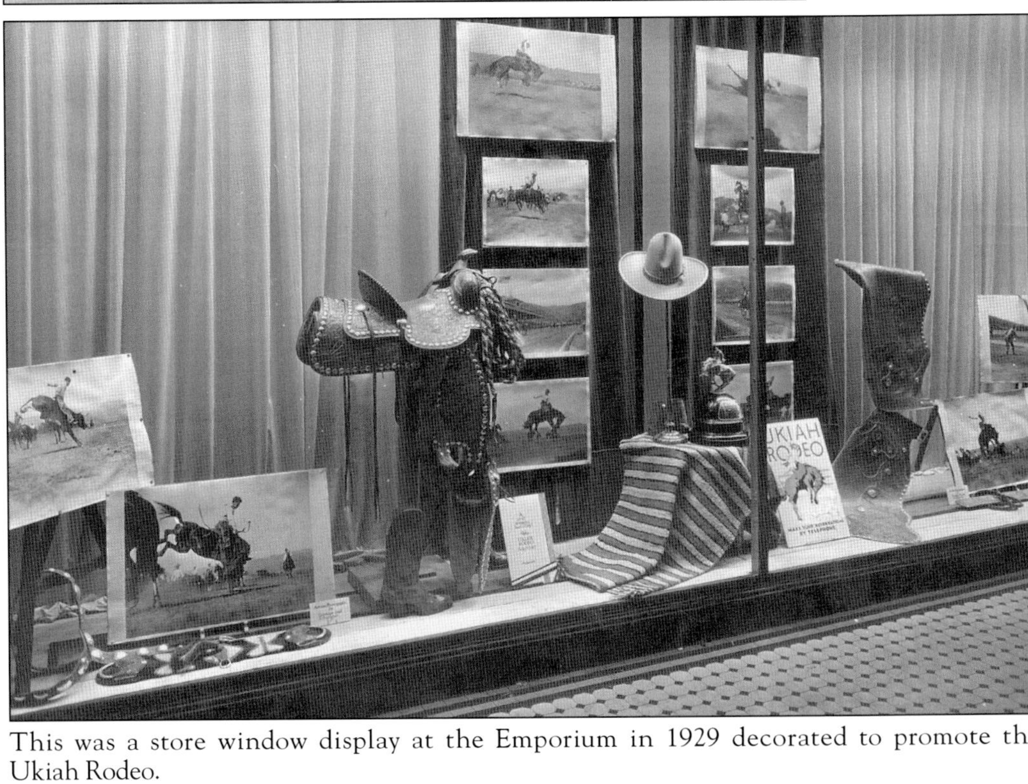

This was a store window display at the Emporium in 1929 decorated to promote the Ukiah Rodeo.

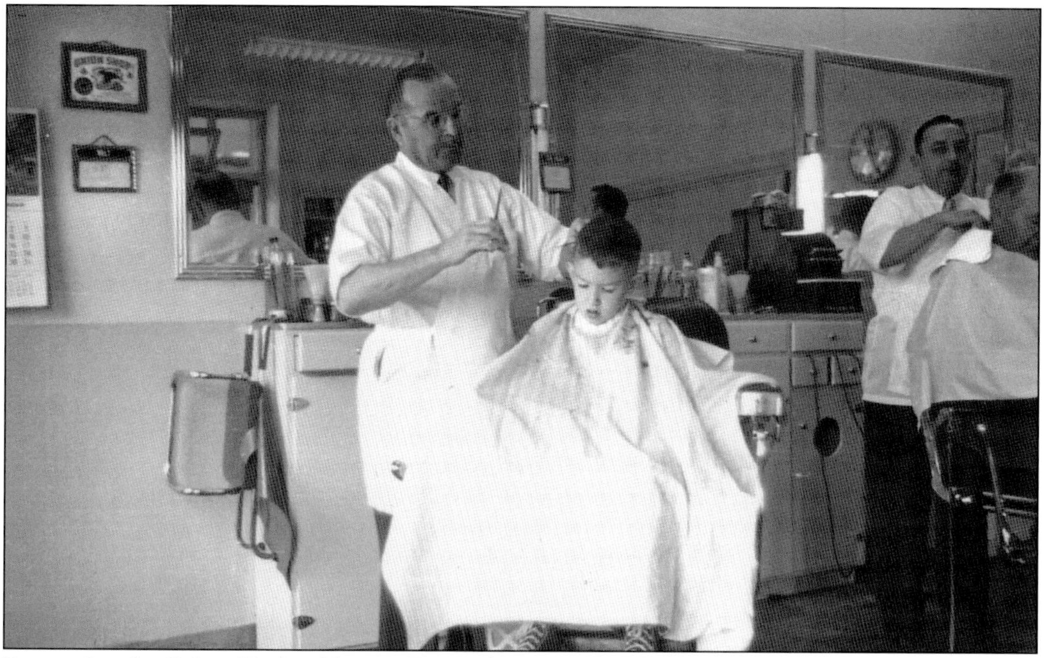

Pictured is the Palace Barber Shop in December 1955. On the left is Walt Sandkulla, and on the right is Carl Wright. The customers are unidentified.

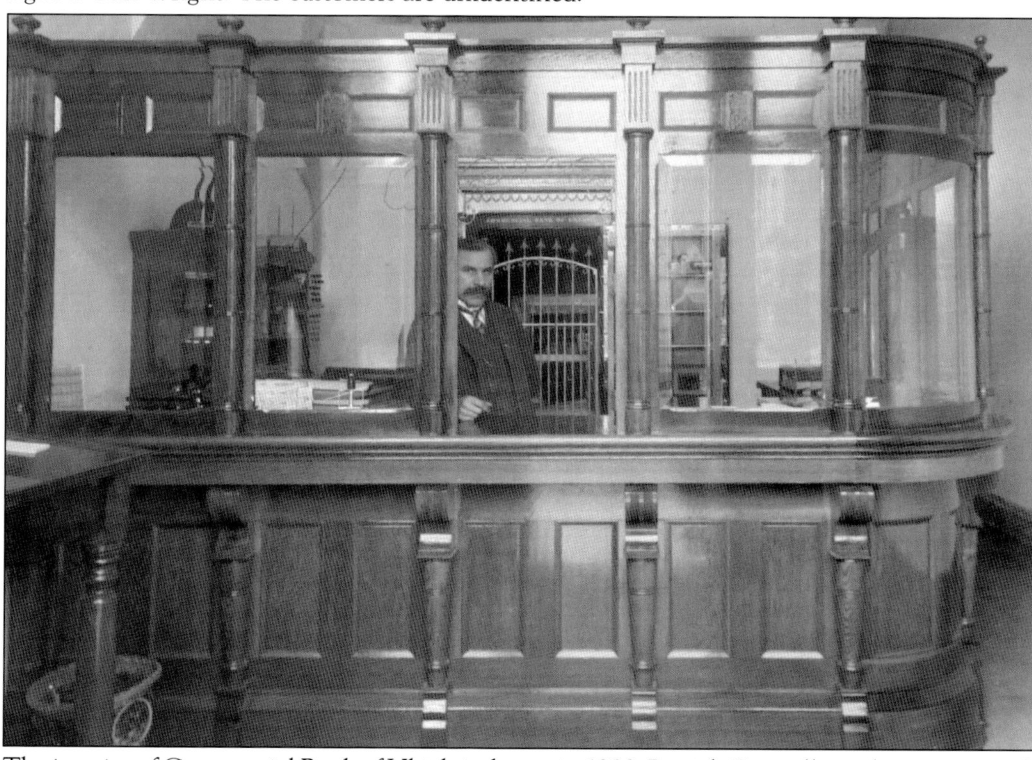

The interior of Commercial Bank of Ukiah is shown in 1908. Patrick Connolly, cashier, is pictured. The Commercial Bank was in this location from January 1902 until October 1909. The bank was located at the northwest corner of Perkins and School Streets.

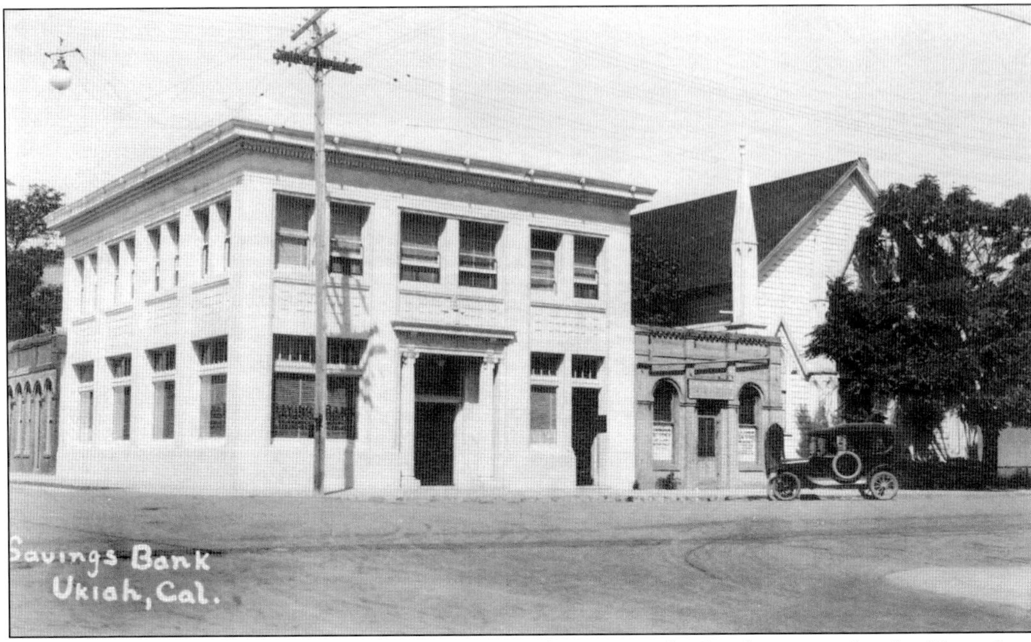

This postcard shows the Savings Bank in the early 1920s. The bank was in this building from February 1917 until December 1992.

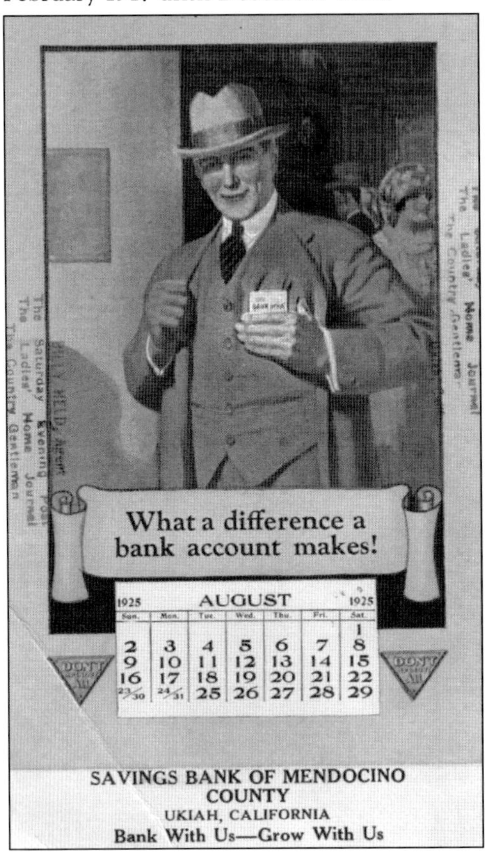

A Savings Bank ink blotter with a gentleman's picture from 1925 is pictured. (Courtesy of Ed Bold.)

Pictured is the Savings Bank Anniversary Book 1903–1953. The Savings Bank of Mendocino County published this anniversary book to advertise their 50th year in business. The book included the history of the bank as well as many pictures and stories on local businesses throughout the 50 years.

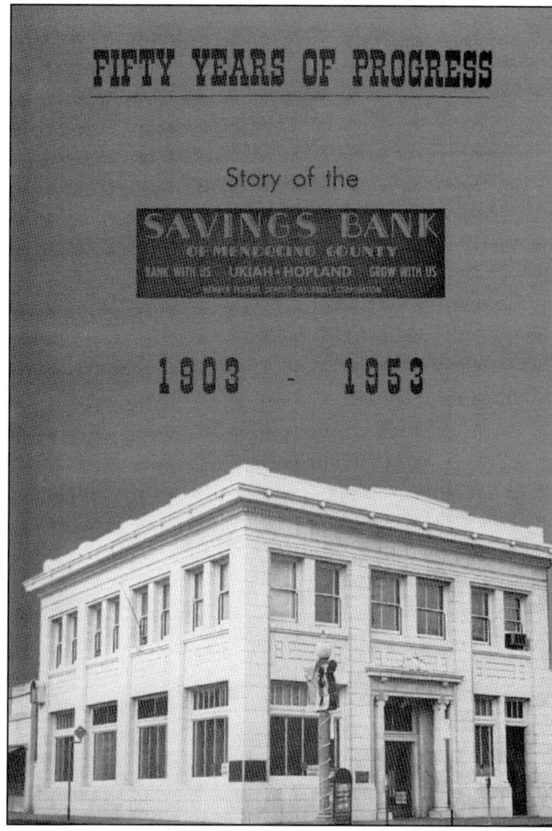

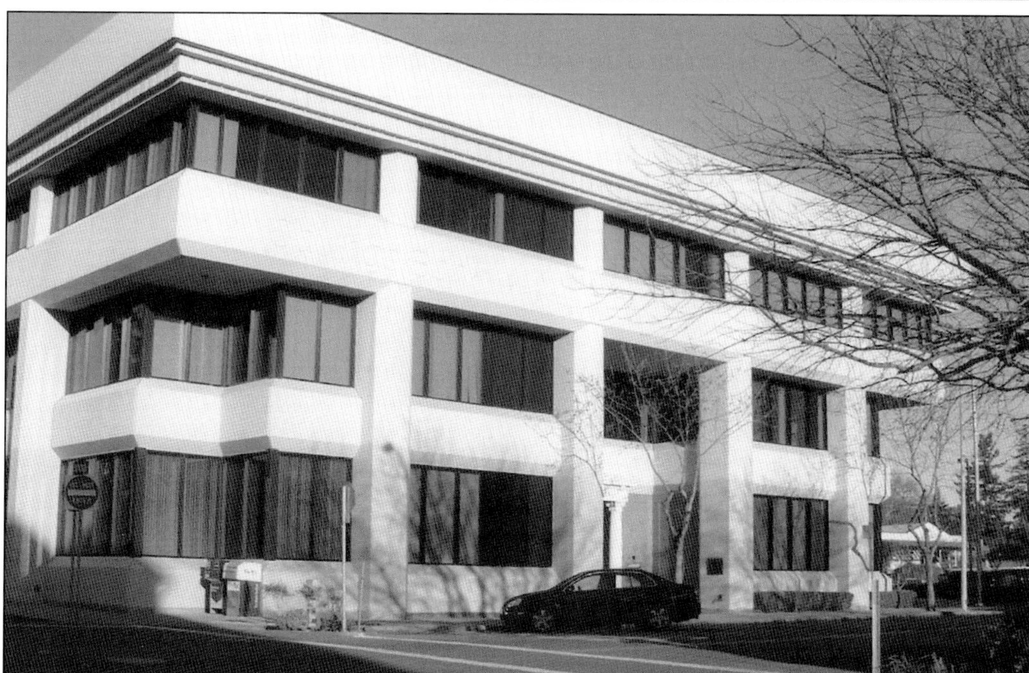

The Savings Bank had a new building dedicated on July 25, 1994.

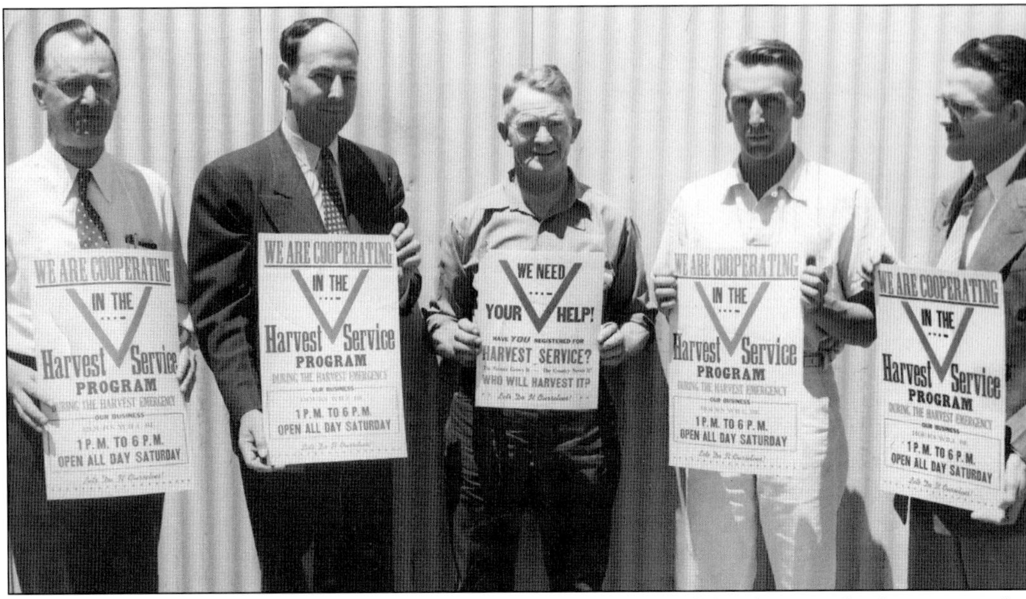

Farmer Roy Yarbrough, representing the agricultural industry of the district, displays a sign that reads, "We need your help! Have you registered for Harvest Service?" in July 1942. Pictured are, from left to right, John MacNab of MacNab's store; Stan Philliber, manager of Montgomery Ward; Roy Yarbrough; Larry Wildberger of Wildberger's; and E. H. Balyeat, manager of J. C. Penney Company.

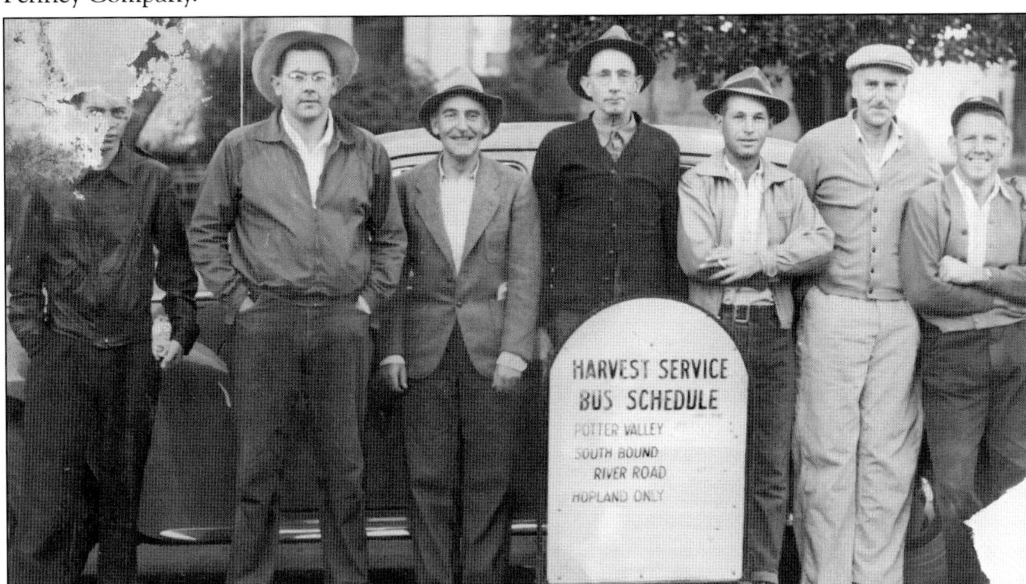

Seen here is the Harvest Service bus schedule from September 6, 1942. The white-collar workers in the community donated their time to assist with the pear harvest. Many prominent local businessmen lined up early at the bus stop to head to the orchards to help harvest the crop. Pictured from left to right are unidentified (damaged area), attorney Hal Brunner, chamber of commerce secretary Phil Kington, attorney Will Van Dyke, attorney Newell Rawles, banker Fred Creen, and banker Charles Shimmin. It was reliably reported the group lost their smiles before the day was over but stayed with the job.

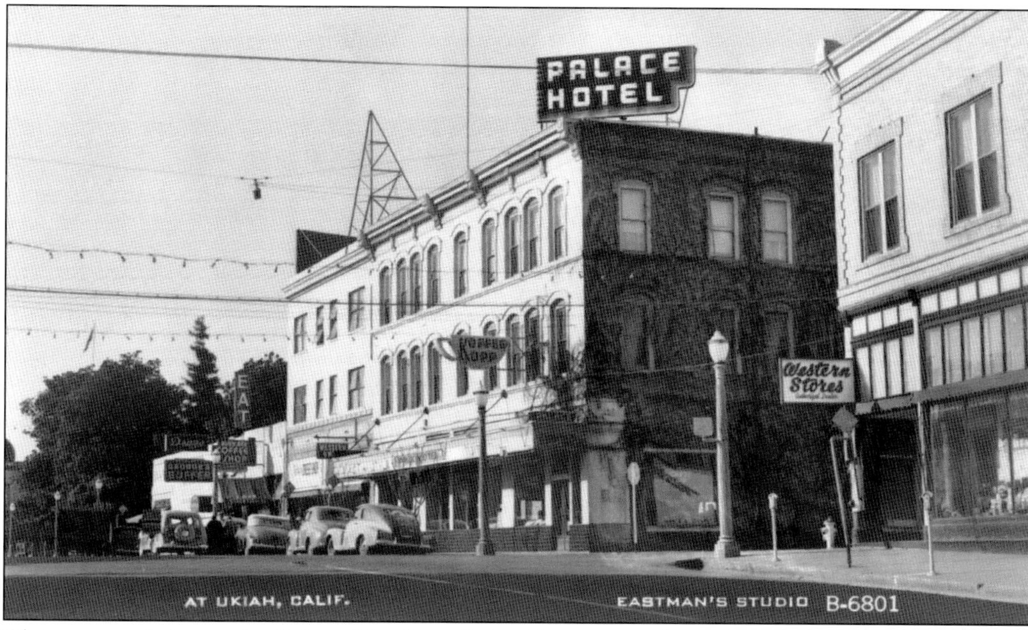

This postcard shows the Palace Hotel in 1949. Also pictured are the Koffee Kupp café and the Western Store.

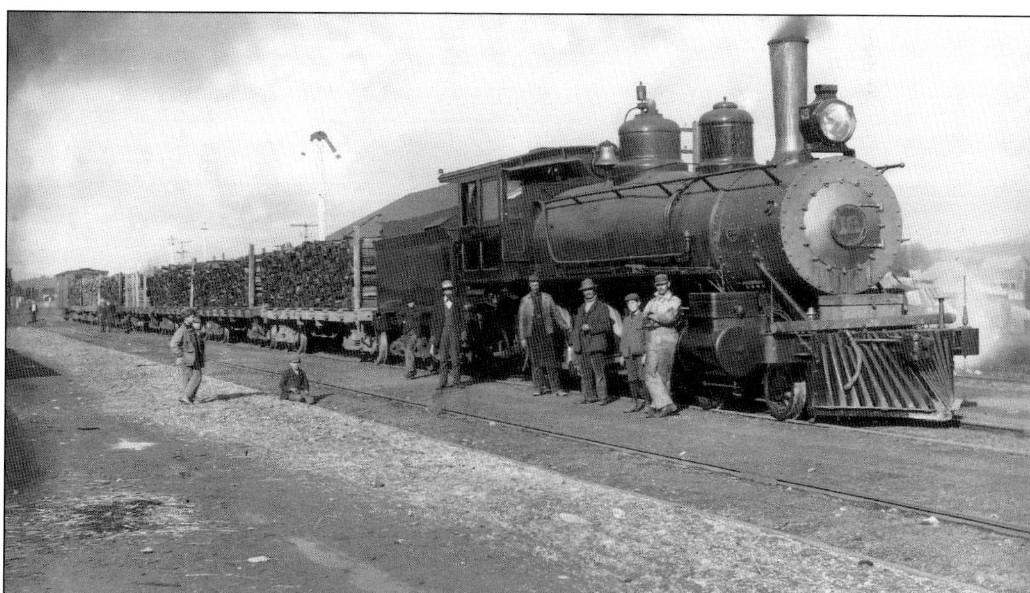

Pictured here is locomotive No. 19 from the San Francisco and North Pacific Railway around 1900. (Photograph by A. O. Carpenter; courtesy of the Grace Hudson Museum.)

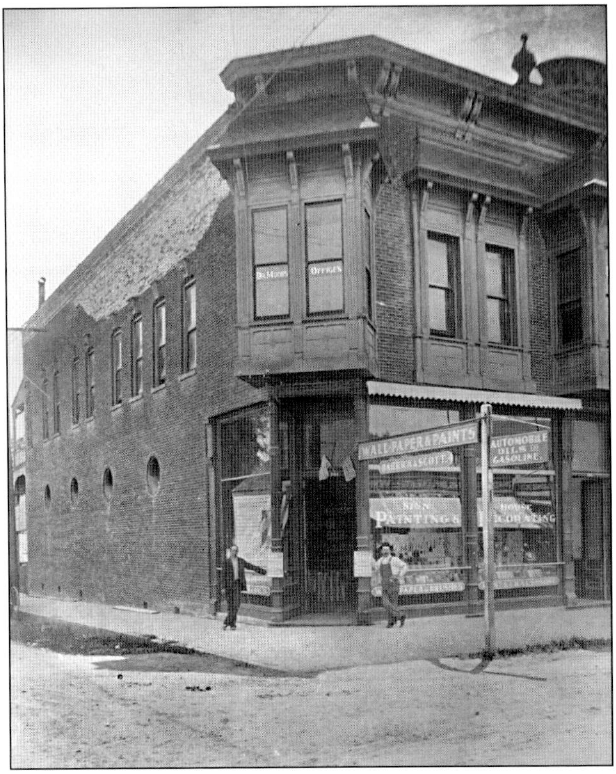

The McGlashan Building is seen here around 1907. The Barrick and Scott Wallpaper and Paint Store was in business at this location from January 1907 until July 1909. Note the damage on the side of the building from the 1906 earthquake.

The Samuel D. McKesson residence is shown here in 1898. The residence at 445 North State Street was later moved to the rear of the property. The real estate was eventually purchased by T. J. and Emma Lamb. After T. J. Lamb's death in 1906, Emma Lamb opened a room and boardinghouse. Another building was erected in the front of the property, which became the Lamb's Inn in 1915.

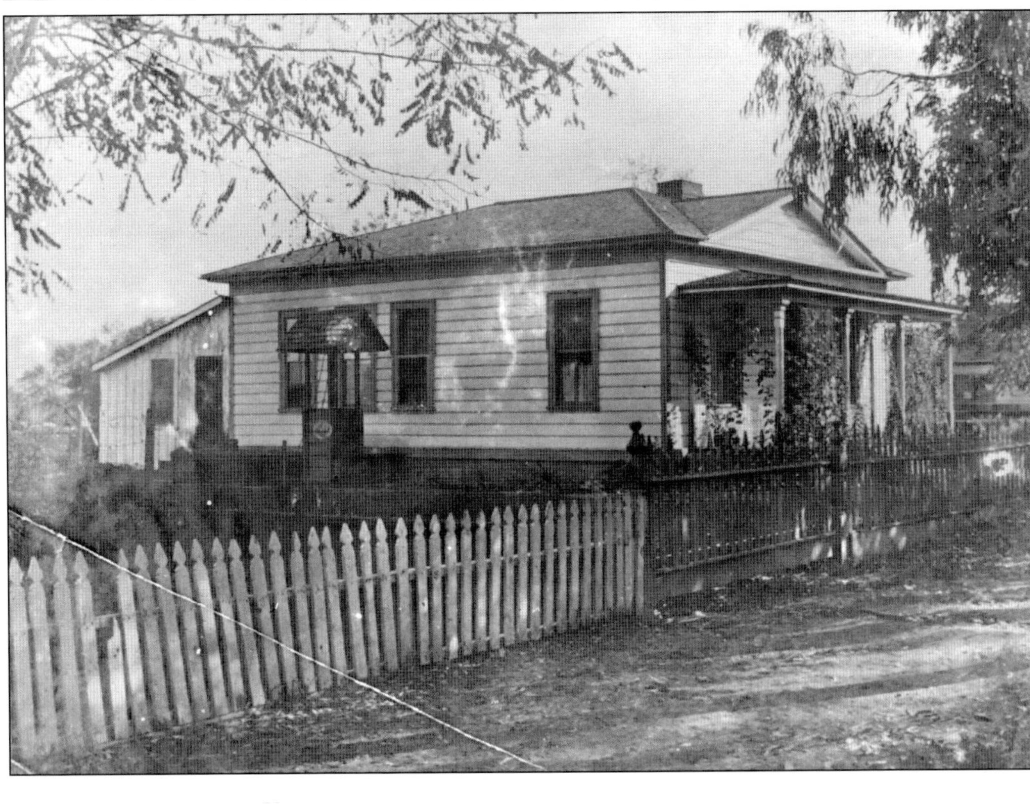

This shows a Ukiah street scene looking north on State Street from Church Street. Henry Marks is pictured standing in front of his store, the City of Ukiah.

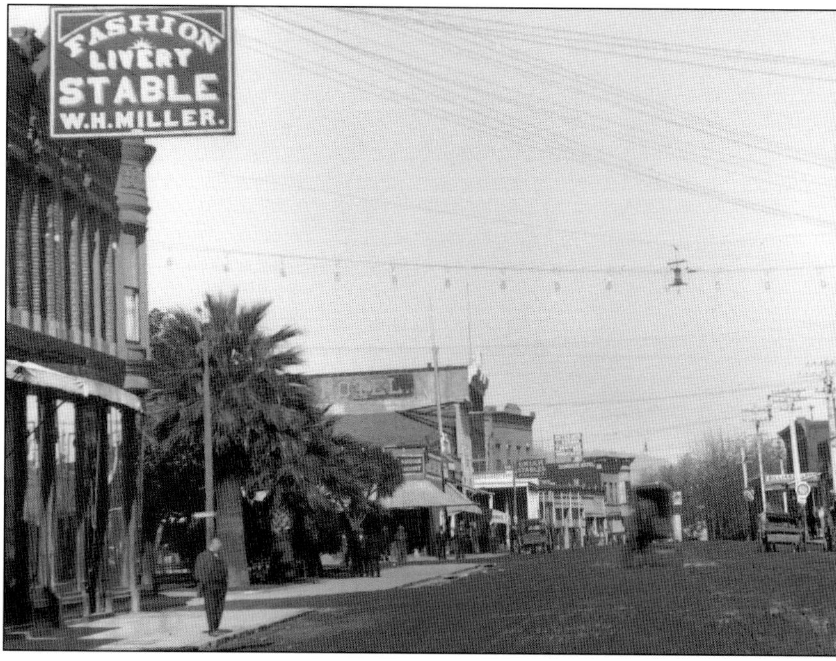

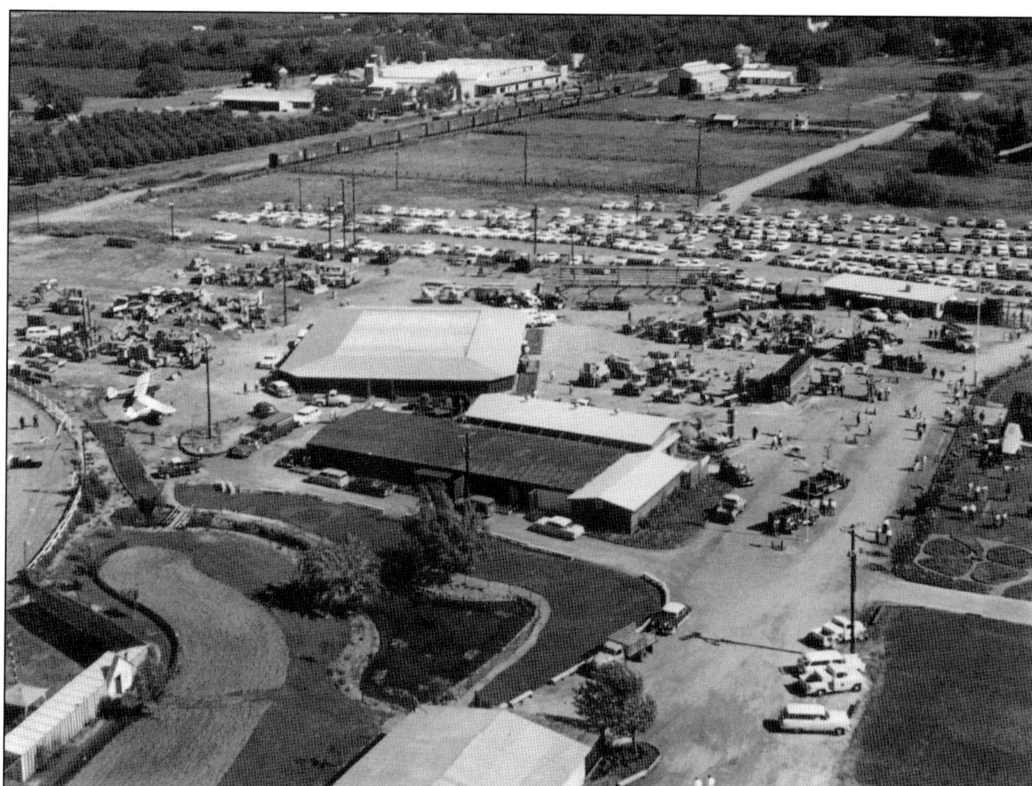

A view is shown of the 18th Annual Redwood Region Logging Conference from May 25–26, 1956. This is an aerial picture of the 12th district fairgrounds.

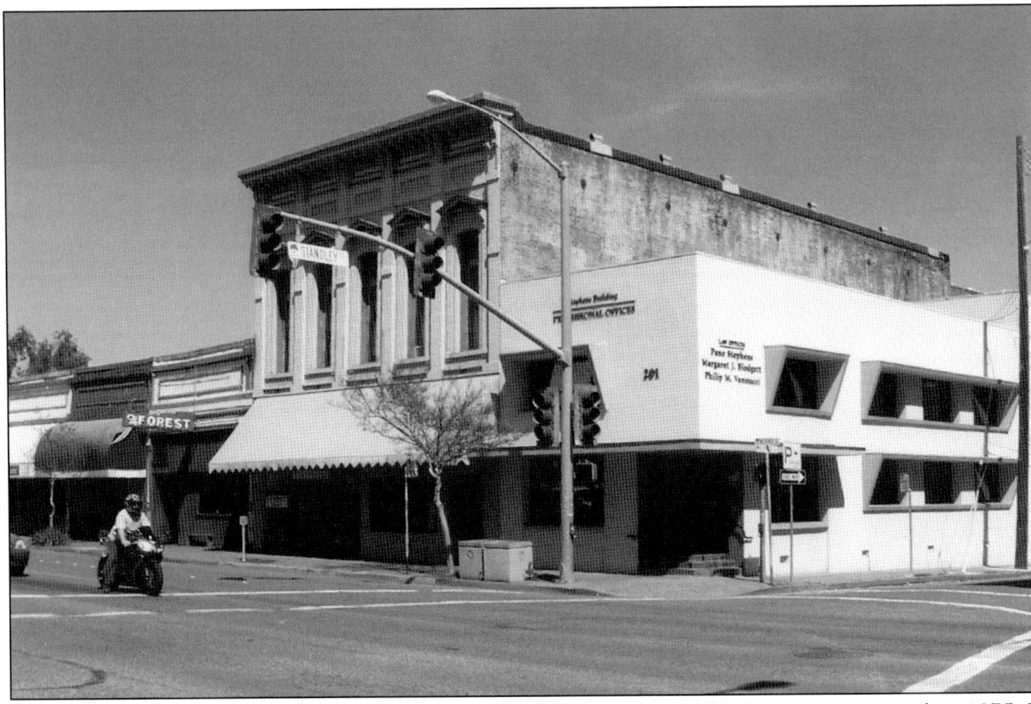

The Pano Stephens Building is shown here in 2009; the original building was erected in 1875. It was formerly the site of the Bank of Ukiah.

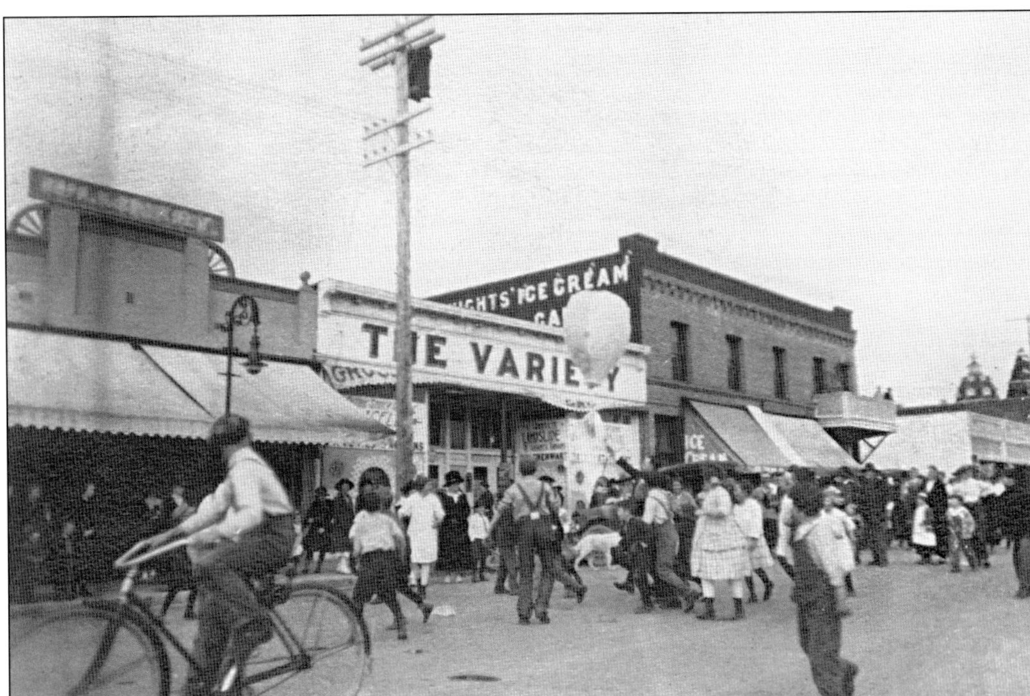

This was a promotion for a sale at Foster's Variety Store. The person finding the balloon could redeem an attached coupon for a prize. Pictured is the balloon ascension on March 22, 1919.

Four

Parades and Festivals

Nothing says small-town America like a parade. For over 100 years, Ukiah has had a Fourth of July Parade. There have been Eagle Fire Department (the previous name of the Ukiah Fire Department) parades and American Legion Drum Corps parades. In 1895, the Second Artillery Unit of the National Guard held a dress parade on State Street.

From the Thrift Stamp parade to support World War I to the annual Lighted Truck parade at Christmastime, where semis and flatbed trucks are decorated with lights and holiday decorations, parades have entertained people in Ukiah. State Street is lined with families from one end of town to the other. Ukiah High School still has a homecoming parade with dozens of floats and a caravan of the candidates from the high school. All the hopeful couples ride down State Street on the backs of convertibles. Each young couple hopes to be crowned king and queen at the homecoming football game that night. The identity of the lucky couple is announced during halftime.

Ukiah is where one could find the Hop Festival in 1912 and 1913. For the past 20 years, the Pumpkinfest, a weekend festival that starts with a weigh-in of giant pumpkins, has been held in downtown Ukiah. The parades and festivals are some of the things that make this small town so enjoyable and such a great place to live.

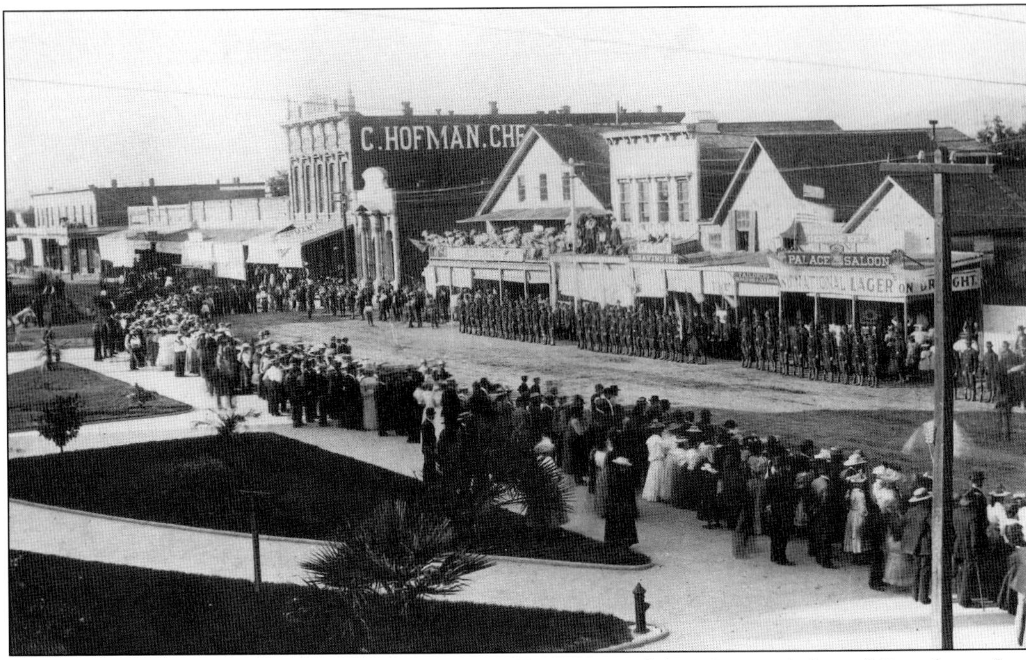

Pictured is the dress parade of the Second Artillery Unit of the National Guard Parade on June 17, 1895. The spectators are lining North State Street awaiting the drill. The photograph was taken from Perkins Street.

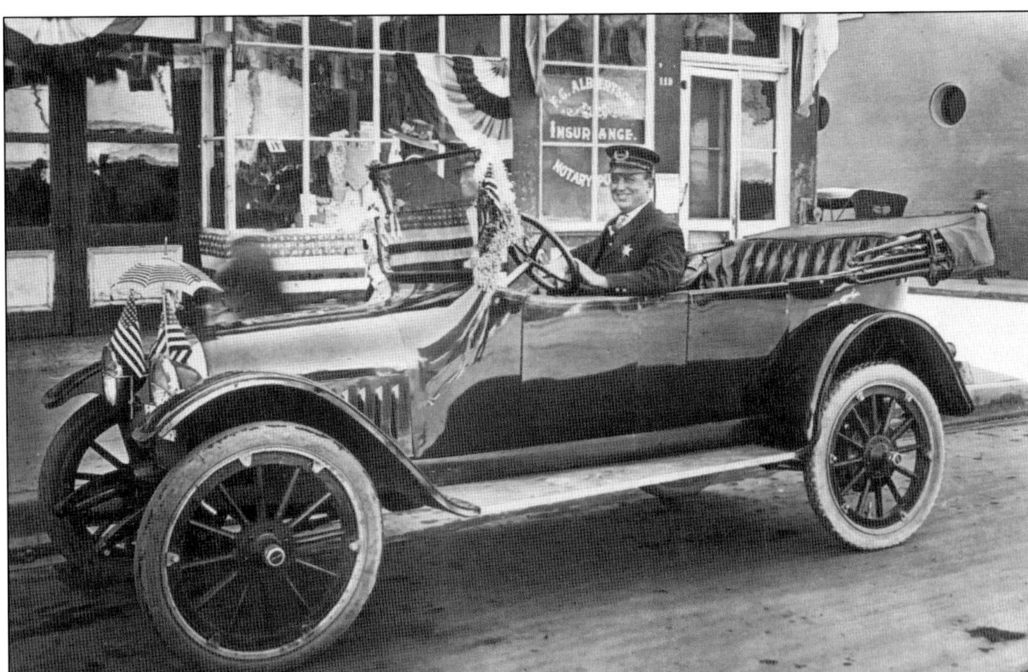

Clyde Brewer, the city marshal, is shown in his new Oakland automobile. The occasion was the July 4, 1916, parade. Brewer was city marshal from April 15, 1912, to November 10, 1918. This picture was taken from the corner of State and Church Streets.

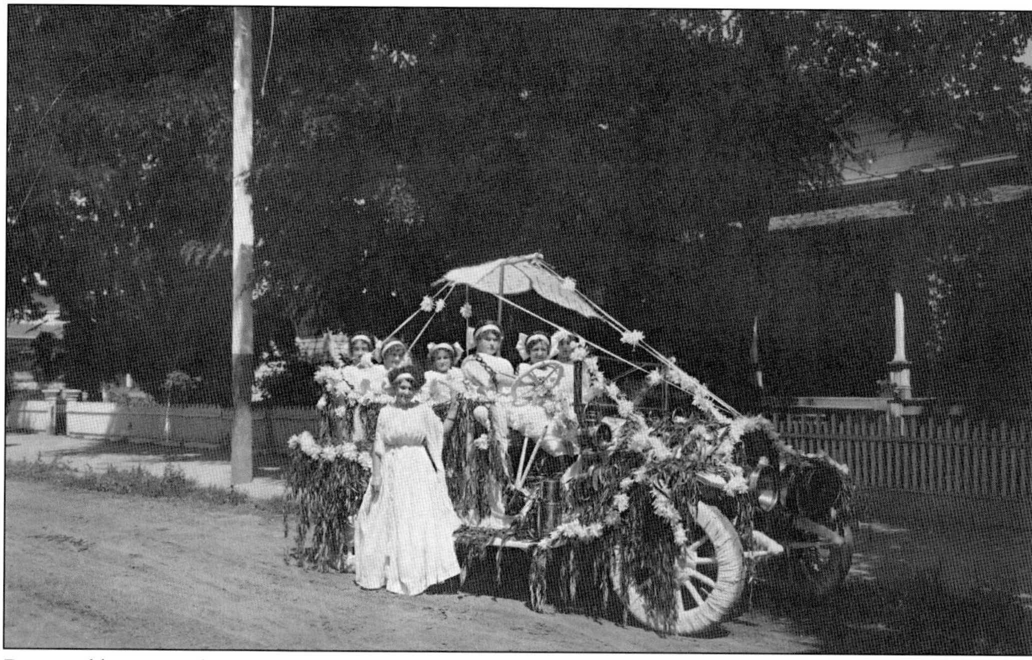

Pictured here is a decorated automobile for the first Hop Festival Parade. The festival was held in September 1912 and was a three-day event. Included in the festival were an auto parade, motorcycle races, and the appearance of the first airplane in Ukiah. Unfortunately the plane crashed soon after taking off, but luckily no one was injured in the crash.

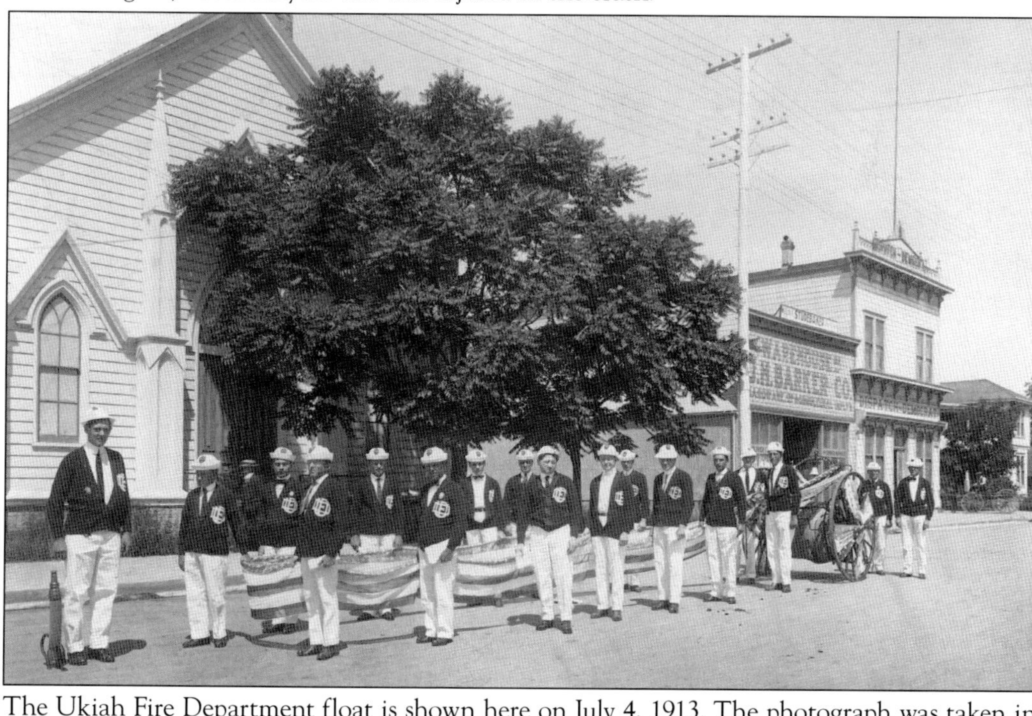

The Ukiah Fire Department float is shown here on July 4, 1913. The photograph was taken in front of the Christian church on North School Street. The gentleman at the far left is fire chief Frank Barker.

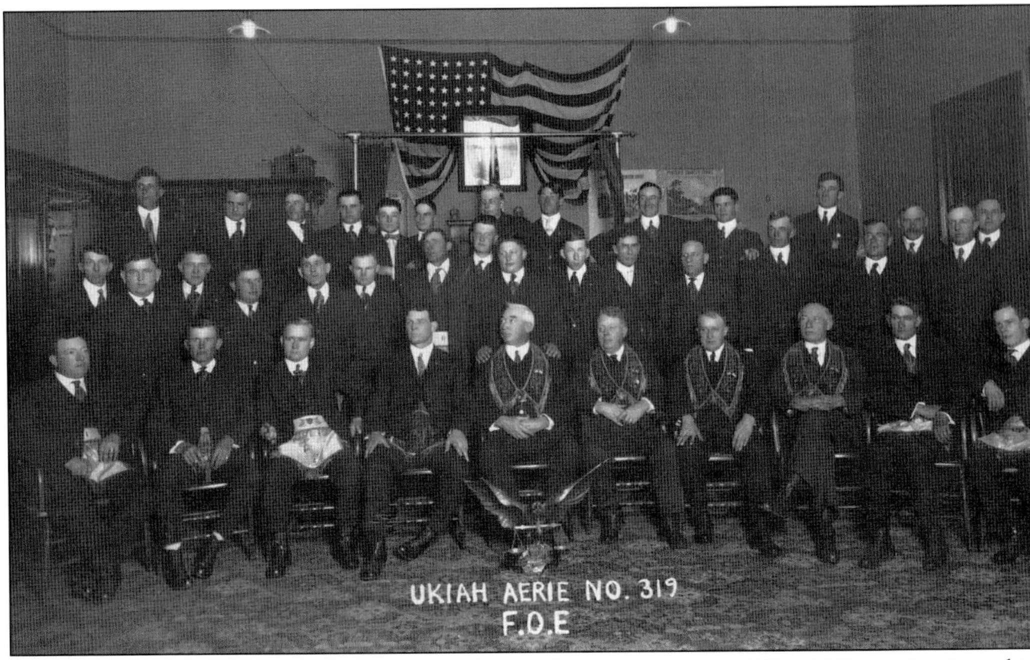

The Fraternal Order of Eagles was a men's benevolent organization. The FOE was instituted in May 1903 and in a few years had over 200 members. Some of the prominent members of the community pictured are Lilburn Gibson, Ed Sanford, Edward Eversole, Ralph Burns, Bernard Saunders, Floyd Banker, Bunt Cox, and Mort Eilers.

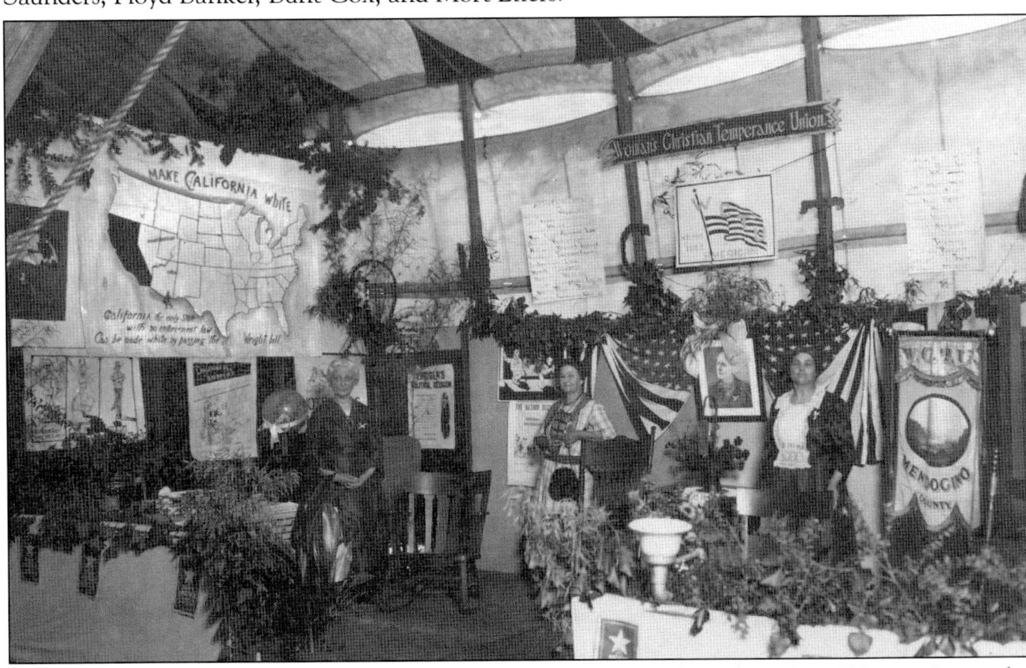

The Women's Christian Temperance Union booth is shown at the Yokaya Pow-Wow in September 1922. The Women's Christian Temperance Union was an organization of women who were against the partaking of alcohol. From left to right are Valma Eversole, unidentified, and Elizabeth Corbett Luce.

This is a scene from the Yokaya Pow-Wow Parade on September 18, 1922. The Eversole family is shown riding in their decorated vehicle.

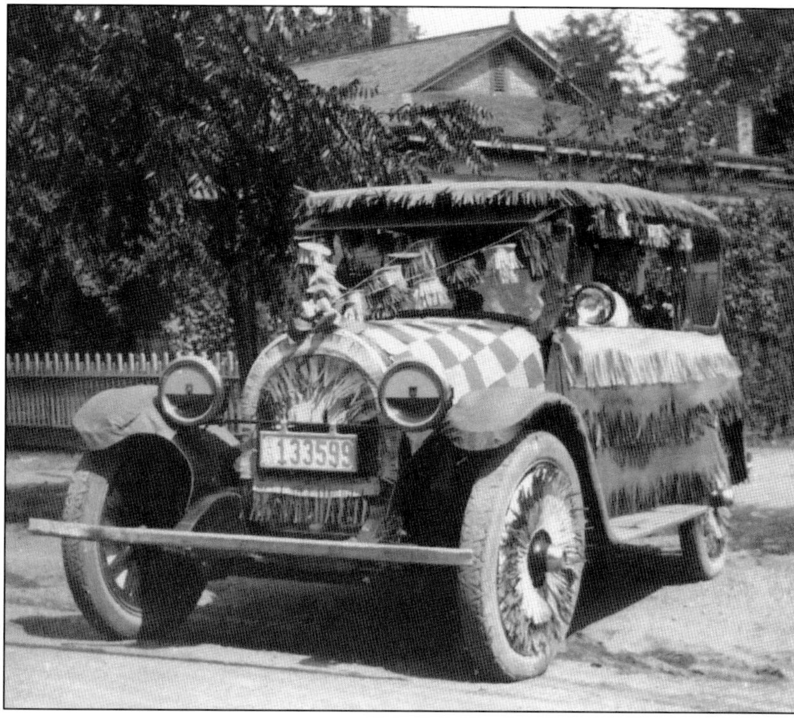

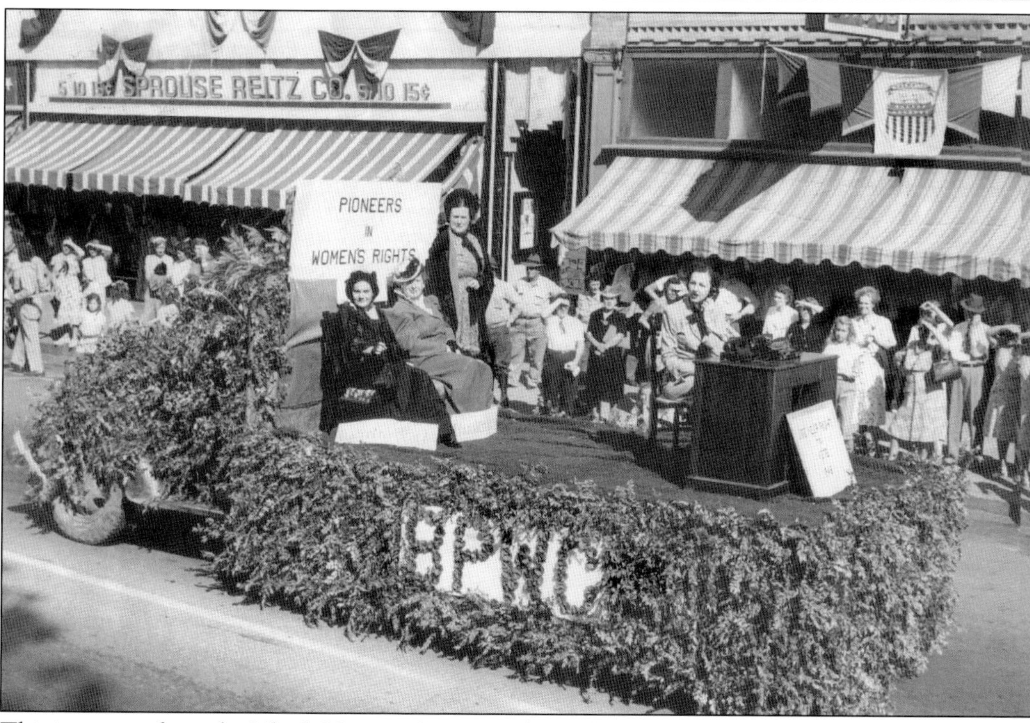

This is a scene from the Ukiah Vintage Centennial Parade on October 9, 1948. The theme was "Use Your Right to Vote in 48." This was the Business and Professional Women's Club float. Pictured are Henrietta Wilford on the telephone with, from left to right, Rena Webb, Nita Hildebrand, and president of the Redwood Empire chapter, Ella Butler. (Courtesy of William French Jr.)

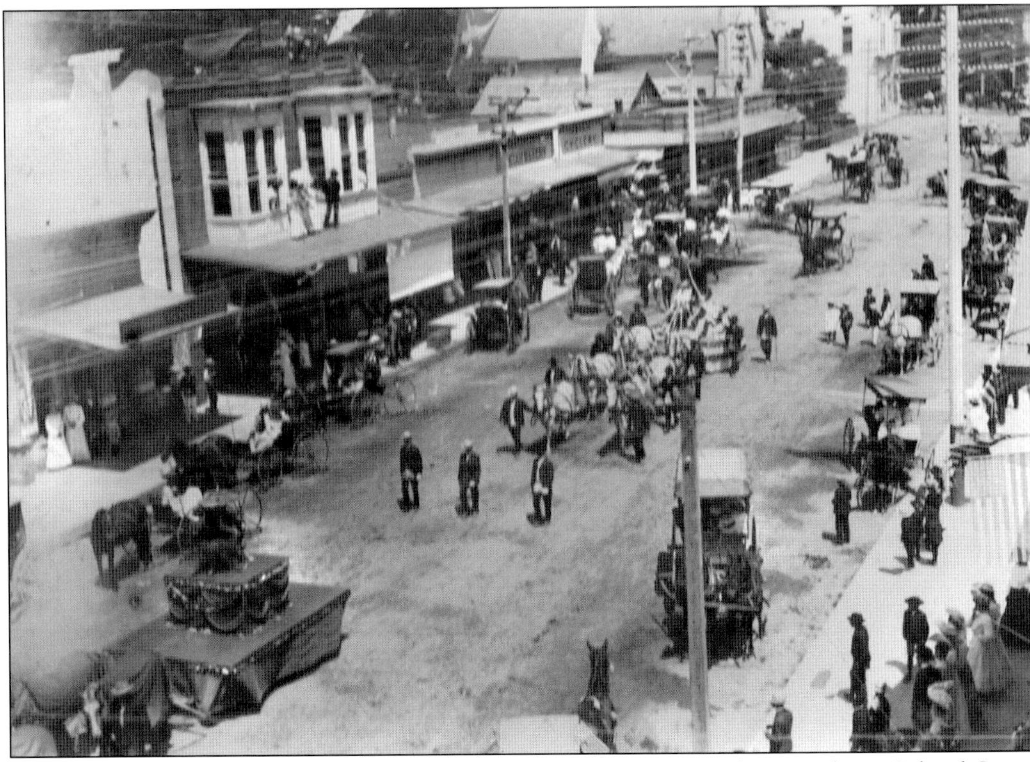

The Goddess of Liberty float and the Eagles float are shown traveling south on School Street on July 4, 1904.

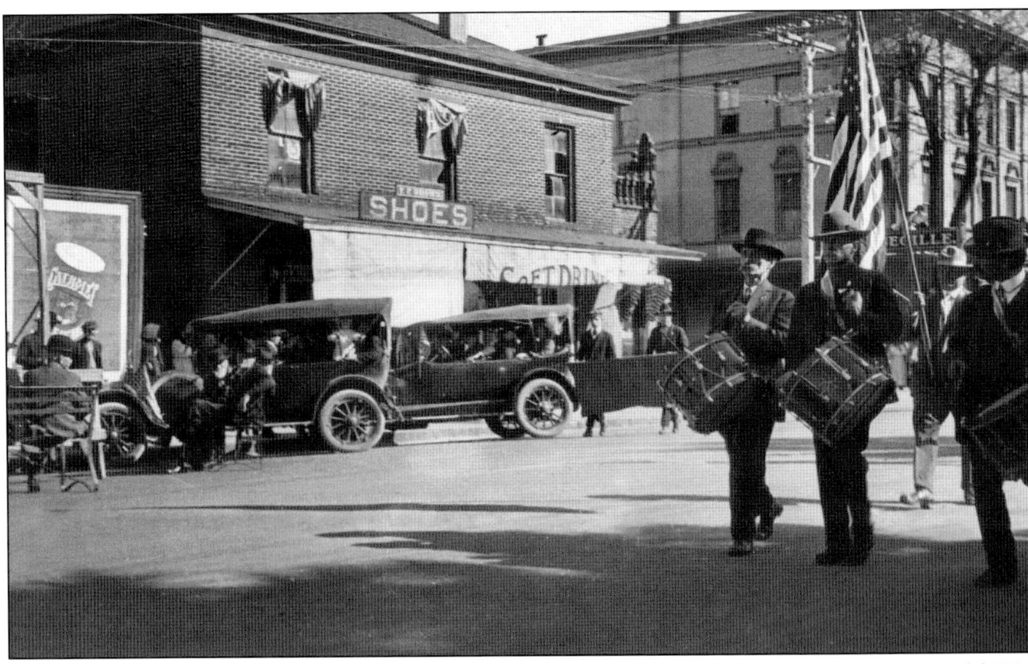

A Thrift Stamp parade is pictured on March 15, 1918. A parade was held to support World War I, and citizens were encouraged to purchase thrift stamps to support the war effort.

A scene at the Yo-Kayo Pow-Wow is shown from June 1939. Paul Poulos, accused of being a non-whisker-grower, was thrown into a makeshift jail. Two princess candidates, Marjorie Nasale (left) and Ruby Zunder (right), are pictured. Assisting were Opal Foster (left) and Katherine Foster (right) dressed in official Pow-Wow costumes.

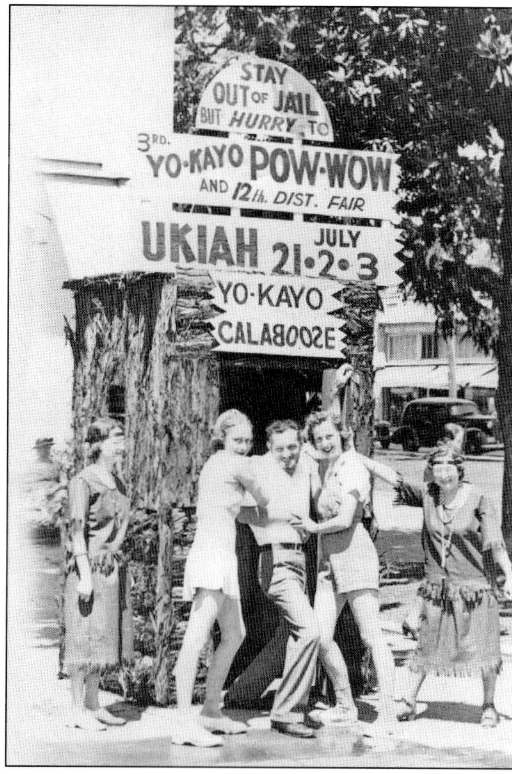

The Fourth of July parade in 1903 is pictured. This view is looking north from the intersection of State and Perkins Streets. Roth and Waugh Groceries, shown in the photograph, were only in business from 1902 to 1903.

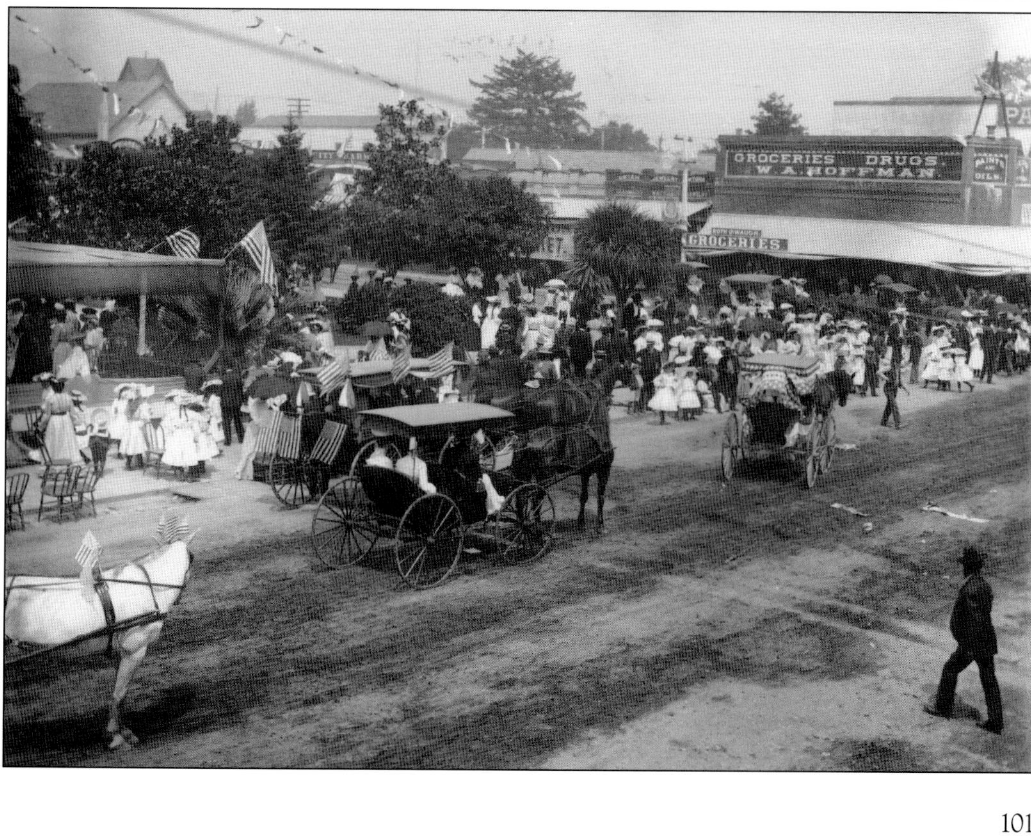

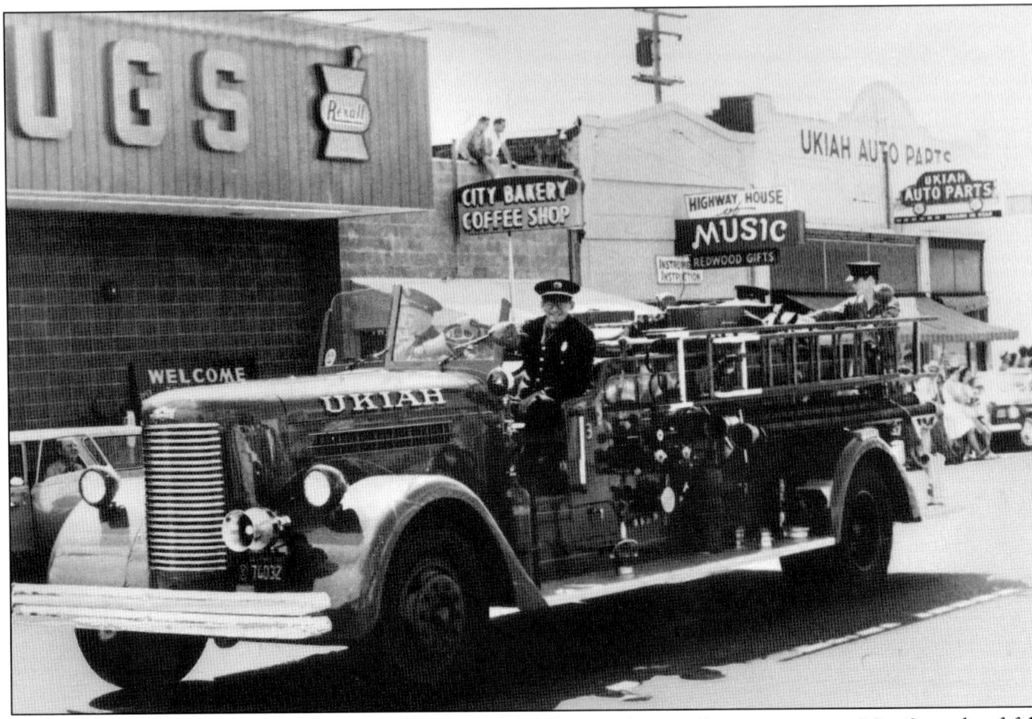

Representing the Ukiah Fire Department, Mark King is shown driving engine No. 3 at the fifth annual Ukiah Valley Rodeo Parade on May 18, 1963.

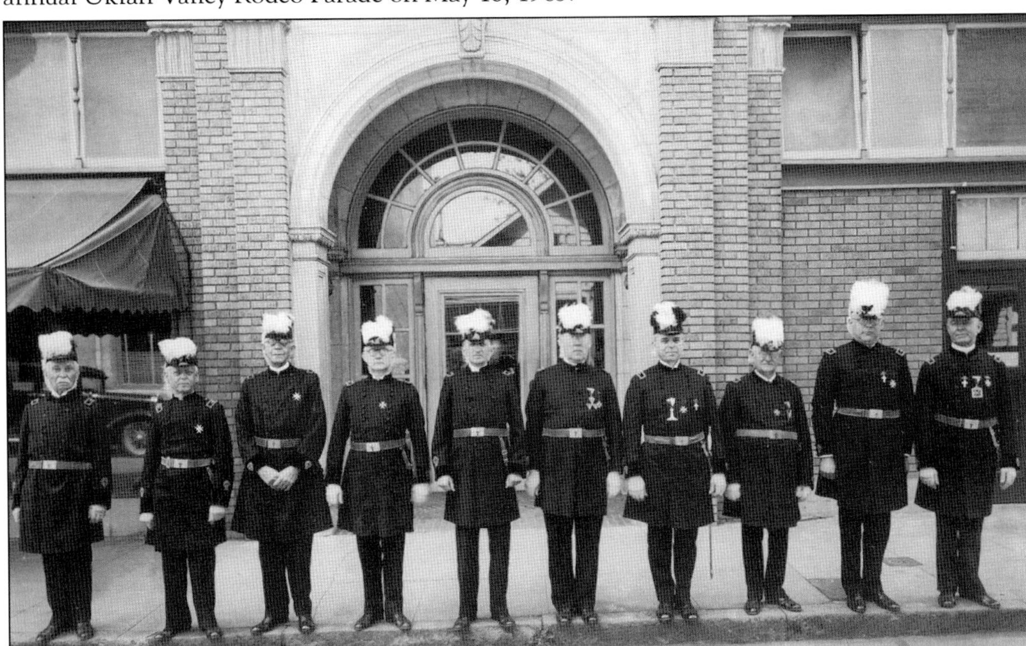

The Knights Templar at the Masonic Temple are shown on April 21, 1935, on Easter Sunday. From left to right are Hale McCowen Sr., W. D. L. Held, Bert Cleland, Judge Charles Mannon, George Anderson, William Bromley, Hale McCowen Jr., Edward James, Walter Sandelin, and Frank Savage.

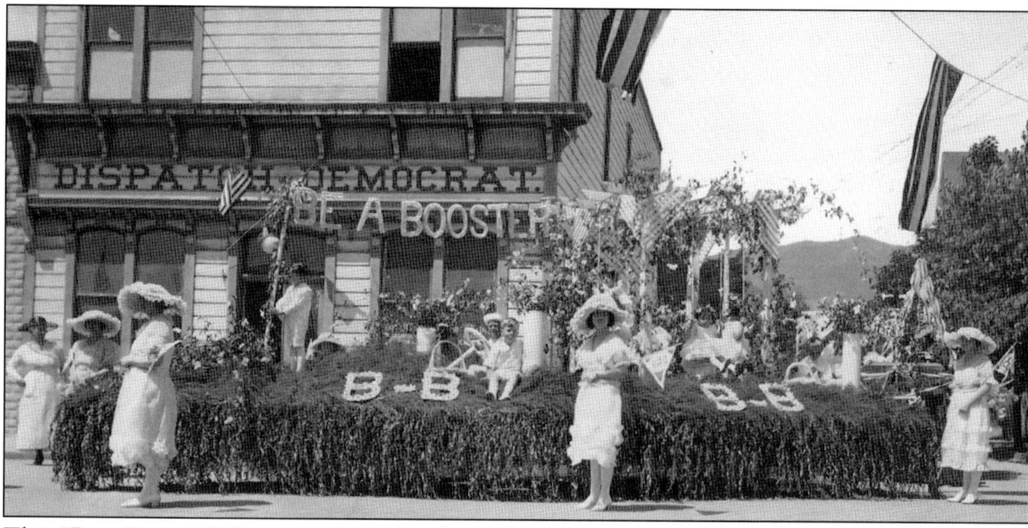

This "Be a Booster" float was from the Saturday Afternoon Club on July 4, 1921. The *Dispatch Democrat* office is seen in the background.

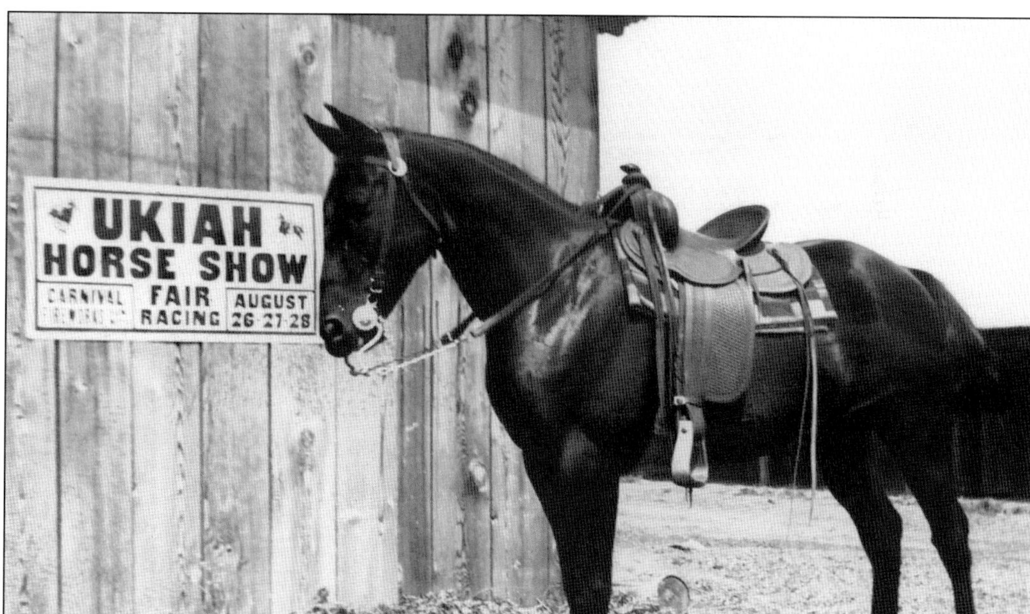

The Ukiah Horse Show and carnival on August 26–28, 1938, is being advertised here.

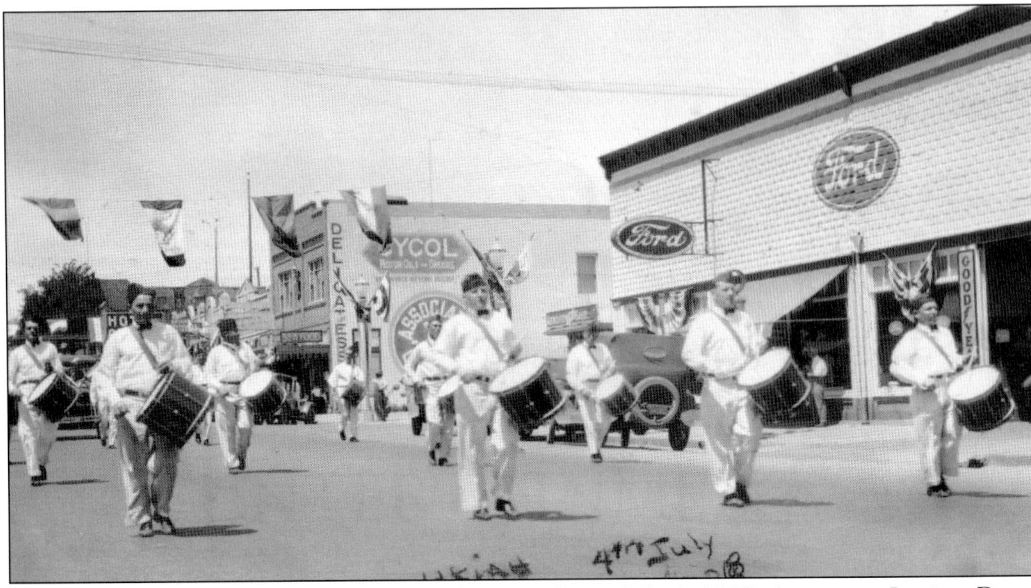

This photograph depicts the Ukiah Rodeo Parade on July 1, 1928. American Legion Drum Corps member Robert Stambaugh is shown in the center of the picture. (Courtesy of William ("Bill") Stambaugh.)

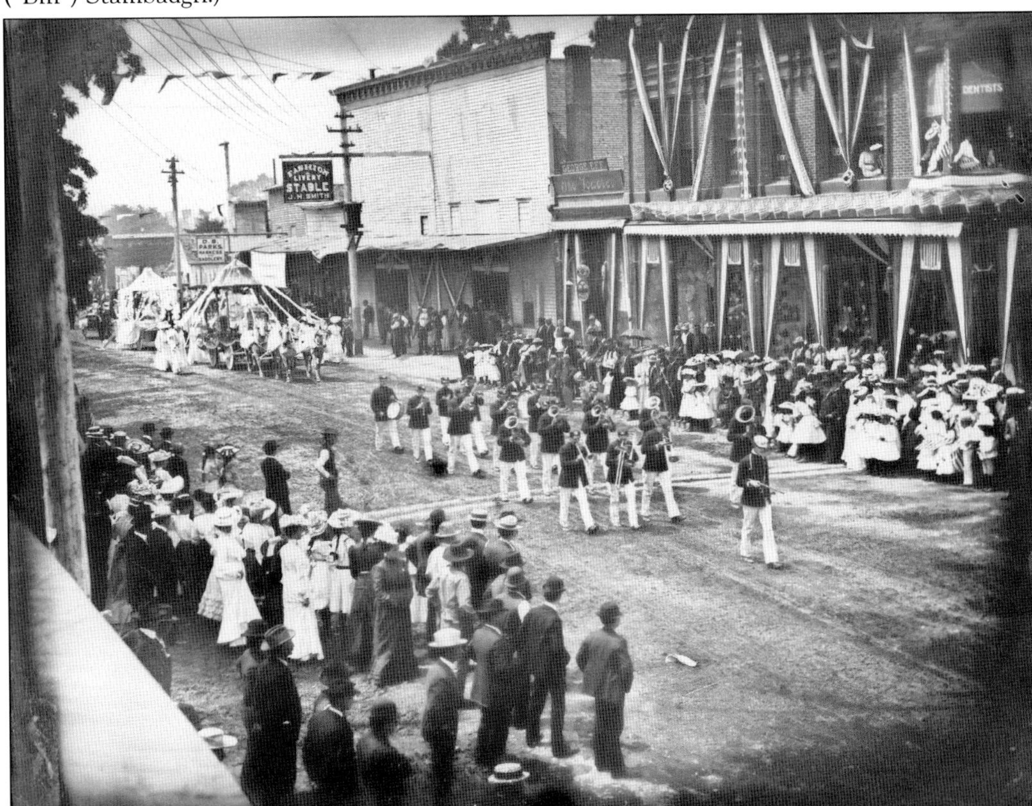

The Fourth of July Parade of 1904 is shown here. The photograph is by A. O. Carpenter. (Courtesy of the Grace Hudson Museum.)

Five

Entertainment and the Arts

Ukiah, although primarily a farming community, is home to a wide variety of entertainment. The Grace Hudson Museum and the Sun House are located in the downtown area and are visited by thousands of visitors, both local and tourists, throughout the year.

During the summer months, Sundays in the Park provide a series of six free concerts. Richie Havens and the David Grisman Quintet are showcased as well as jazz, Latin, and country music performers. Residents can bring a picnic basket and settle back to listen to the music and dance. The fall brings the county Pumpkinfest and the Early Iron Club's Fabulous Flashback Car Show. During the Christmas holidays, an antique trolley car provides free rides around downtown Ukiah. Ukiah Players Theatre presents several drama productions every year. SPACE (School for the Performing Arts and Cultural Education) provides lessons for children of all ages in dance, voice, and clowning. Performances are presented throughout the year.

The Ukiah Civic Light Opera, in conjunction with Mendocino College, provides musical productions and sponsors a local "Ukiah Idol" contest at the county fair. Ukiah Community Concerts, started in 1947, bring musicians from all over the world for concerts of classical music and jazz. Tierra Art Gallery and Tasting Room has changing art exhibits each month. First Friday, a group of local art galleries, have an open house the first Friday of each month, presenting oil, ceramics, and metal sculptures by local Mendocino County artists. There is something for everyone looking for art and entertainment in Ukiah.

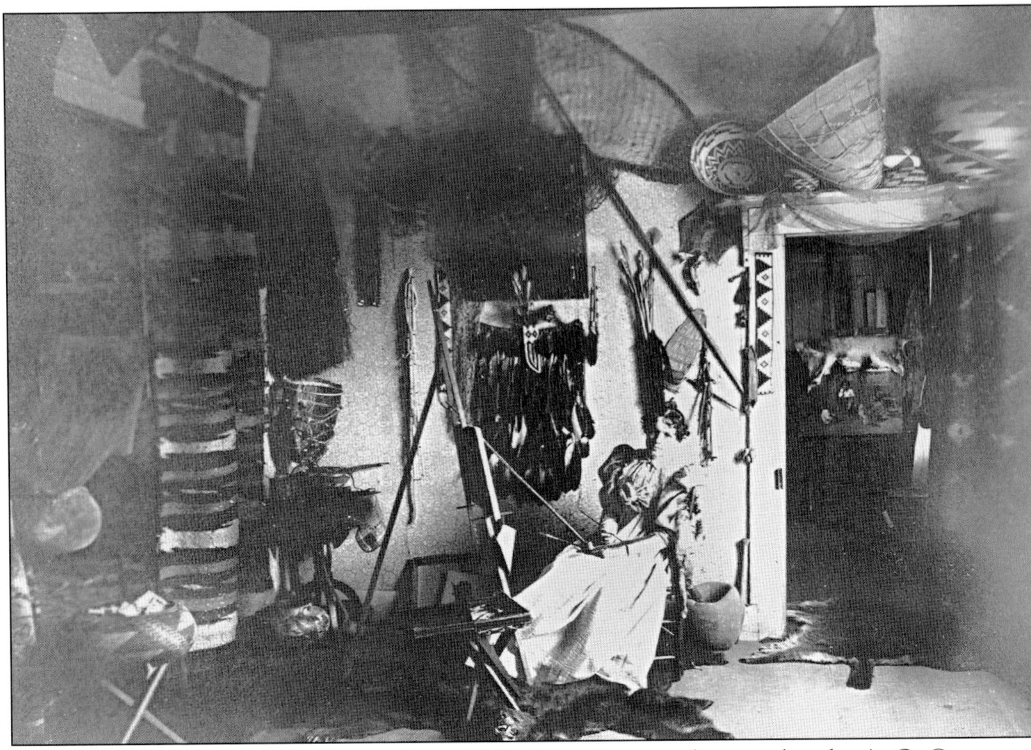

Grace Hudson is pictured in her studio in 1895. The photograph was taken by A. O. Carpenter. (Courtesy of the Grace Hudson Museum.)

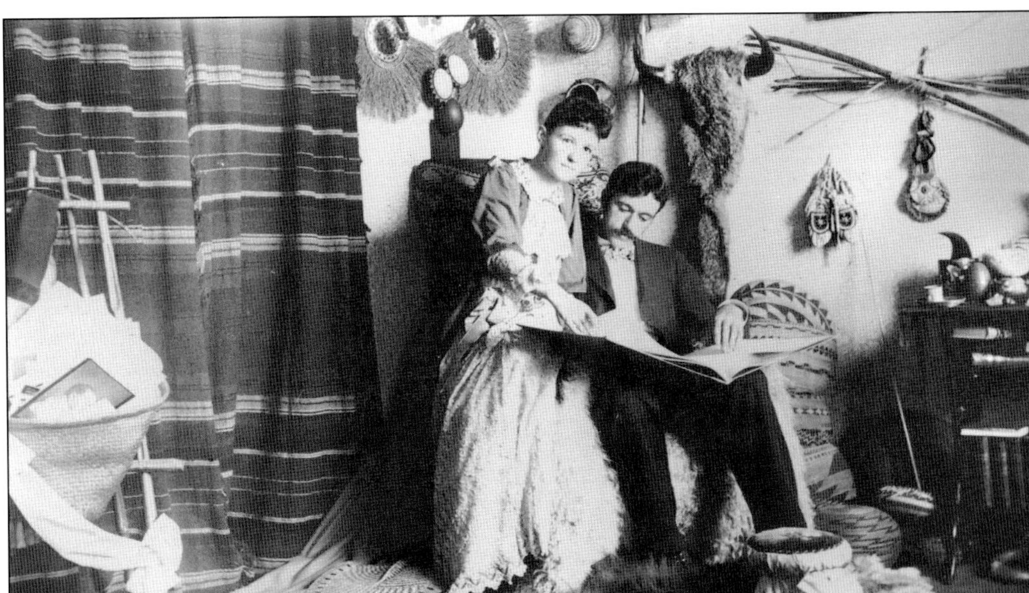

Grace Hudson and John Hudson are shown in Grace's studio in 1890. This photograph is from a 4.5- by 7.5-inch vintage print. (Courtesy of the Grace Hudson Museum.)

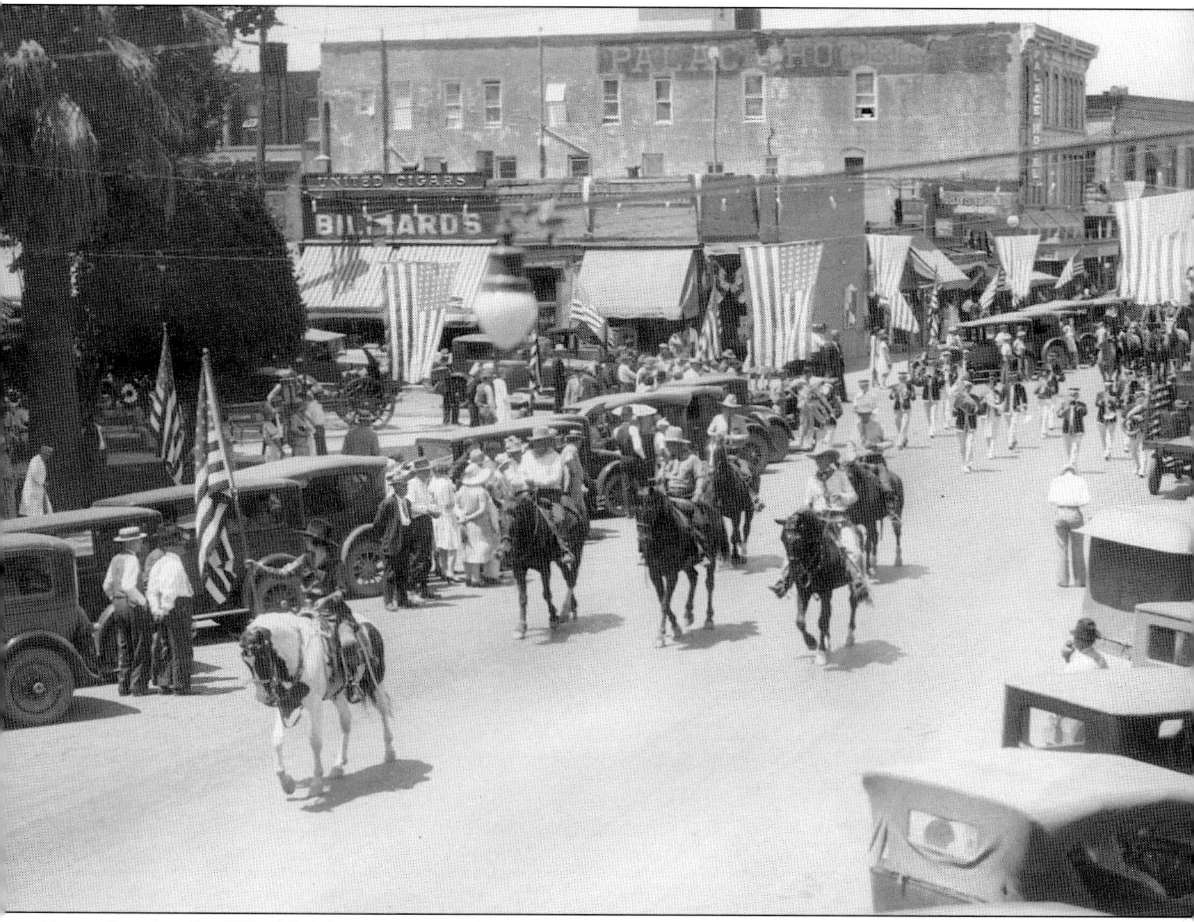

Rose Smith, the World Champion Trick and Fancy Rider Champion, is leading the July 1927 Ukiah Rodeo Parade.

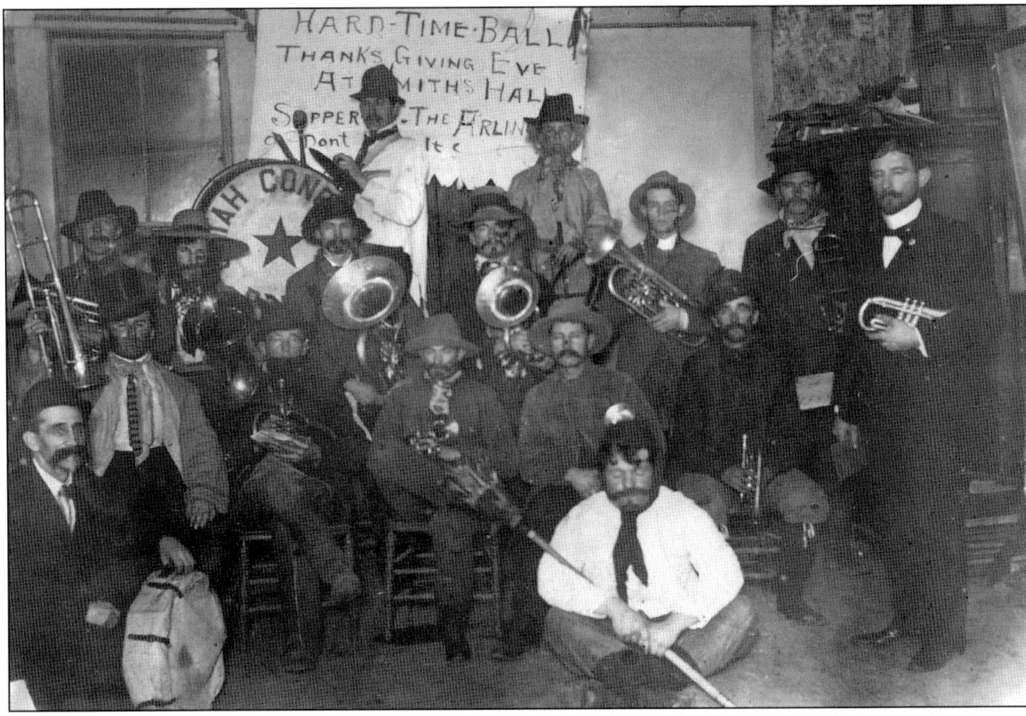

The Hard Times Ball was held November 26, 1902, at the Arlington Hotel. It was a fund-raiser to purchase new instruments for Keller's Band. Couples were charged 50¢, spectators 25¢.

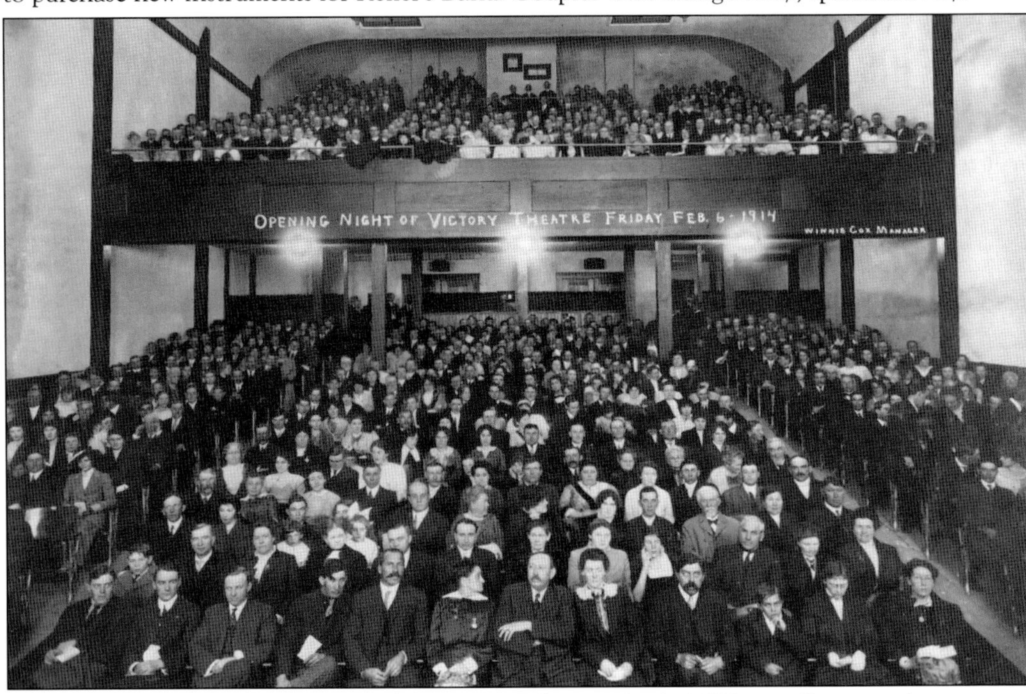

The opening night at the Victory Theatre was February 6, 1914. Winnie Cox was the manager. The Victory Theatre became the State Theatre in March 1923. The building was declared to be unsafe and was closed in March 1948.

This performance program for "A Night at the Opera" is for the Ukiah Civic Light Opera in 1994.

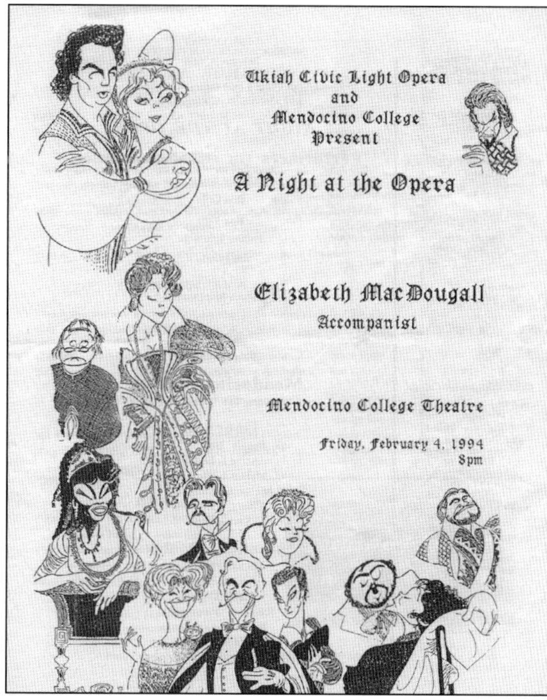

The Mandolin Club is shown on May 1, 1896. From left to right are (first row) Florence Handy, Felice Cerf, and Lena Johnson; (second row) William Kahler, Celia Hofman, Rudolph Brunner, and Ernest Wheeler.

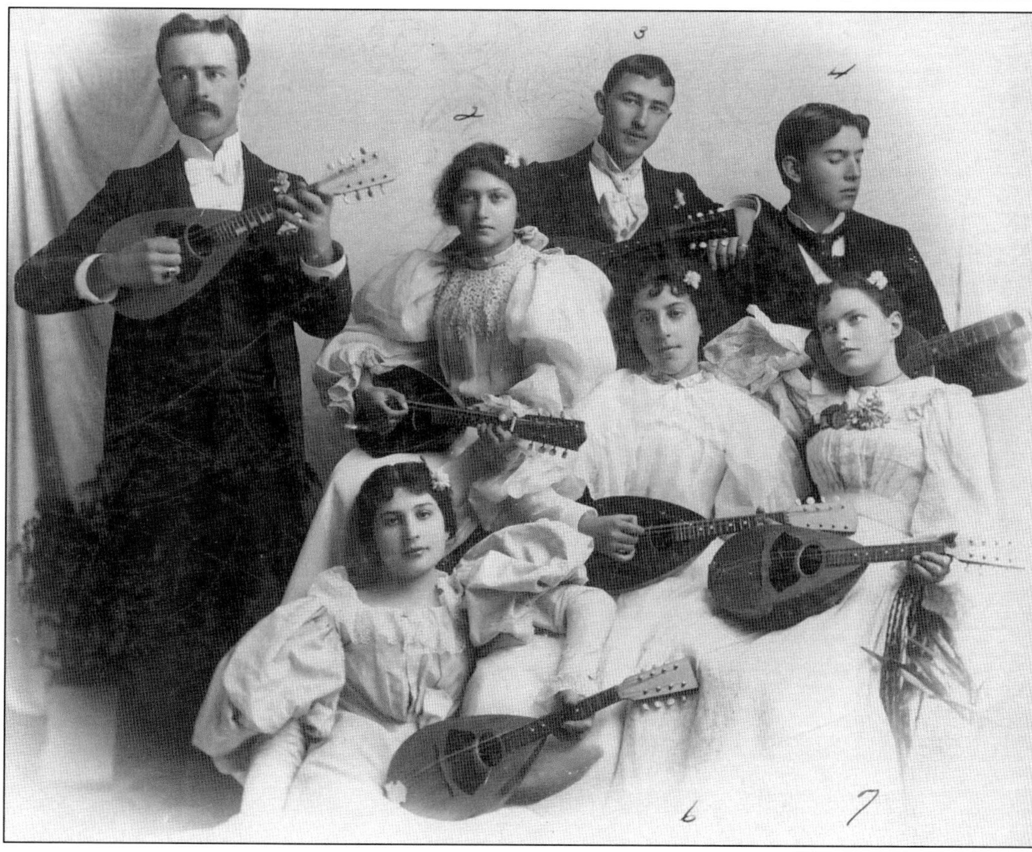

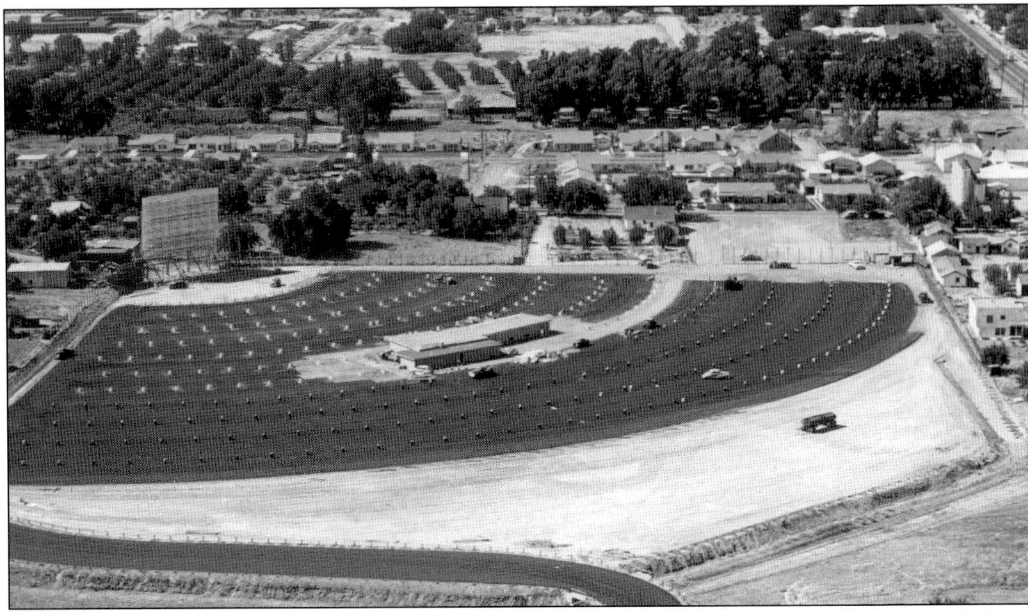

The State Drive-in Theatre is shown in June 1950. The theater opened July 6, 1950, and closed October 27, 1979.

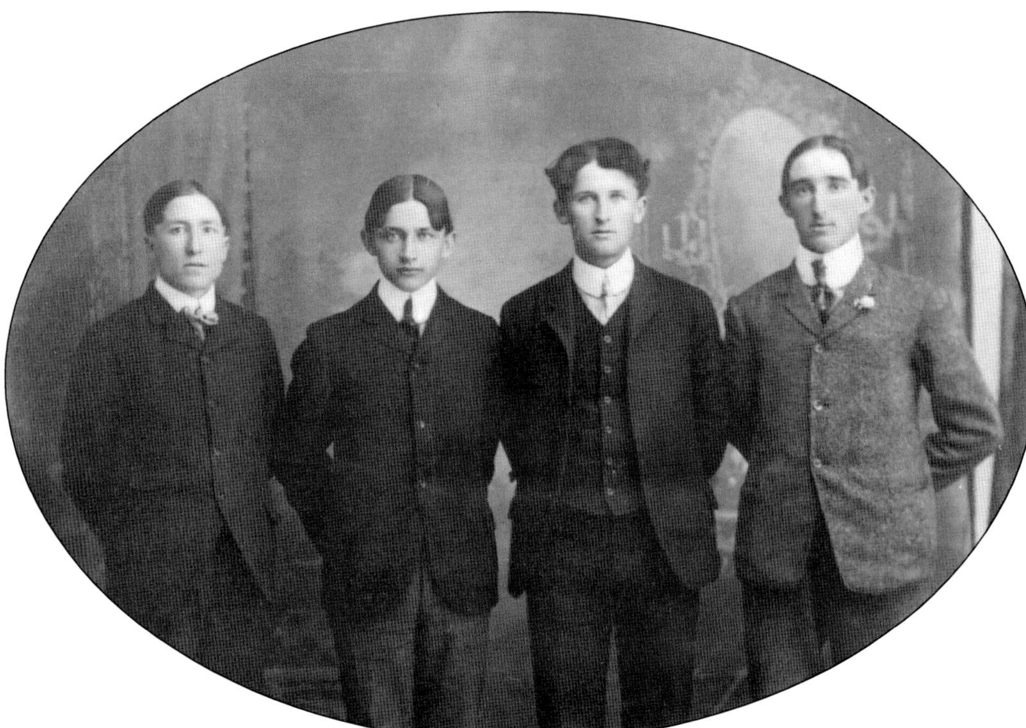

The Ukiah Minstrels are shown in this *c.* 1905 photograph. From left to right are Ralph Vernon, Bill Shattuck, Bud Meyers, and Gus Angle.

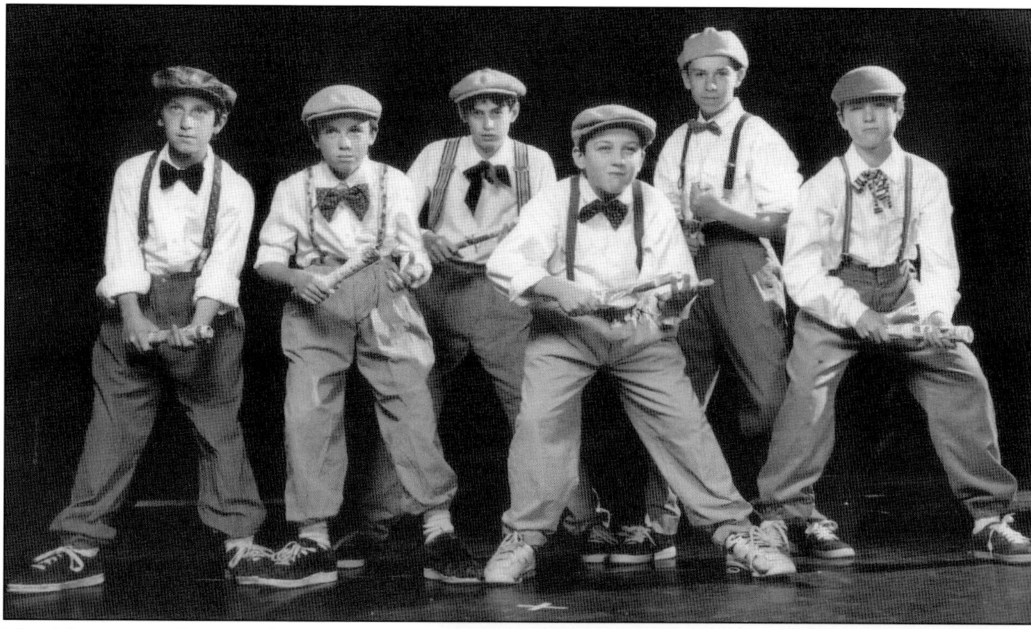

The Newspaper Boys, with an all-male dance troupe, was a 1995 production as part of the School of Performing Arts and Cultural Education "Strictly Streets" cultural performance project. (Courtesy of SPACE.)

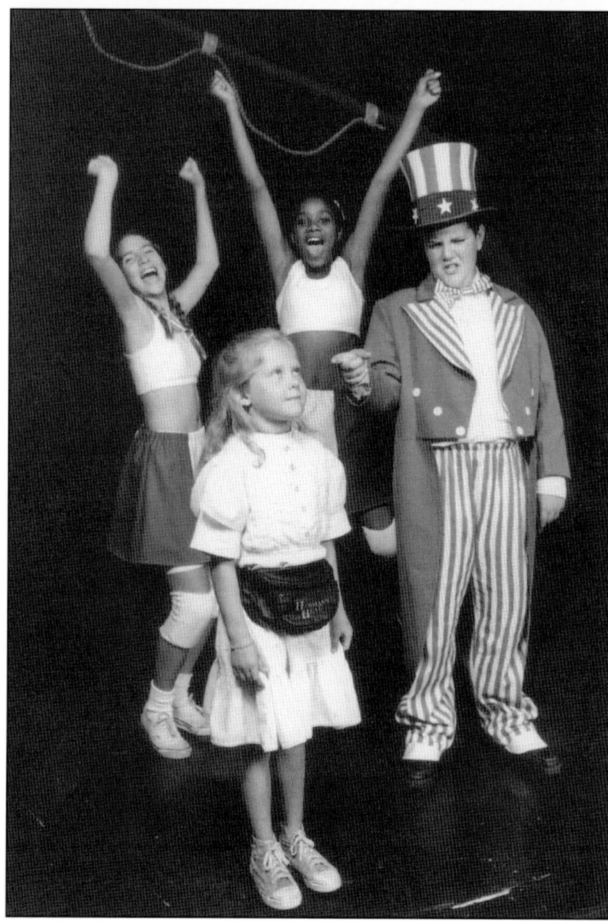

Fruitcakes was produced in 1999 at SPACE's Performing Arts Summer Camp by 70 children. It was written by Paulette Arnold, Kate Magruder, and Laurel Near in collaboration with David Lincoln. (Courtesy of SPACE.)

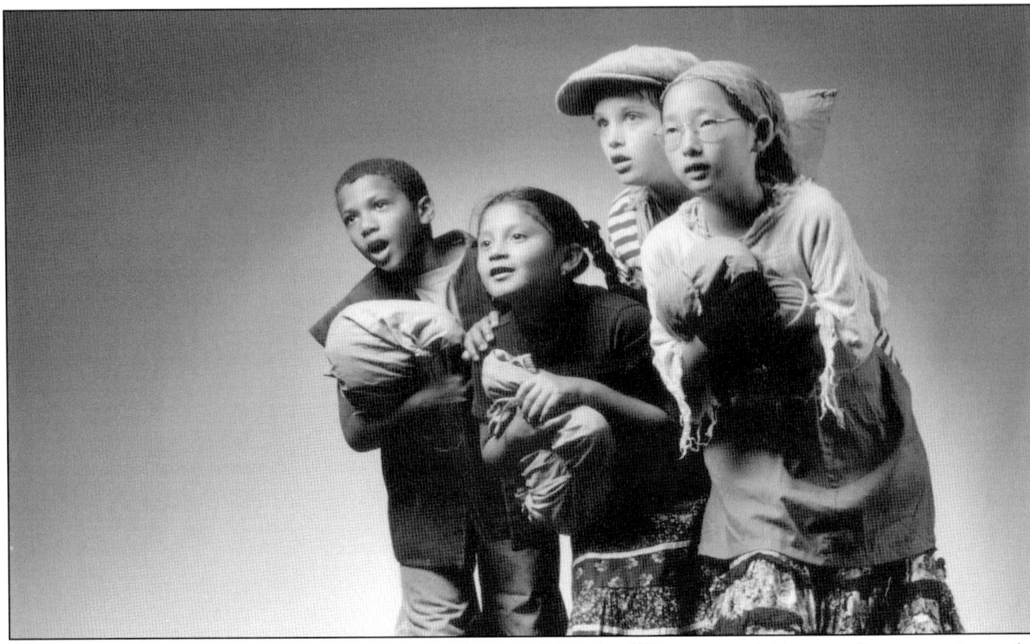

The "If You Believe" production in 1998 featured *Basket Woman and Coyote*. It was written by Paulette Arnold, Kate Magruder, and Laurel Near in collaboration with David Lincoln. (Courtesy of SPACE.)

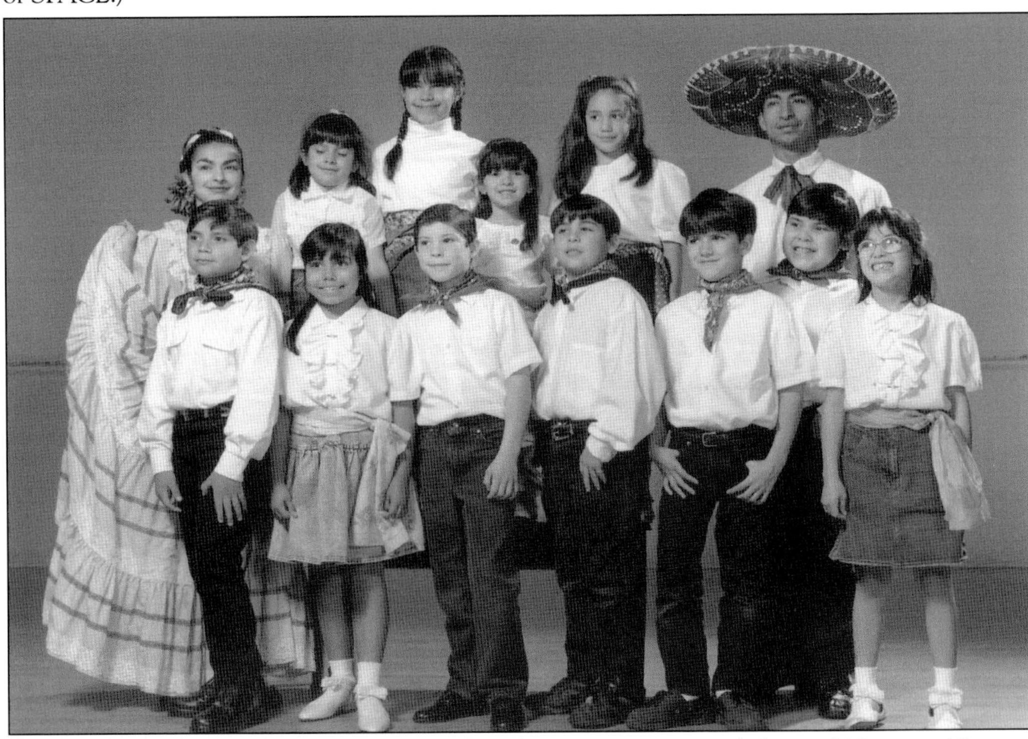

The Ballet Folklorico in 1994 was a cultural performance project with Juvenal Vasquez. This was the first time dancers from widely diverse communities came together to perform at the Ukiah Playhouse under the direction of Laurel Near. (Courtesy of SPACE.)

A Grand Open Air Ball was held on April 8, 1899. It was given by the Talmage Social Club at Camp Ringrose in Talmage.

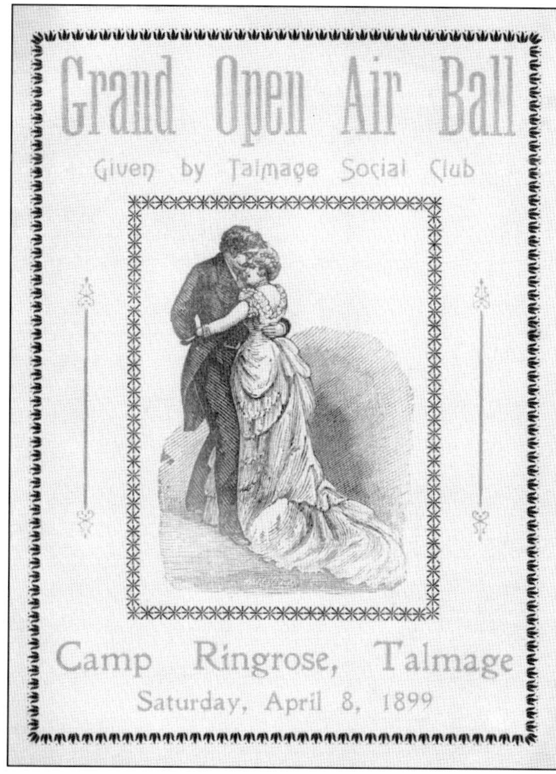

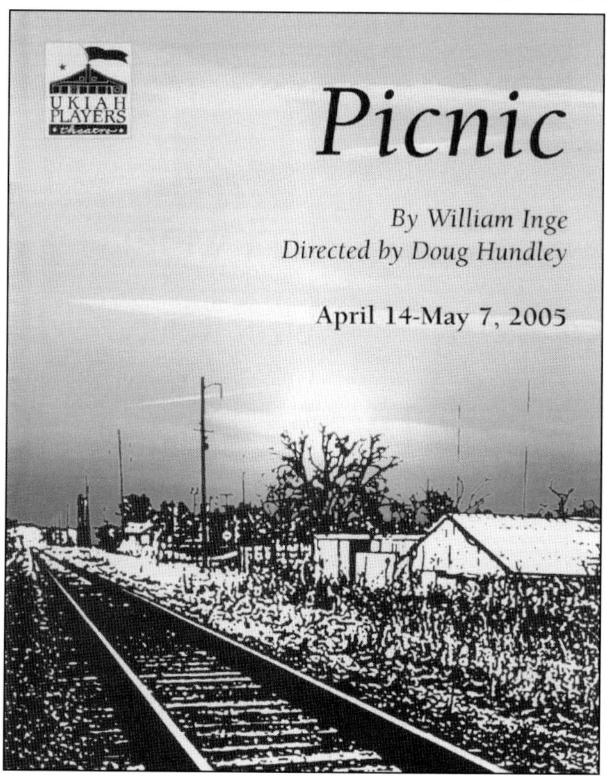

The Ukiah Players Theatre performed William Inge's drama *Picnic* in the spring of 2005. In May 2005, UPT hosted a fund-raiser called "Walk on the West Side." The event featured a tour of homes on the west side of Ukiah. Each residence had a host or hostess who led visitors on a tour of the house.

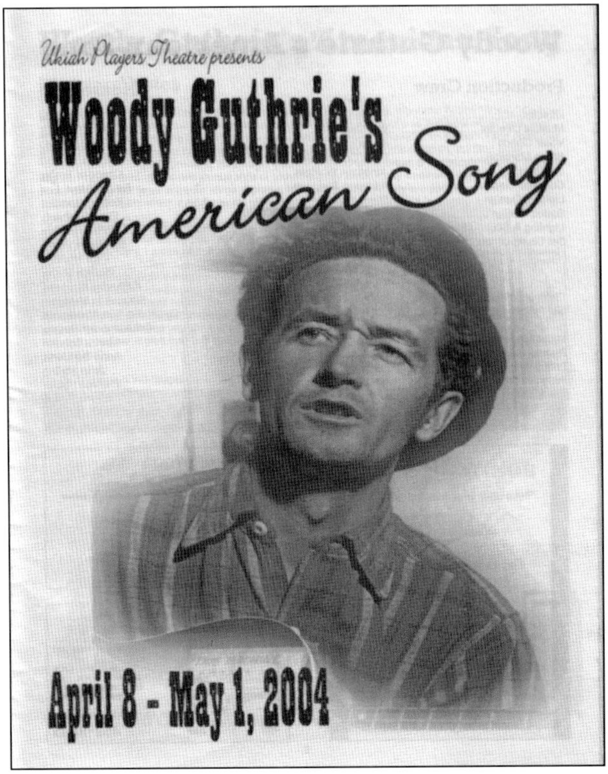

Woody Guthrie's *American Song* was presented in the spring of 2004. Songs from the 1930s, 1940s, and today made up the program by the Ukiah Players Theatre cast. Woody Guthrie songs spoke of the "real people" who lived through the Oklahoma oil boom, the Dust Bowl migration, and the Great Depression.

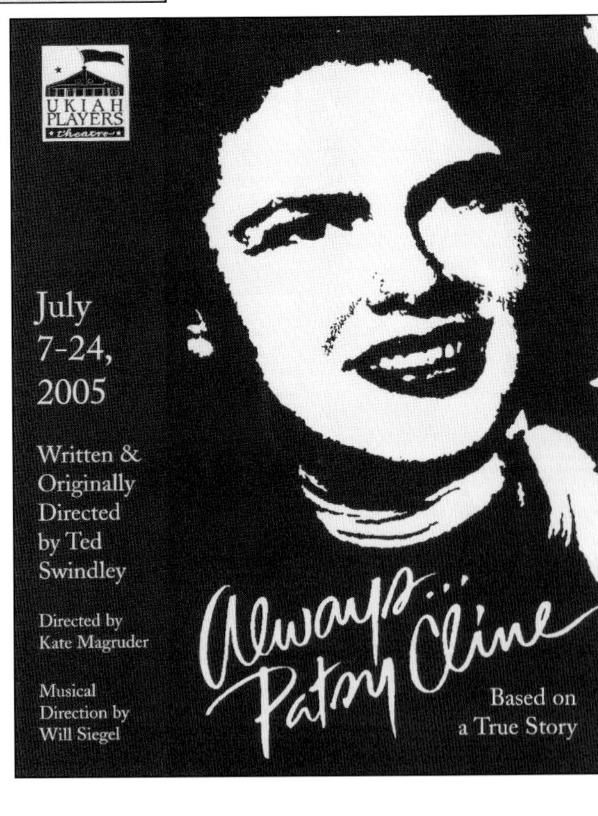

Always . . . Patsy Cline was presented by the Ukiah Players Theatre cast in the spring of 2006. The Ukiah Players Theatre began in the summer of 1977 when a small group of local actors and actresses came together to form a production company. UPT has produced hundreds of plays, musicals, readings, and special projects with community members of all ages. The company is known nationally for its pioneering work in projects that explore local history and contemporary issues.

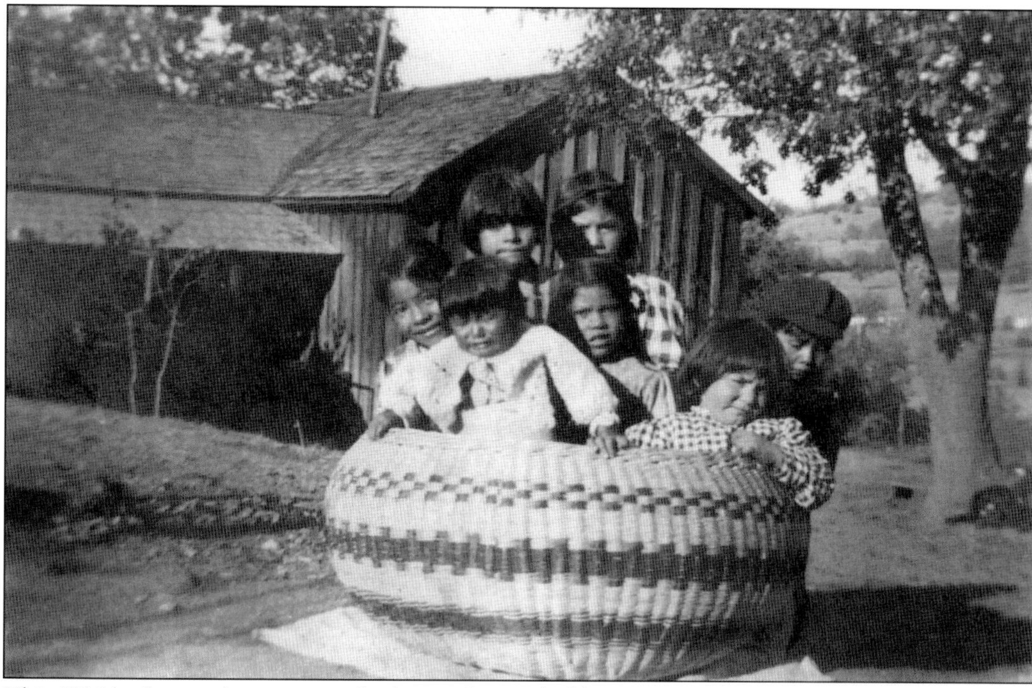

This 1910 basket is a large storage basket in the yard of famous Pomo Indian basket makers William and Mary Ben's house at the Yokayo Rancheria. The basket was most likely the handiwork of William Benson. (Photograph probably by William Benson; courtesy of the Grace Hudson Museum.)

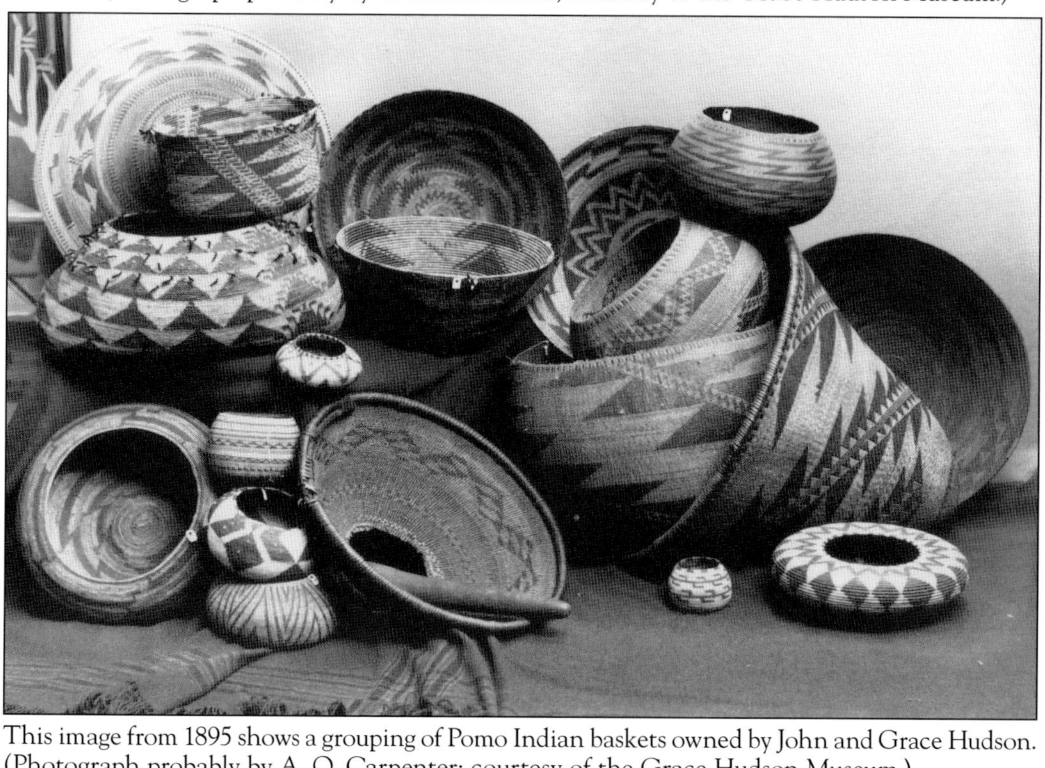

This image from 1895 shows a grouping of Pomo Indian baskets owned by John and Grace Hudson. (Photograph probably by A. O. Carpenter; courtesy of the Grace Hudson Museum.)

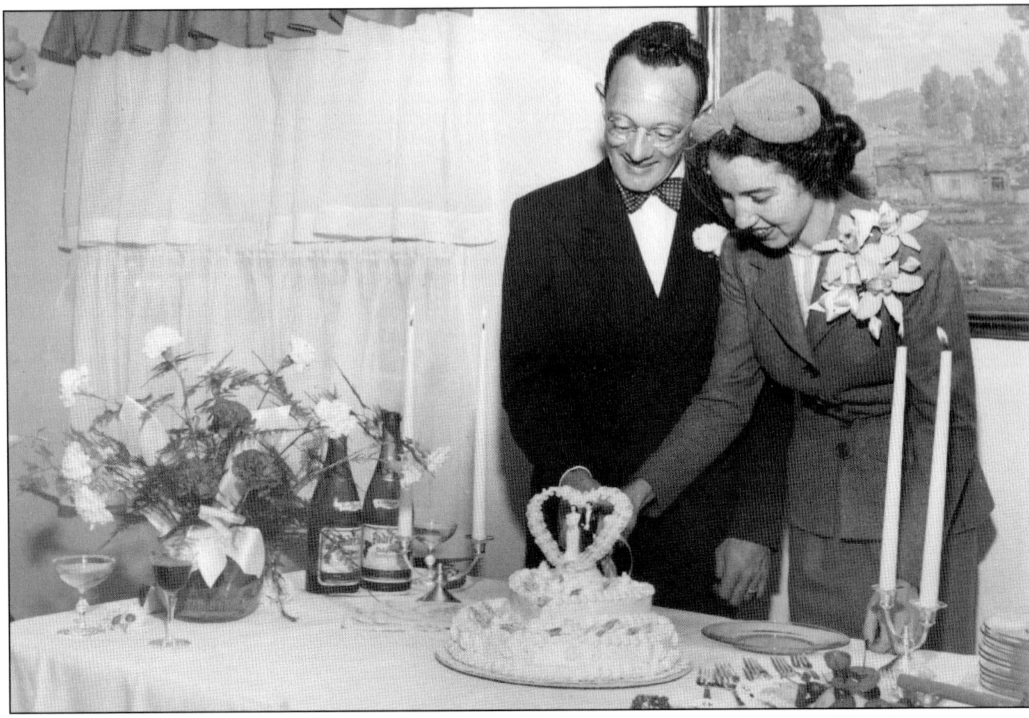

This image is from James and Virginia Williams' wedding on November 18, 1951. Virginia served on the first board of directors of Community Concerts and remains on the board.

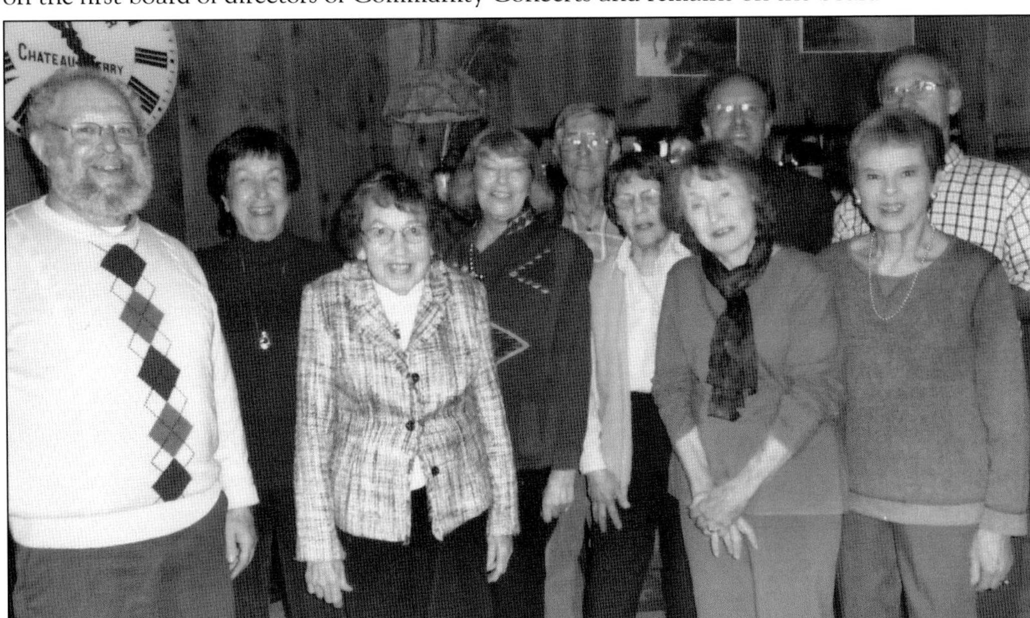

The Community Concerts board of directors is shown here. From left to right are Dr. Steven Pasternak, Kay Sause, Virginia Williams (vice president), Francine Bearden, All Bellon (second vice president), Maggie Cooper, Frances Stevens, Dr. Geoffrey Rice (president), Joyce Murray (recording secretary), and David Crew. The group has presented classical concerts since 1947, featuring groups from the United States and Europe.

An example of a Community Concerts program is pictured here.

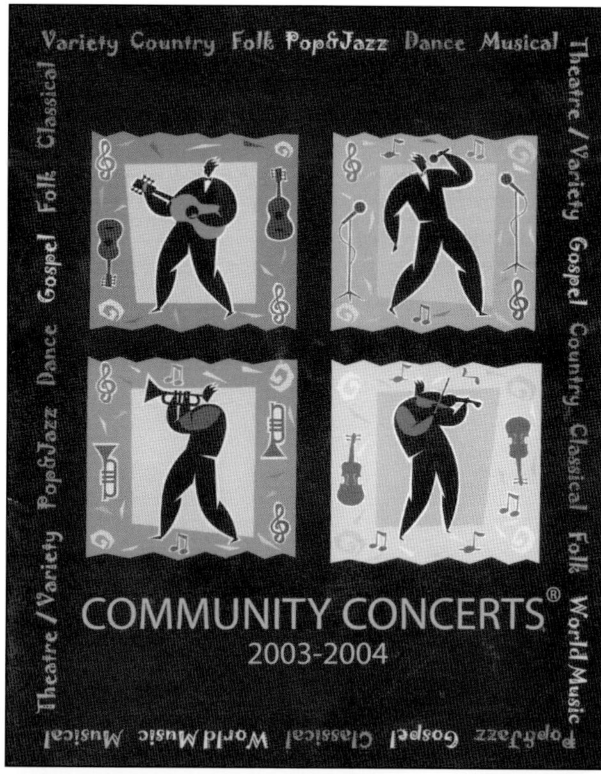

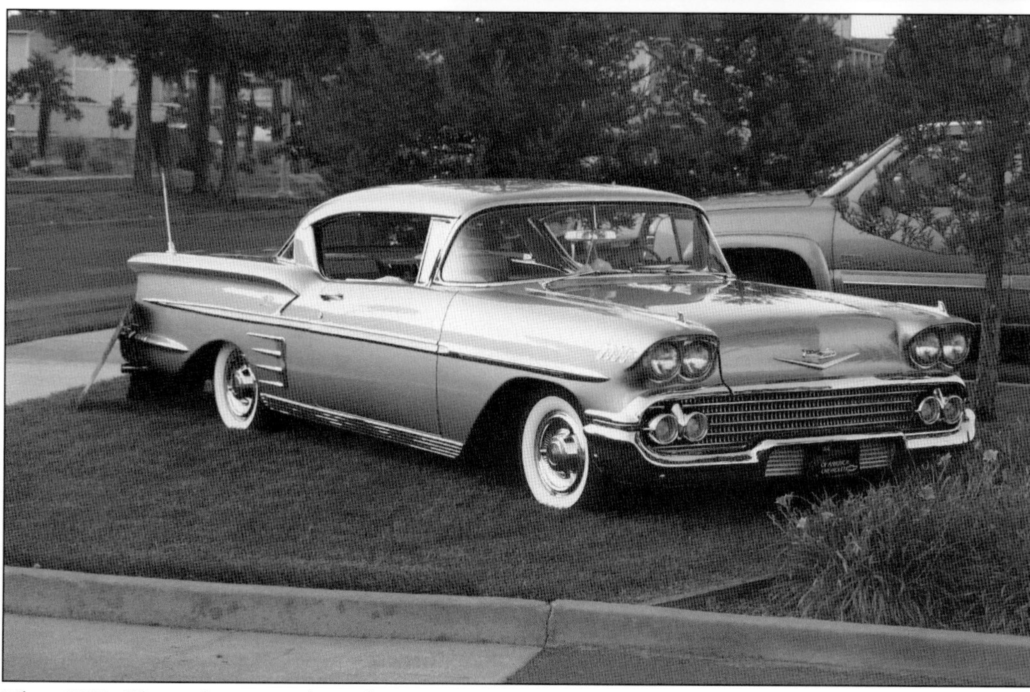

This 1953 Chevrolet was selected as Best of Show at the September 2002 Fabulous Flashback vintage car show. The Early Iron Club was started in 1980 by several couples who were involved in restoring old cars and trucks as a hobby. (Courtesy of the Early Iron Club.)

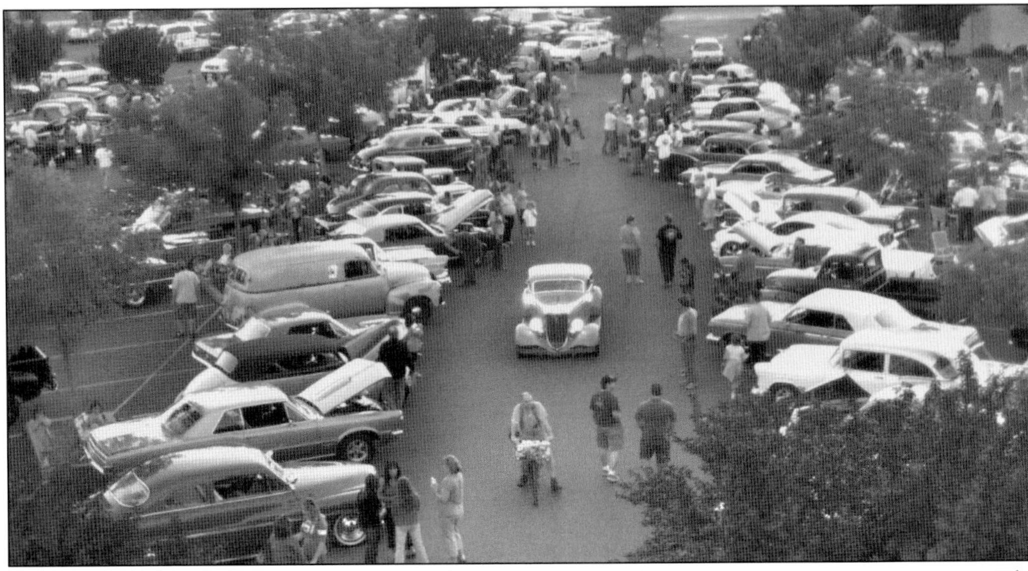

Every year since 1990, the Early Iron Club has sponsored an exhibition of antique cars. The Fabulous Flashback weekend starts on a Friday evening with a sock hop. On Saturday, School Street is closed and the cars are lined up for the show. The owners are available for anyone who wants to talk to them, and a street party provides fun for young and old alike. On Saturday evening, there is a parade to Todd Grove Park, and on Sunday, a poker run ends the weekend. The club raises money to provide scholarships to high school students who show an aptitude for automotive shop skills. (Courtesy of the Early Iron Club.)

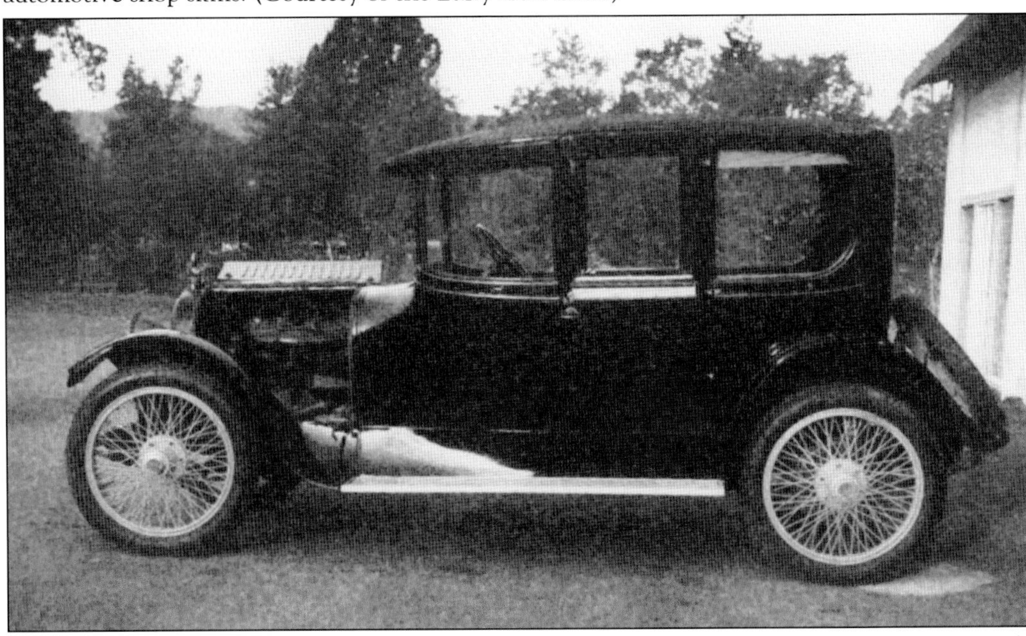

The Moline Knight was the featured car at the 2007 Fabulous Flashback show. The Moline Knight was manufactured by the Moline automobile company, which was formed in 1904 as a subsidiary of the Root and Vandervoort Engineering Company, a company that built gas engines. There are only about 31 Moline Knight cars that have survived until today. The owners of this vehicle are Richard and Julie Martin of Ukiah. (Courtesy of the Early Iron Club.)

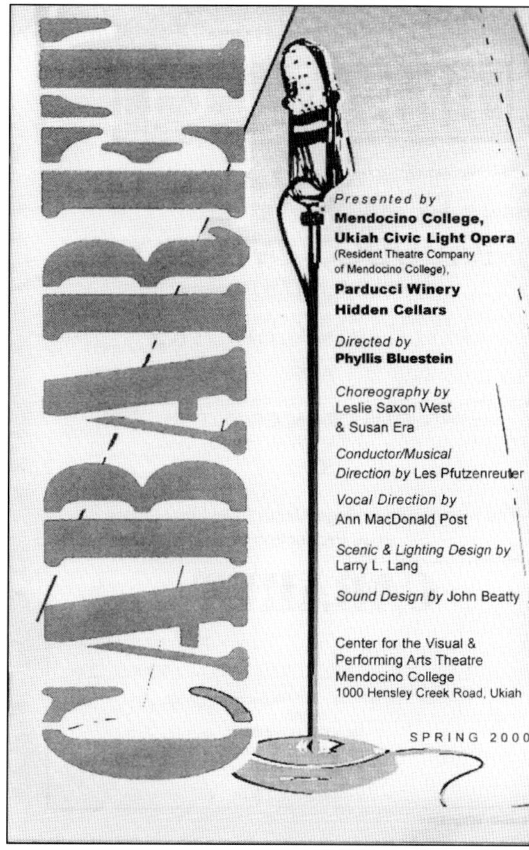

Cabaret was performed in the spring of 2000 as a collaboration between the Ukiah Civic Light Opera and the resident theater of Mendocino College. The musical played to sold-out audiences every evening.

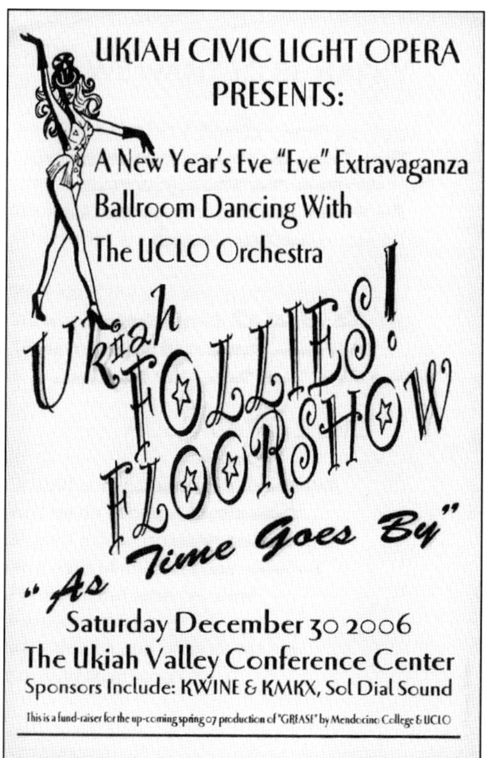

The Ukiah Valley Conference Center and the Ukiah Civic Light Opera combined forces to present the Ukiah Follies. The follies were a takeoff on the Palm Springs Follies, which requires performers to be 55 years of age or older. The musical was written by Paula Samonte and directed by Dawn Senften. Old favorites from the 1930s, 1940s, and beyond made up the program.

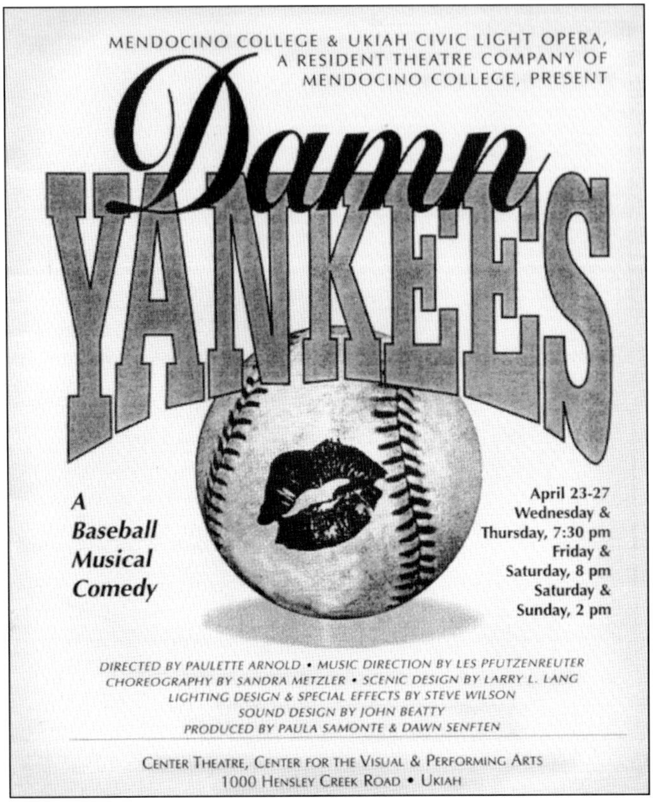

The Ukiah Civic Light Opera presented the award-winning musical *Damn Yankees* in April 1997. The comedy was originally presented in the 1950s in Washington, D.C. It was written by George Abbott and Douglass Wallop with music and lyrics by Richard Adler and Jerry Ross.

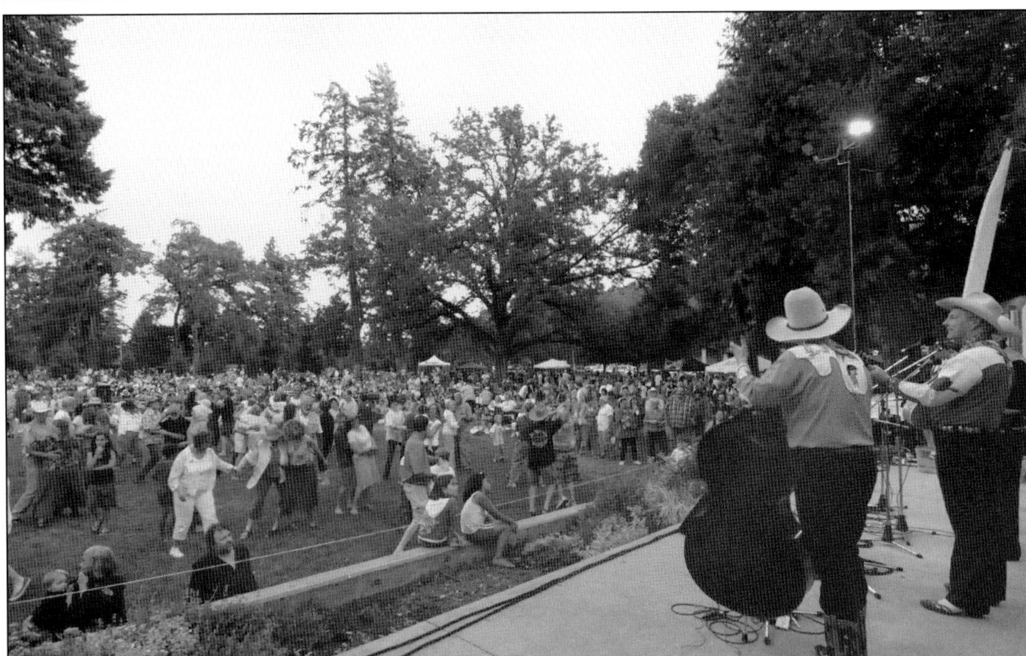

The Sundays in the Park concerts bring in thousands of people in the summer for a picnic, dancing, and just enjoying the music. (Courtesy of Spencer Brewer.)

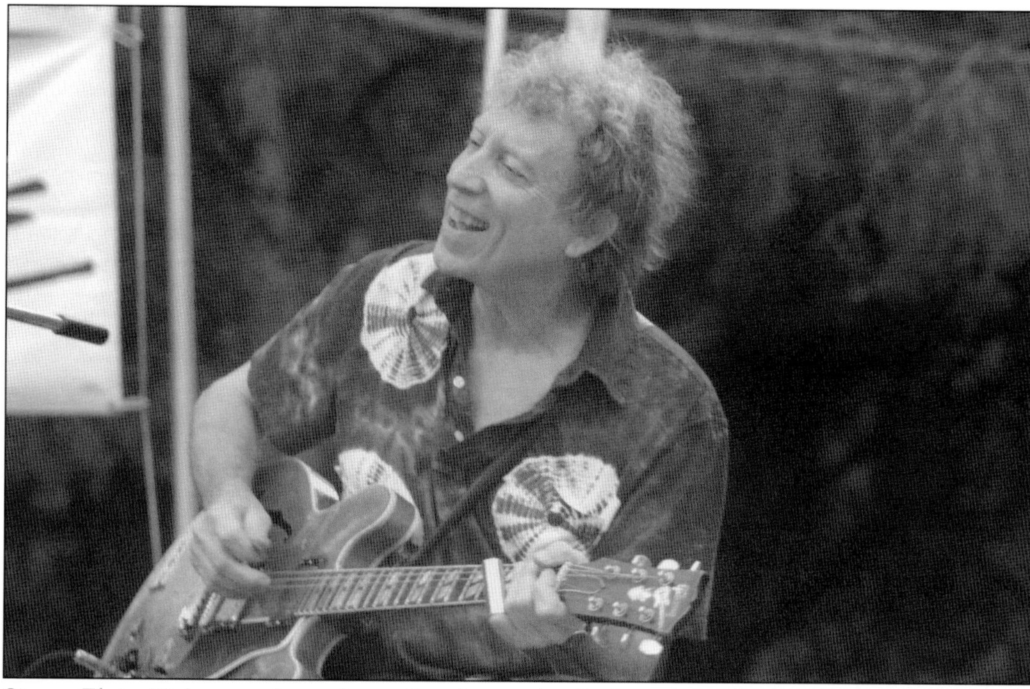

Singer Elvin Bishop performed at a Sunday in the Park concert during the summer of 1994. (Courtesy of Spencer Brewer.)

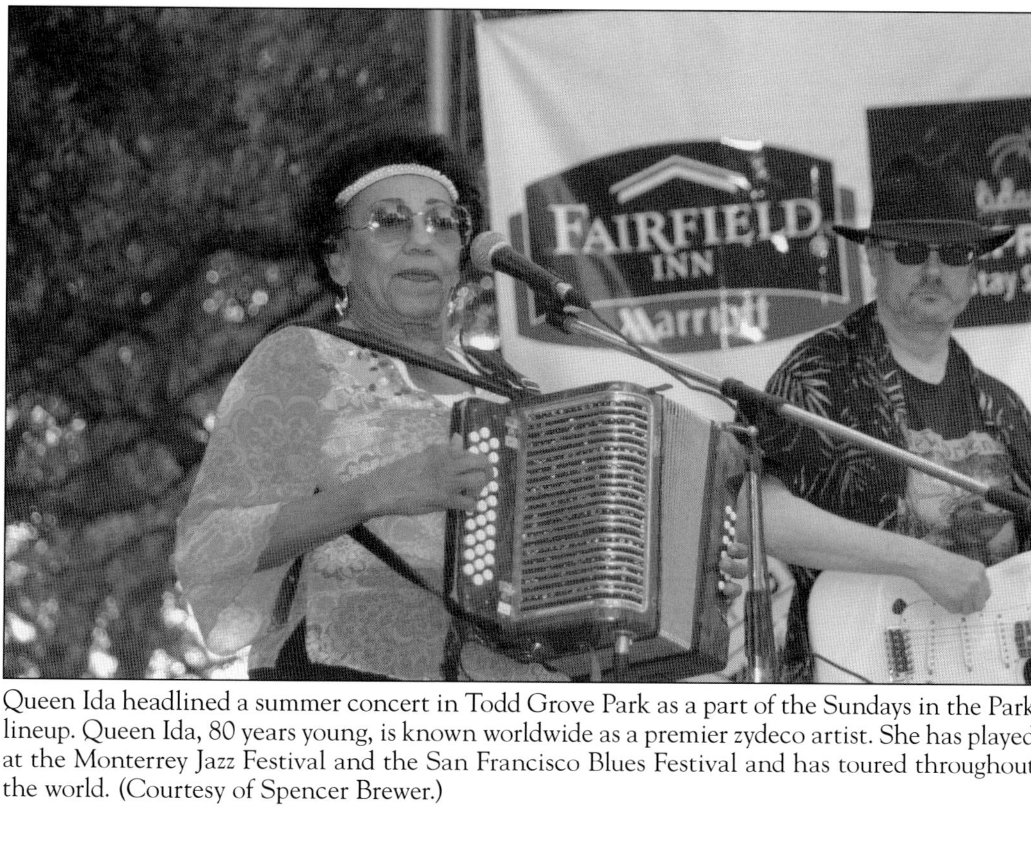

Queen Ida headlined a summer concert in Todd Grove Park as a part of the Sundays in the Park lineup. Queen Ida, 80 years young, is known worldwide as a premier zydeco artist. She has played at the Monterrey Jazz Festival and the San Francisco Blues Festival and has toured throughout the world. (Courtesy of Spencer Brewer.)

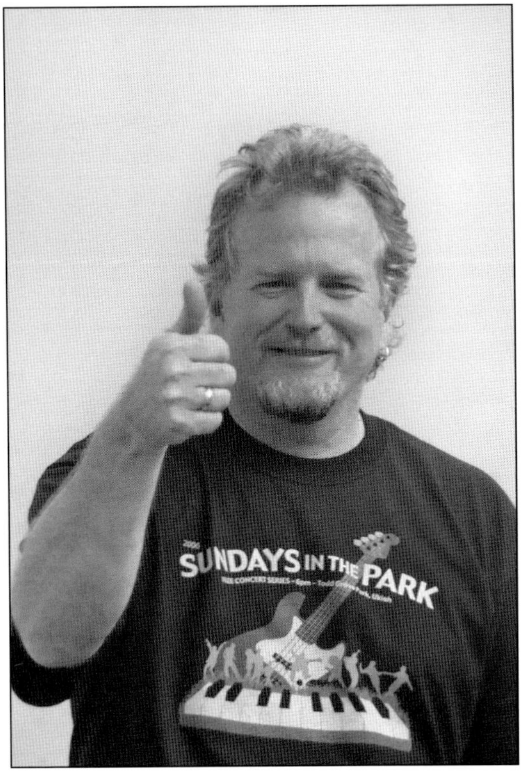

Spencer Brewer, a multimillion-selling composer, pianist, and producer, started the Acoustical Café in 2006 as a venue for regional musical talent in an acoustic-type setting. He was also the driving force in starting Sundays in the Park, which, under his guidance, has grown to an audience of thousands. (Courtesy of Spencer Brewer.)

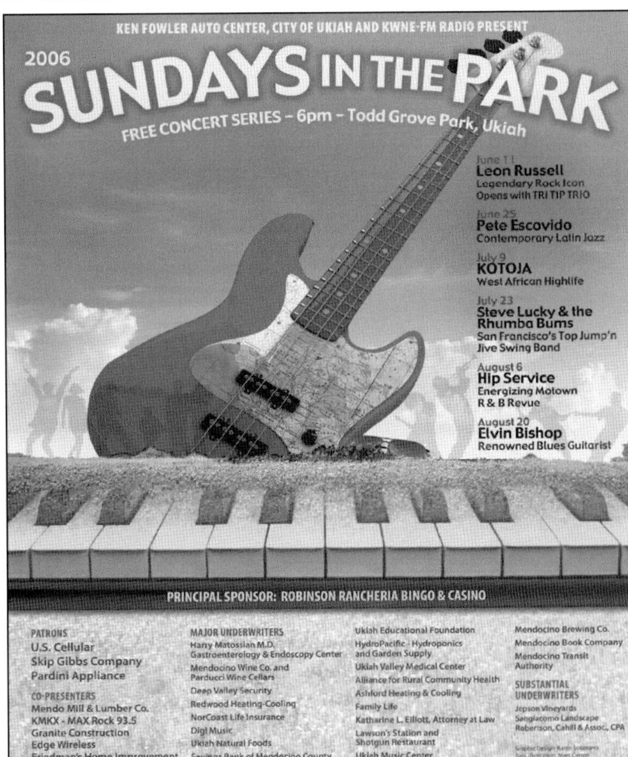

Maria Muldaur, known for her rendition of "Midnight at the Oasis" and "I'm a Woman," led off the summer series of Sunday in the Park concerts in 2000. In the late 1970s, she was a member of the Jerry Garcia Band. (Courtesy of Spencer Brewer.)

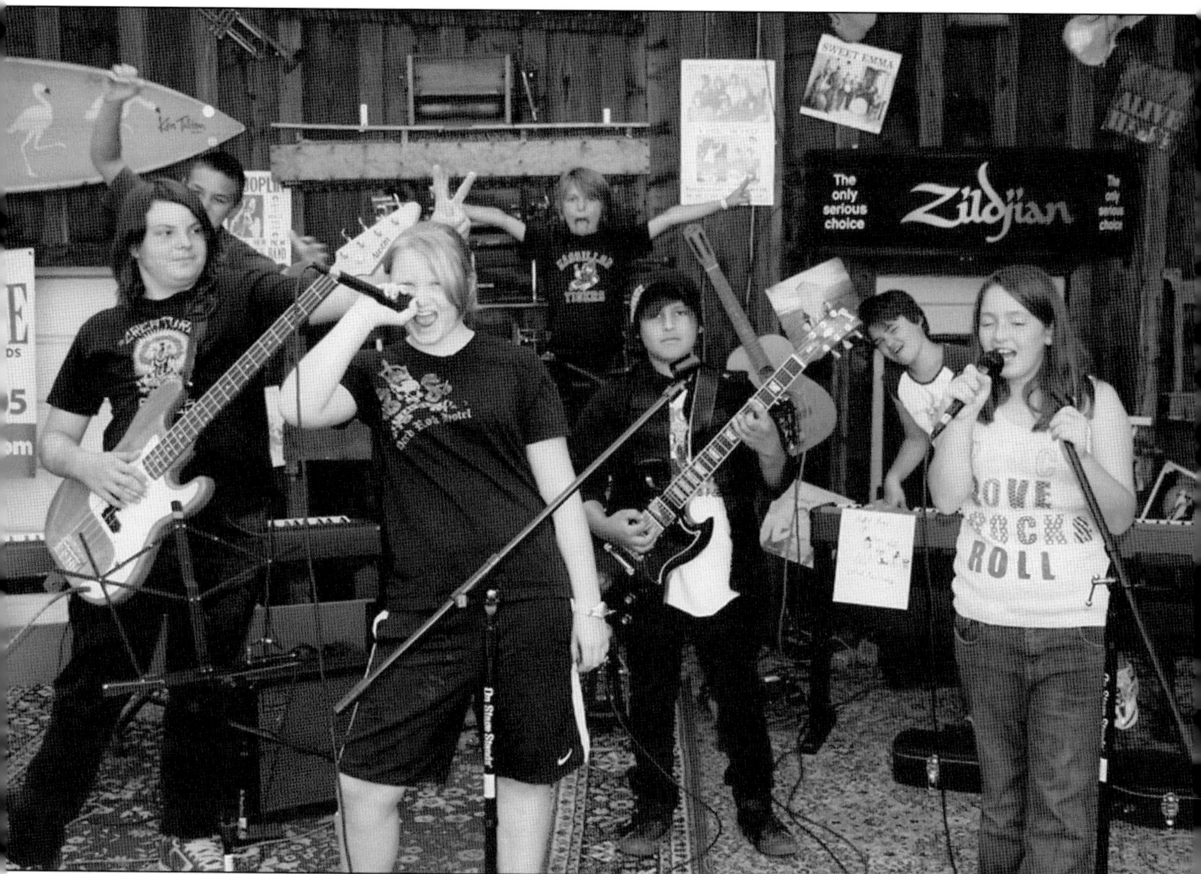

Rock Camp is a summer music camp for children and young adults. Spencer Brewer started this summer music camp to further their musical education in a focused setting during the summer months. (Courtesy of Spencer Brewer.)

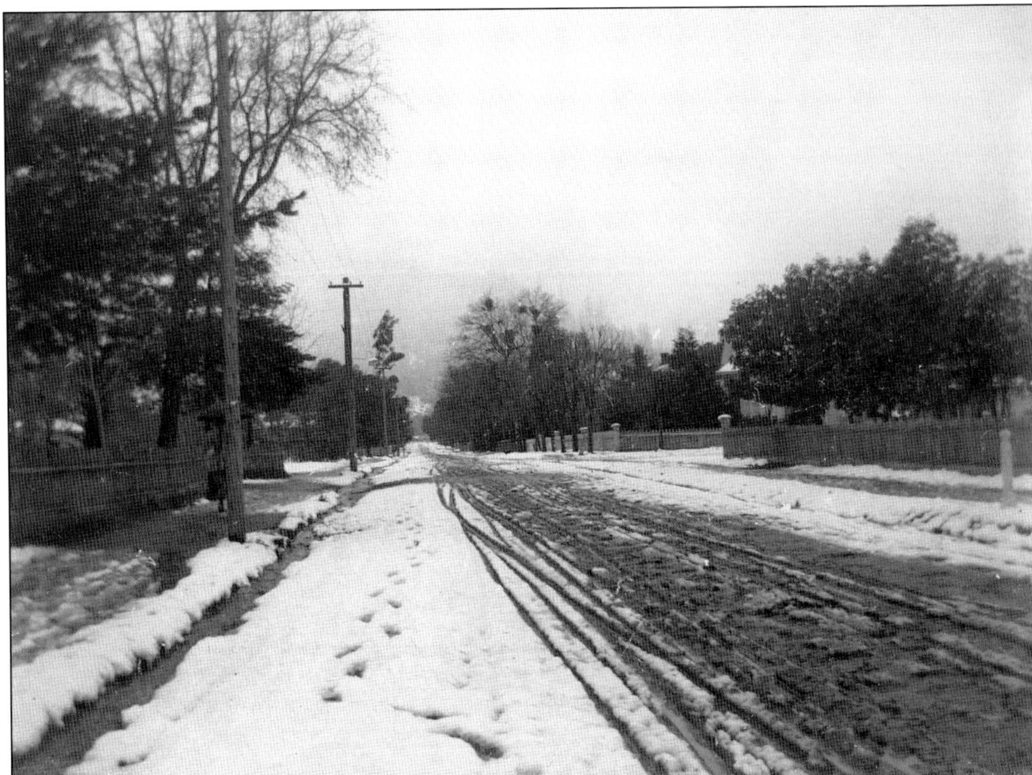

A Ukiah street snow scene is shown in the early 1900s.

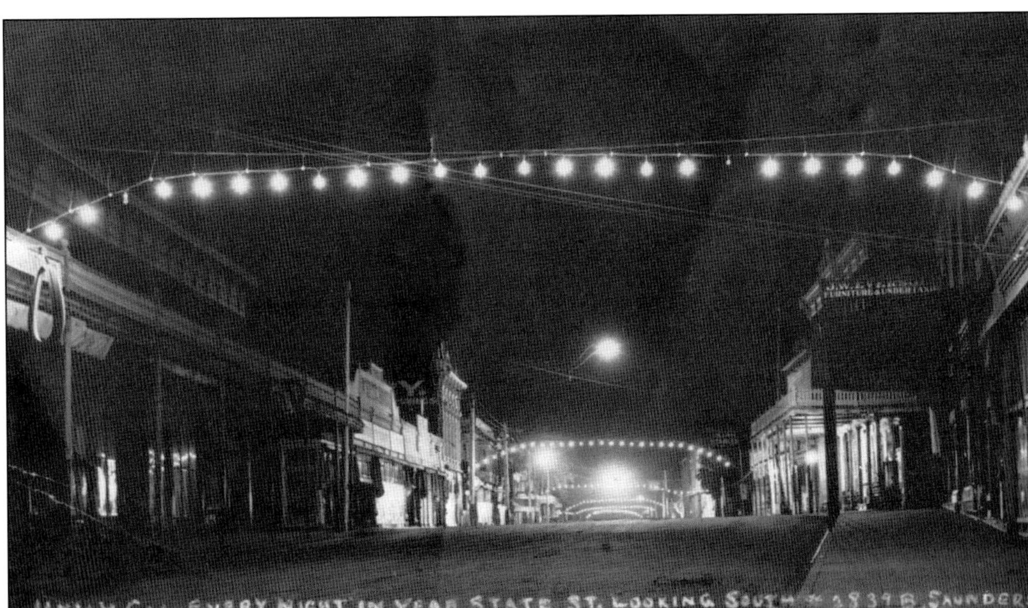

This State Street night scene postcard, around 1912, is looking south on State Street from Henry Street. This is the earliest known night view of Ukiah.

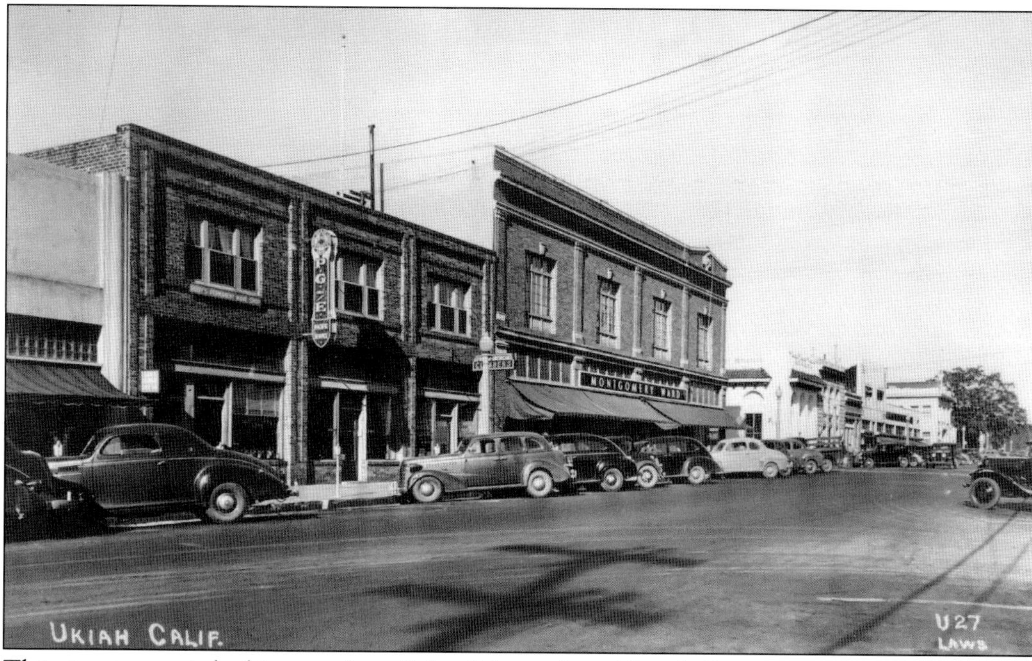

This street scene is looking north on School Street from Church Street around 1948. PG&E and Montgomery Ward are shown in the background.

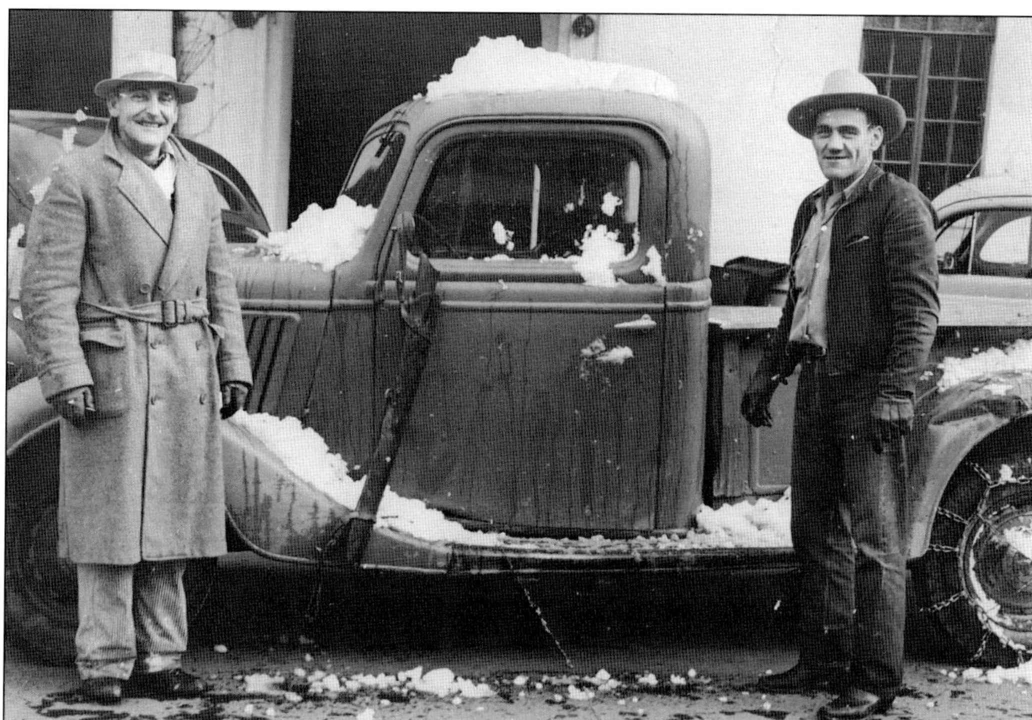

Phil Kingston (left) and Al Tatman are shown when they arrived in town on Christmas morning 1941 from a lookout station on top of the mountains west of Ukiah. There was 7 inches of snow covering their pickup truck.

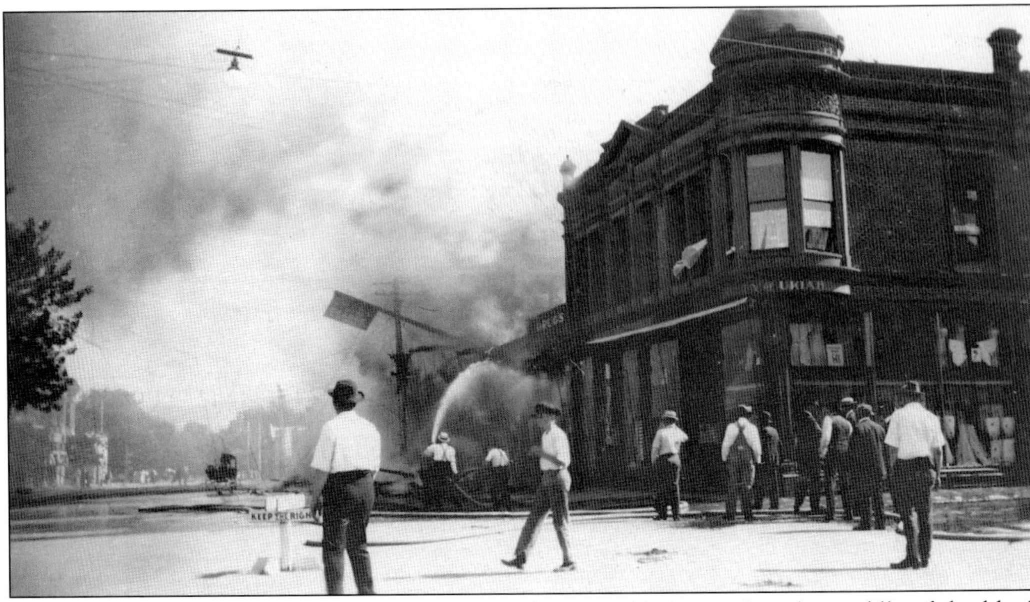

A fire in Ukiah on June 18, 1917, started in the livery stable located in the middle of the block south of the Marks Building.

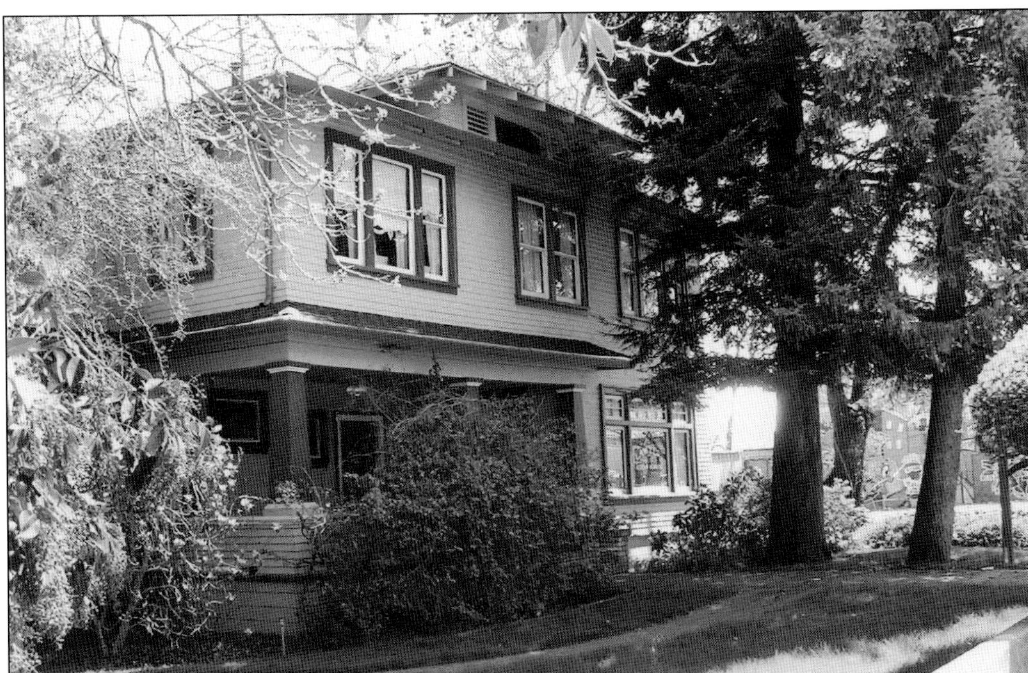

Pictured is the Lamb's Inn in 2009. The original home was moved to the rear of the property, and the Lamb's Inn was built in 1915. In 1918, Alice Lamb took over management of the inn and ran it until her death at the age of 95.

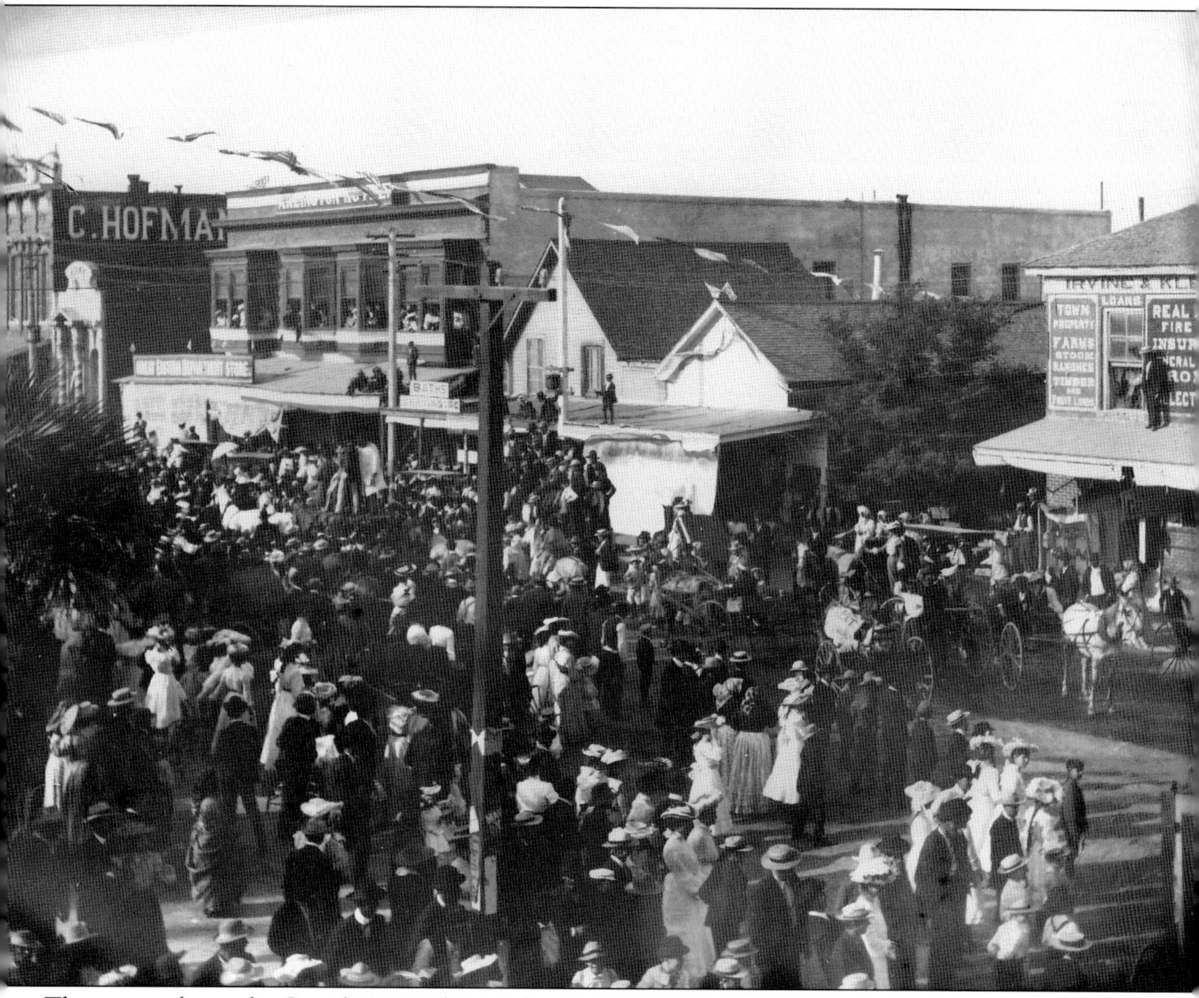

This image shows the Growler's Parade on July 4, 1903, on State Street in front of the courthouse plaza. The Growler's Parade was a mock celebration of a parade held earlier in the day. The Growlers were making fun of local businessmen of the era. A quote from the local newspaper at the time stated, "To see the Growler's was to laugh."